Lunch with the FT

Alongside the colour pink and the Lex column, Lunch with the *FT* is an indelible part of the *Financial Times*. Over 25 years, the formula has remained deceptively simple: a conversation-cum-interview over an agreeable lunch, usually in a convivial setting (one exception being an encounter in a Bogotá police station with the Colombian police chief who hunted down Pablo Escobar, the notorious drug lord).

Lunch is an opportunity for fine food, but above all fine writing. Our gastronomic guests have included many world leaders and other men and women of renown in business, finance, the arts and entertainment worlds. Together these personalities highlight the global reach of the modern *FT*.

In this our 131st anniversary year, when we surpassed our target of 1 million paying readers and returned to our old headquarters at Bracken House opposite St Paul's Cathedral, we wanted to mark the occasion with something special. What better than a second helping of *Lunch with the* FT?

The 1 million milestone marks our successful transition from a purely print business to a truly 21st-century digital operation delivering words, graphics and the moving image to a worldwide audience. This is a tribute to the spirit of innovation which animates everyone at the *FT*. It also serves to underline the importance of quality journalism epitomized by Lunch. *Bon appétit!*

Lionel Barber

Lunch with the FT
A Second Helping

Edited by Lionel Barber

Foreword by Alec Russell

Illustrations by James Ferguson

BUSINESS

PENGUIN BUSINESS

UK | USA | Canada | Ireland | Australia
India | New Zealand | South Africa

Penguin Business is part of the Penguin Random House group of companies
whose addresses can be found at global.penguinrandomhouse.com.

First published 2019
001

Copyright © *Financial Times*, 2019

The moral right of the authors has been asserted

'Letters to the Editor' reproduced by agreement with the authors

Additonal artworks reproduced by agreement with the artists: Alex Hedworth, Patrick Morgan, Seb
Jarnot, Ciaran Murphy, Sam Kerr, Vanessa Dell, Luke Waller

Set in 10.15/14.75pt MillerText
Typeset by Jouve (UK), Milton Keynes
Printed in India by Replika Press Pvt. Ltd.
Colour reproduction by Rhapsody Ltd, London

A CIP catalogue record for this book is available from the British Library

ISBN: 978-0-241-40068-5

Contents

THINKERS AND CREATORS

'You can't walk down the street without thinking about things that men generally don't have to think about'

THE ART OF MONEY

'I was selling this shitty product and it embarrassed me'

STARS OF PAGE, STAGE AND SCREEN

'I'm becoming a bit of a recluse. I like solitude. I like silence'

THE REVOLUTIONARIES

'A lot of people who care about me tell me
to shut up'

SPORT'S GREATS

'You can buy everything except passion'

Foreword

One of the great privileges of being editor of *FT Weekend* is receiving the weekly reader mailbag. Every weekend in come the emails – and letters too – from around the world commending, questioning and sometimes excoriating anything from our choice of front-page picture to our ballet coverage. Our readers have varied tastes and interests but if there is one feature that unites their fascination, it is Lunch with the *FT*.

Lunch was dreamed up in 1994 by Max Wilkinson, an idiosyncratic predecessor of mine whom I recall with trepidation and admiration as an editor. The interview has been running every Saturday since without pause – and with the same formula: the guest chooses the destination and the *FT* pays. This has led to some headaches for our managing editor who has to juggle the *FT*'s budget (see 'The Art of Expenses' by Henry Mance on p. xiii).

A few years ago David Pilling, our Africa editor and one of our outstanding regular Lunch interviewers, went to settle up after lunch with the South African populist Julius Malema and found he was paying for the firebrand's five-strong security detail. In June 2015 the loudmouth British newspaper tycoon Richard Desmond was more brazen still. As my colleague Mance wrote: '"We'll have that one," Desmond says, before I can intervene. As the sommelier skips away, the sum of £580 lingers on my retina. So this, I think, is how it feels to be screwed by Richard Desmond. It took less than 10 minutes.' In 2017 Mance won the Interviewer of the Year award in the British Press Awards. One of his entries was another bibulous lunch – and with another loudmouth, Nigel Farage. The bar bill encompassed six pints, a bottle of wine and two glasses of port . . . Alcohol is not essential of course for a good lunch; we appreciate that the art of lunching has changed in recent years. But if my correspondence with readers is anything to go by, they groan when too many lunches in succession unspool over mineral water or Diet Coke.

When would-be interviewers ask me for the critical ingredient for a 'good Lunch' I reply 'electricity'. The only thing that really matters is that it has to be an arresting conversation.

Scoundrels tend more easily to deliver more 'electric' copy. Filleting or roasting them can be more readily absorbing than the probing of, say, a literary legend. But it's not that we only interview scoundrels, far from it. This selection includes mesmerizing encounters with the wonderful writer Edna O'Brien and the madcap football philosopher Eric Cantona. We also include a lunch with an inspiring junior citizen, Bana al-Abed, the Syrian girl who became known as the 'Face of Aleppo' during the city's siege by government forces. There are plenty of people we would not lunch. There is always a risk you will provide a platform for a charlatan or crook. I hesitated before agreeing to fly to Harare to have lunch with 'the Crocodile', Zimbabwe's new president, in January 2018 but then concluded that the chance of a scoop with his first interview since he succeeded Robert Mugabe was too tempting.

At the annual *FT Weekend* festival in London, I asked for a show of hands from a boisterous crowd about our philosophy for choosing Lunch guests. Readers had come from as far as Berlin, Singapore and New York. What did they think of lunching sleazebags? Briefly I worried that an age of earnestness might have taken hold. But no. The near-unanimous answer was yes to sleazebags!

We have now lunched well over 1,000 people. There were tough choices for the final selection for this line-up. Of political titans, Jean-Claude Juncker made the cut, sharing, yes, wine as well as lunch with the *FT*'s Editor, Lionel Barber. Of the thinkers and millennials shaping our world, we have the brilliant Demis Hassabis and Whitney Wolfe. Our sybaritic lunchers are represented by Isabelle Huppert and Carlo Ancelotti.

Timing with Lunch, as with all journalism, is everything. Donald Trump's encounter with the *FT*'s former deputy editor Martin Dickson in 2013, three years before his election as US president, is riveting and revealing in equal measure – and after publication led to a gloriously testy exchange with his office. So, too, our Lunch with Sheryl Sandberg is worth a second read now, in light of the fresh controversies raging over Facebook.

Among the considerations when I meet my colleagues to finalize the week's Lunch is our global range. In these pages you will meet the North Korean refugee Hyeonseo Lee. You will encounter Edward Snowden, hidden away in a Moscow hotel room. You will go to a scruffy San Francisco flat to have takeaway Thai with the then 23-year-old billionaire Vitalik Buterin, founder of the Ethereum cryptocurrency. Chloe Cornish, also in her early twenties, an *FT* graduate, asked him about everything from the bitcoin bubble and his homeland Russia to his quest for eternal life. It is a kaleidoscopic cast, reflecting the eclecticism of our journalism and the interests of our readers.

Accompanying almost all of these Lunches are the illustrations by the brilliant James Ferguson (see page xv). I have lost count of the number of times readers have asked if he too is allowed to eat! Finally I would like to thank my colleague Natalie Whittle who has overseen this second volume with her customary clarity, determination and wit.

Alec Russell
Editor, *FT Weekend*

The Art of Expenses

By Henry Mance

Yes, I got screwed. I took British media baron Richard Desmond out for lunch, and he ordered a £580 bottle of Bordeaux. The tip on the wine alone was £72. I sat shell-shocked through the rest of the meal, which was probably Desmond's intention. It was my first ever Lunch with the *FT*, and I was certain it would be my last. I waited weeks before breaking the news to my editors. They were sympathetic; the *FT*'s expenses system was not, and blocked my initial request for repayment.

Some guests, however, object to the *FT* picking up the tab. 'Usually, we just leave, right?' exclaimed Donald Trump, after a 2013 lunch at the Trump Grill. He did allow the *FT* to pay, but motor-racing billionaire Bernie Ecclestone did not. 'I never stopped breaking the rules,' Ecclestone said, unfurling £50 notes to settle the bill at London's Mandarin Oriental. This brings its own form of embarrassment for the journalist. It's another way for the guest to assert themselves: success breeds largesse.

Canny guests sometimes seek to disguise their power. Facebook's Sheryl Sandberg chose to eat at a standard Mexican restaurant on the tech company's campus; Spotify's Daniel Ek settled for a sandwich on New York's High Line. But if they think *FT* journalists are impressed by simplicity, I have bad news. We can have a sandwich any day. Expensive lunches tend to make good interviews. The humility tactic only works if it reflects the guest's actual habits. The beauty of interviewing someone over food is that you can quickly sniff out inauthenticity.

Not all the *FT*'s interviewees are people for whom you would normally reach into your pocket – I'm thinking of figures such as Martin Shkreli, the pharmaceutical price-gouger. Journalists – and readers – are forgiven for thinking: why are we helping this person become even richer?

On other occasions, it's a pleasure to pay the bill, because the guest has given so much in return. The actor Isabelle Huppert ate 12 courses over three-and-a-half hours at L'Arpège, the Michelin-starred Paris restaurant. Who cares that it cost £412?

Or take BBC's Alan Yentob, who joined me for Lunch at London's River Café. The restaurant is practically his second home, and revealed his character. (Although I could have done without him insisting that I buy the in-house cookbook: I knew the *FT* expenses system would really draw a line there.)

As for Desmond, I have seen him occasionally since we shared that wine. He never fails to argue that the *FT*'s most expensive lunch to date was all a misunderstanding, and that he had offered to pick up the tab. That is not how I remember it. And I have the tape.

A Note on the Illustrator

James Ferguson is the third guest at every Lunch with the *FT*. Our veteran staff illustrator has been painting egos, icons and rogues on to sheets of cotton paper for Lunch with the *FT* since 2004.

The routine is the same for presidents, financiers and Hollywood stars: the reporter takes a picture of their guest at the lunch table, which Ferguson then works up on paper, after a close read of the interview for clues on character. There is 'no secret', he says, to his weekly task. 'Just observe and interpret.' The beauty of the subject can make the job tougher, however. The hardest person to draw in this collection, Ferguson says, was the luminous Gwyneth Paltrow.

Ferguson describes himself as an 'artodidact'; he did not study fine art formally, he was simply 'good at drawing'. Quality paint and paper are important to the end result, but he is liberal with his materials: 'I use anything. Watercolours, gouache, acrylics, inks, crayons, knives [to distress the paint].'

All this work takes place silently at his *FT* desk, until the deadline looms and the illustration needs to be handed to the designer. Which is when a sound familiar in the office ignites: the 'Ferguson hairdryer', giving a blast of hot air to dry off the famous faces. Lunch with the *FT* would be half the meal without him.

Natalie Whittle

Power and Politics

'I have met two big destroyers: Gorbachev and Cameron'

Jean-Claude Juncker

'I have met two big destroyers: Gorbachev and Cameron'

By Lionel Barber

Four black-and-white photographs line one wall in the private dining room of the president of the European Commission. Each pays homage to past office-holders: Roy Jenkins, Labour party reformer and *grand gourmand*; Gaston Thorn, plucky Luxembourger; and Jacques Delors, the French philosopher king who helped to build the single market and the euro.

The fourth picture catches the eye. The year is 1966. Walter Hallstein, German law professor, diplomat and first Commission president, is entertaining President Habib Bourguiba of Tunisia. Here is a snapshot of the original, intimate club of Six in the European Economic Community. Today's sprawling, squabbling European Union of 28 members, soon to be 27 with the departure of the British, seems a world apart.

This week marks the 60th anniversary of the founding Treaty of Rome. The clinking of champagne glasses will be muted. Europe remains battered by low growth and high unemployment, a migration wave from the Middle East and north Africa, not to mention Brexit and Donald Trump. If Jean-Claude Juncker is feeling depressed, he masks it well. The current president of the European Commission, another Luxembourger in the top job, has agreed to have lunch to mark the Rome anniversary. He arrives on time at 12.30pm, all smiles behind a sober dark suit, white shirt and dashing pink tie.

'How come it has been so long?' he says in French, embracing me warmly. It's been 15 years since we last met. Back in the 1990s, when I was the *FT*'s bureau chief in Brussels. Juncker was his country's prime

Illustration by James Ferguson

minister, a mini power broker between France and Germany, and a trusted source.

At 62, he has been near the centre of power for more than three decades, present at the creation of the modern EU. Today, he is the last man standing.

'I've been elected 14 times in my life, nine times to the Luxembourg parliament, four times to the European Parliament,' he says, omitting the last controversial vote when 'Buggins's turn' dictated he was the centre-right's candidate for the Commission job. 'Being described as a stupid bureaucrat with no link to representative democracy is difficult to take. We are not in an iron tower.'

As we take our place at a pristine dining table set for two, I begin with a few short sharp questions: What went wrong with Europe? Was enlargement a mistake? What about the original mission, to exorcise the demons of nationalism and war?

Juncker says enlargement was an inevitable consequence of the end of the cold war. More than 20 new countries took their place on the European map. Border conflicts posed a huge risk. Yet he admits the message of war and peace no longer resonates with the younger generation.

'I [also] explain Europe with a future perspective . . . we are losing weight economically and demographically even if we think we are still masters of the world. By the end of this century, we will be 4 per cent of Europeans out of 10 billion people. This is not the time for new divisions. We have to stick together.'

The president sips from a glass of wine, a crispy white from Languedoc. 'My father was a steelworker and he told me about a new beginning in Europe [in the 1950s]. He had been forced to join the German army, along with three of his brothers. That was a terrible period in the lives of my father and uncles, which impressed me for the rest of my life.'

His father was wounded in Odessa on the eastern front and taken prisoner by the Russians. During the Brexit referendum campaign, British tabloids reported that his father was a Nazi, a slur that deeply upset the president and his father, who passed away shortly afterwards. 'It was unjust and disgusting,' says Juncker, 'even [Nigel] Farage [leader of Ukip] apologized.'

Now in the twilight of his career, Juncker has been criticized as low-energy, a relic of a bygone era who delegates too much to Martin Selmayr, his Machiavellian chief of staff, and who spends too little time in the 'newcomer' member states in central and eastern Europe. ('I accept this,' he says of the last point.)

Over a two-hour conversation, he is determined to show he is on top of his brief, rattling off statistics ranging from the minimum wage in Bulgaria to the declining number of telephone kiosks in Germany, all delivered effortlessly in English, French and occasionally German. Food is a tiresome distraction. The president barely touches his starter, a tasty if stringy Carpaccio de Saint-Jacques in sesame and soya oil.

A waitress arrives with a bottle of red wine, a 2005 Pomerol. 'No, no,' says the president, waving away the claret. 'I cannot mix white and red. We will have major events.'

The president's weakness for alcohol is well known. Today, he is on best behaviour. I ask him how he survived all those late-night councils. By his account, the worst was a budget meeting in Brussels in late 1985 ahead of Spain and Portugal joining the EU.

'I was chairing the meeting. It started on Monday morning at 11am and finished on Thursday at 11pm, without going to the hotel, without having a shower. They [still] sent me the bill.'

'So what's the secret of getting through the all-night sittings?' I ask.

'Coffee and water.'

'You can't be serious.'

'No whisky, nothing of that kind.'

'No brandy?'

'No, no, no.'

With one eye on Brexit, I ask the president to name the most brutal negotiations he was involved in.

'Greece continuing to be a member of the euro,' he shoots back.

Between 2004 and 2013, Juncker was on another Brussels jobs merry-go-round, chairing the Eurogroup, which by 2011 comprised 17 members. 'I had to be supportive of Greece because no one else was. I had to take in my compromise . . . and I had to tell the third group [the Slovaks and Slovenes]: "I will no longer listen to you because you are not in the right mood." Those were really difficult moments.'

In 2015, the same drama played out, this time with the new Greek government led by Alexis Tsipras, the radical left-winger. By now Juncker was

Commission president and keen to cut a deal on Greek debt restructuring. 'It took a moment to convince him I was partly on his side. All this was very difficult because the Commission was not really in charge; it was the Eurogroup. We were taking all the initiatives. And the Germans and others were saying: "What are you doing there? This is not your job."'

Juncker has irked member states by insisting he is running a 'political' Commission not a bureaucracy. They fear a power grab but the president has a point: the Brussels-based executive has the right of legislative initiative, it enforces the rules, it keeps the show on the road.

I first witnessed Juncker in action in Dublin Castle in 1996 when he helped to broker a deal over the German-inspired Stability Pact to enforce budgetary discipline in the future eurozone.

'Chirac started the meeting by saying the pact was an invention of German bureaucrats, pointing very directly at Theo Waigel, then finance minister, who refused to speak to Chirac. It was the very first time I played a role at head of state level. And when I could say to myself: without me, it would have been a collapse.'

Helmut Kohl was even more influential. Juncker describes the German chancellor as 'a modest giant, a little saint in a great church' who understood the 'secret psychology' of making the smaller countries feel he was listening. 'When everything went wrong, he would say: "Listen, friends, I am going to be strongly attacked in Germany. But it does not matter; I am doing this for European reasons. I am not playing the national card; I am playing now the European card. Please do the same. Today and next time." That happened three or four times. And the others were in fact ashamed.'

The waitress brings more Pomerol to wash down the veal fillet that is tender, if a little overcooked. By now, Juncker is dropping his diplomatic mask. France's inability to stick to budget discipline was a big problem and 'it still is'. Those who believe the Dutch elections show populism has peaked are wrong. '*Fruchtbar ist der Schoss* [the womb is still fertile],' he says, citing Brecht's warning about fascism returning to Europe in the 1950s.

Can Marine Le Pen win the French presidential election?

'I don't think so . . . I cannot imagine the whole of France shifting to the extreme right. But they have a solid *Sockel* [pillar] of support.'

I suggest the danger lies in the collapse of the traditional centre-left and centre-right parties. Juncker agrees: 'That is the problem of France . . . the French are not used to coalitions. They hate each other.'

By contrast, post-war Germany has a different political tradition. 'The German system was never driven by extremists, whereas the French system was driven by communist extremists and now by the extreme right . . . the best thing to happen in France would be bridging these abnormally huge differences. Will it happen? I don't know.'

This hints at a preference for Emmanuel Macron, the centrist newcomer with no party, but Juncker says he has no intention of meddling.

The coffee and chocolates arrive. It is time to tackle Brexit, which he describes as 'a tragedy, and people do not know that this tragedy will lead to conclusions'.

Before last year's referendum the then UK prime minister, David Cameron, and his close ally and then chancellor of the exchequer, George Osborne, were desperate to appease Tory hardliners. 'Cameron always said: "I have one major problem. If Theresa May [the then home secretary who succeeded him as prime minister after Britain voted last June to leave the EU] publicly says that she is for Brexit, then we are lost."'

Juncker describes May as a Brexiter and predicts Cameron will not be judged kindly by history. 'I have met in my life two big destroyers: Gorbachev, who destroyed the Soviet Union, and Cameron, who destroyed the United Kingdom to some extent, even if there is no wave of Scotland to become independent.'

The exit bill for the UK will be at least €60 billion and Britain's departure will also change the balance of power in Europe, says Juncker. The UK always defended new members from central and eastern Europe. Germany cannot replace the British nor can it supplant Britain's role in the transatlantic relationship.

Juncker is visibly agitated about President Donald Trump's delight in Brexit. When US vice-president Mike Pence paid a recent visit to Brussels, he did not mince words. 'I told him: "Do not invite others to leave, because if the EU collapses, you will have another war in the western Balkans." The only possibility for this tortured part of Europe is to have a European perspective. If we leave them to themselves – Bosnia and Herzegovina, Republika Srpska, Macedonia, Albania, all of these countries – we will have a war again.'

Will Trump galvanize Europe to be more united? Juncker is cautious. Trump has made Europeans think twice about American intentions, especially given the 'very serious, though overestimated' threat from Russia. 'When it comes to security, Trump is pushing them more and more in the direction of European integration.'

With two-and-a-half more years left in his five-year term, Juncker knows that any new political initiative must await the outcome of this September's German election. Still, the president does hint that there may be moves in 2018 to a more formalized 'multi-speed' Europe where, say, a euro core group moves ahead with greater integration. He rejects the notion of a new 'Iron Curtain', which segregates the 'newcomers', the slightly ambivalent term he repeatedly uses to categorize the central and east Europeans.

He also condemns the idea of a united federal Europe built against the nation states. 'Forgetting the importance of national landscapes, cultures, national behaviours, reactions and reflexes is a big, big mistake. I am against nationalists, but I am very much in favour of patriots.'

As we sip our coffee, I remind Juncker that he once said that power had an erotic quality. After 35 years of Euro-building, does he still find power erotic?

'I find it more and more exciting and less and less erotic.'

How so?

'You are enthusiastic because the challenges are there and because you are part of a system trying to give a response. But after several years you stop being irrational. Eroticism is irrational; explicable but irrational. Why are you in love with a person? The day you know means that you have stopped being in love.'

But surely there is always room for intuition, whether in love or politics?

European Commission
Berlaymont, Rue de la Loi 200, 1049 Brussels

....

Carpaccio de
  Saint-Jacques
Noisette de filet de veau
Crêpe caramélisée à
  l'orange
Moka et mignardises
Mas Champart
Château L'Hospitalet de
  Gazin, Pomerol

....

Total – Complimentary

'Yes,' says the president, 'these are the fucking moments.'

Whether this refers to a Euro summit or something else is left unsaid. We adjourn to the president's spacious office down the hall. He is a ferocious reader (especially newspapers, much to the frustration of his staff). He tells me he is thinking in retirement of writing a history of the euro, based on 50 metres of original documents he has accumulated since 1986.

And he has one more story to tell.

Back in the early 1990s, when European monetary union was still a distant prospect, the Luxembourg government secretly ordered the printing of a new national currency, 50 billion new notes as an insurance policy. The Grand Duchy was part of a monetary union with Belgium but clearly did not have full confidence in the Belgians staying the course to the single European currency. On the launch of the euro on 1 January 1999 Juncker had the notes destroyed, keeping one for himself and the other for the Grand Duke.

The president chuckles, checks his watch and rises from his chair. We walk out of his office, past photographs of all the Commission presidents, ending with José Manuel Barroso of Portugal. There is one last space for Juncker's own portrait, next to a large exit door.

Après lui, le déluge? Let's hope not.

Ellen Johnson Sirleaf

'The integrity issue is systemic'

By David Pilling

Ma Ellen is not happy. Then again she is not exactly angry, either. She looks at me sternly from behind her spectacles with a glint of weary amusement. 'You're meddlin' now,' she says, in what sounds like a southern American drawl. 'I'm meddling? Is that what you said?' I ask, checking that I've heard correctly. 'Yes,' she says, as though that settles it.

We're not in the Deep South, though the ornate furnishings, home-cooked food and her rich, lilting accent might suggest otherwise. We're in Liberia, the west African country founded by emancipated slaves from America. My guest is the president, Ellen Johnson Sirleaf – 'Ma Ellen' to many Liberians – the first woman to be elected head of state in Africa when she took over 11 years ago, and, at 77, a dogged survivor of her country's brutal past.

The subject of my meddling is the coup of 1980, when Samuel Doe, a master sergeant in the army, overthrew the government of William R. Tolbert to become Liberia's first indigenous leader. Since it was first settled by African-Americans in 1822, Liberia had been run by and for Americo-Liberians, the elite that traced its ancestry back to the US. It was rumoured that Doe's soldiers, venting pent-up anger at years of exploitation, gouged out Tolbert's right eye and disembowelled him.

Thirteen members of the government were subsequently taken to the beach, where the rough grey waters of the Atlantic pound against the African coast. There, they were summarily shot before jeering crowds. Sirleaf was finance minister at the time and one of only four cabinet members to be spared. My question is: where was she that night? 'There's no big secret. I was at a private home with a friend. People were listening to gunfire and passing the news around.' Did she fear for her

Illustration by James Ferguson

life? 'I had concerns,' she says matter-of-factly. 'I was called in [by Doe] and, in the end, I was protected.' And you served briefly in his administration, I prompt. 'Yes, if you say president of the Liberian Bank, that's correct.'

The events of 1980 were the start of Liberia's descent into a murderous hell, first under Doe himself and then, in the 1990s and early 2000s, under Charles Taylor, the warlord who overthrew Doe and plunged the country into civil war. During this time, Sirleaf spent long periods abroad, but never abandoned her political ambitions. In 2005 she was finally elected president, in a contest overseen by US peacekeepers brought in to help enforce a ceasefire and re-establish democratic rule.

'We've done a lot to restore Liberia's credibility, Liberia's reputation, Liberia's presence,' she says of her presidency, the commas almost audible. Certainly abroad, the Harvard-educated, former United Nations technocrat is seen as a near miracle worker who has brought stability to her impoverished, war-ravaged country. Until 2014's catastrophic Ebola outbreak, the country's GDP was growing at an average of 8 per cent a year, and in 2011 Sirleaf was awarded the Nobel Peace Prize. At home, her image is of an 'iron lady' who has – literally and figuratively – dodged several bullets on her way to the top.

When I suggest that she is less popular in Liberia than in Washington or London, she points out that she has been elected twice. 'History will challenge that. I'm not talking about what you hear from 5 per cent of the population on the radio, in the papers,' she says. 'I don't pay attention to it. I travel around the country. I'm happy I have a good relationship with the people.'

We're in the long, private dining room of a restaurant in the Congo Town part of Monrovia, the scrappy capital scythed out of malarial jungle in the 19th century. On a side table are several local specialities including pepper soup with pig's feet, fufu (cassava flour pounded into a smooth paste) and 'check rice', which is 'beautified' with okra. There are dishes with meats, as well as vegetables including 'bennie' sesame seeds, 'parched in a skillet and pounded', according to one of Sirleaf's assistants.

I'm seated next to Sirleaf at the head table, which is laid with a regally red tablecloth and set with ornate gold-coloured underplates. She is dressed in a deep-blue headscarf, a striped jacket of local fabric and a long scarf decorated with the Liberian flag, a derivative of the Stars and Stripes.

Flanking us at the top table are the president's press secretary and information minister. Perpendicular is a long table with 18 chairs, at which are sat a smattering of aides and officials, also eating. Behind them are photographers and pen-pushers. Rather than an intimate lunch, it feels like we're being ogled by whispering courtiers.

I concentrate on Sirleaf. She is eating fufu and bitter leaf, a green vegetable commonly served in west Africa. It's the first time that I've seen anyone eat the former, a white sticky paste normally rolled into balls with one's fingers, with a knife and fork. No one had asked my preference, but I have been served the green-tinged check rice with a spicy curry sauce containing fish and the most succulent of shrimp. While Sirleaf is talking in her deliberate style, I busy myself prising off the translucent orange shells, popping the flesh into my mouth. 'I'm glad you like it,' she says when I signal my appreciation. 'Those are river shrimps. They're good.'

We're still discussing the past. The country had peculiar beginnings, I say of the freed slaves who came to Africa only to impose a form of quasi-slavery of their own. 'Very peculiar,' she agrees. 'That beginning has shaped some of our values, even today. The ostentatious lifestyle. A lot of socialization. The Antebellum South.'

On her paternal side, Sirleaf's grandmother was one of eight wives of a Gola chief. Her maternal grandmother was a market woman married to a German trader. Both women were 'totally illiterate', she says. As was the custom of the time, her mother and father were sent as 'wards' to families of the Americo-Liberian elite in Monrovia, the only plausible path out of poverty. Her father grew up to become a 'poor man lawyer' and, later, the first indigenous MP in Liberia's history. Her mother was a teacher and a preacher.

'She had an education, and my father had an education. And so they stressed education,' says Sirleaf. Born in 1938, she was ethnically indigenous, but socially she was considered part of the lighter-skinned ruling elite who once wore top hats and tails to distinguish themselves from the locals.

'If "Americo-Liberian" is defined as having a heritage in America, then definitely I'm not,' she says, taking a sip of water. I had been told she might order a beer, but she has not. Reluctantly, I join her in abstemiousness, no small sacrifice given the punishing humidity.

She was married at 17. 'There was just a handsome young man who came [back] from the United States,' she says wistfully, chewing on the algae-coloured bitter leaf. 'He had come home and we met at a party. That was it. My mother was a disciplinarian. She believed that when young girls start to go out with young boys, they get married.'

The couple had four boys and moved to America, where Sirleaf began studying accounting. 'I worked tables and did other types of things. I got back to school with determination to catch up with my former classmates and become a professional.' Sirleaf and her husband, who turned out to be abusive, eventually divorced: 'Of course, it puts strain on a marriage. That was to be expected,' she says, with deliberate understatement.

After a stint in Liberia's treasury in the early 1970s, she returned to the US, completing a masters at Harvard in public administration. By the end of the decade she was back in Liberia, where she rose to become finance minister, the position she held on the night of Doe's coup. Five years after those traumatic events, Doe sought to legitimize his repressive administration by holding elections. Sirleaf, who had been working for the World Bank in Washington and Citibank in Nairobi, returned to run for the senate. She was twice thrown in jail, once when she objected to what she said were rigged results, and later after a failed coup attempt against Doe. Released after eight months in July 1986, she headed back to the US.

It was around this time that she made a bad mistake: she helped fund rebel leader Charles Taylor, who unleashed a violent civil conflict in which 250,000 people – one in every 10 Liberians – were killed. Because she had backed him, Sirleaf was banned from politics for 30 years by Liberia's Truth and Reconciliation Commission, although the verdict was never enforced. 'I don't think $10,000 is what financed the war,' she tells me, referring to the size of her donation.

In fact, in 1997 Sirleaf lost a presidential election to Taylor, who ran on the slogan, 'He killed my ma, he killed my pa, but I will vote for him' – surely one of the most chilling appeals in electoral history. War raged until 2003, when Taylor fled the country. He was eventually convicted at The Hague for crimes against humanity.

I've made quick work of my shrimp and fancy trying the bitter leaf. While the waitress goes off to get some we talk about the 2005 presidential elections, in which Sirleaf defeated the country's footballing idol George Weah. She took charge of a destroyed country, one virtually bereft of roads and electricity and with an army of unemployed youth. 'We've done a lot to restore basic services,' she says, adding that she negotiated successfully to write off much of the national debt and to attract investment. The country began to rebuild and to grow quickly, albeit from a desperately low base.

Yet she's not happy. 'We have not changed the mindset. We have not changed attitudes toward honesty, integrity, hard work. Maybe our educational system has failed us,' she says, almost to herself. 'I don't know. Maybe we've had too much turmoil. It's a history of boom, bust,' she says of an economy whose fortunes have been almost entirely dependent on the vagaries of the weather and commodity prices. 'Things are moving up. All of a sudden, boom.' Her hand explodes over the table. 'Something happens. Whatever it is. Boom. Then we start to climb again. Boom.'

Of late, Liberia has been knocked sideways again, this time by the collapse of rubber and iron ore prices and by the eruption of Ebola, which sent fear around the country as it felled nearly 5,000 victims. 'When are we going to have that continuous climb that will produce enough jobs, that will reduce tensions in society?' she laments.

Doesn't her government bear some responsibility, I ask? After all, stories of corruption are rife. They can't all be made up. 'We hear it and we know it,' she says. 'We've dismissed a lot of people. People are being prosecuted now.' But has anyone senior gone to jail? 'Yes, people have gone to jail. There may not be a minister as yet, but people have been to jail.'

I'm eating the bitter leaf. It's not what I had expected. Underneath the foliage are lurking dark meats, too strong for my taste. Later I read on the menu that they included cow skin and cow foot. I slurp some water to take the taste away.

'The integrity issue is systemic,' she says. I tell her I was stopped by police, only a few days before, at a makeshift roadblock. 'Somebody wanted money from you,' she snorts. 'Integrity is a long-standing issue in this country. What contribution does deprivation make to this? What contribution does poverty make to this? What contribution does dependency make to this?'

Isn't Liberia itself in a permanent state of dependency, I say, pointing to its constant need for donor cash. 'We've been too dependent for too long on giveaways,' she concedes, adding that the country has been a rubber exporter for decades but has never produced a single tyre. 'Our budget should be at a much higher level,' she says of the tiny amount at her government's disposal.

Suddenly she is pointing menacingly at a young waitress. 'Do you pay taxes?' demands the president, eliciting a nervous giggle from the startled girl.

'You're terrifying her,' I say.

'She's smiling,' says Sirleaf without amusement, as if to say that of course she doesn't pay taxes. Finally, she releases the waitress from her gaze.

If she's so down on corruption, I say, why does she not counter accusations of nepotism when it comes to her own sons, one of whom is head of national security, another the interim governor of the central bank and a third the chair of the board of the national oil company – until it went bust? 'I will make no apologies for any of them,' she says, after giving me a detailed explanation of why each was suited to the job. 'I don't have a long list of qualified people.'

But doesn't it look terrible? 'I trusted them. They had the skills. And I knew that they shared my values,' she says, unrepentant.

Terra Cotta Bar & Restaurant
Oldest Congo Town,
Tubman Boulevard,
Monrovia

....

Bitter leaf with fufu, chicken and dried fish	US$50
Pepper soup with fresh fish and pig feet	US$50
Check rice with fish and prawn	US$50
Fufu and soup	US$50
Hall rental	US$100

....

Total (inc. tax) –	US$321
	(£220)

Sirleaf has finished her food and turns down a second helping. The waitress, recovered from her ordeal, brings me sticky fried plantains. I'd like coffee, but none is offered.

Her presidency ends after next year's election, but is she tempted to stay on? 'Our constitution forbids it,' she replies. That's not been much of an impediment for other African leaders, I say. 'Our people wouldn't take it. And my age wouldn't allow it,' she replies. 'I think we're ready for succession. We just must try to do it right.'

I end by asking about her autobiography. The title, *This Child Will Be Great*, doesn't suggest disappointment with the outcome of her life. 'When I was born, this old man went into the room where I was lying on the bed, and he just looked at me and said: "Oh, this child will be great,"' she says. 'And so we all laughed about it and, over the years, with the ups and downs, we used to tease my mother and say: "That old man didn't know what he was talking about."' Then she adds, regretfully, of her mother's death in the mid-1980s: 'She didn't live long enough to see it come to pass.'

She pauses. 'Maybe he was a prophet. Because I'm confident that I've done a good job. I know that history will judge me the best president up until this point.' Better than Samuel Doe and Charles Taylor, I tease. It's hardly a high bar. She's looking at me again with that piercing gaze. It's hard to tell whether she's annoyed or amused. Then she smiles at me indulgently. 'That's fair,' she says.

Nigel Farage

'For God's sake, I am what I am'

By Henry Mance

Nigel Farage has an adjective for the good things in life: 'proper'. Proper blokes, proper jobs, proper markets. And when we meet at The Lamb, a pub in London's Leadenhall Market, he clearly is in the mood for a proper lunch. 'Have we got an order in?' the leader of the UK Independence Party exclaims within two minutes of our arrival. 'A man could die of thirst in here.'

This was Farage's local pub when he was a trader on the London Metal Exchange. When he started in the 1980s, the City was a fantastic gentlemen's club. 'Now it's like being a battery chicken,' he sighs.

Farage, in contrast, is a free-range bull. He once labelled the European Council president a 'damp rag', and said Britons should be 'concerned if a group of Romanian people suddenly moved in next door'. Supporters call him the boss man; opponents call him a racist. He is, undoubtedly, Britain's most effective Brussels-basher, the man without whom there would be no EU referendum in June.

Ukip is the biggest new party to emerge in Britain since Labour a century ago. It won 3.8 million votes in last year's general election, as many as the Scottish Nationalists and Liberal Democrats combined, and is likely to gain dozens of seats in local elections in May.

Yet as Farage jovially plunges into his pint of ale, there is a sense that he may be losing his touch. Academics argue that his rhetoric puts off the very moderates whose votes will decide the in/out referendum. Ukip has also slipped into civil war. Farage is not on speaking terms with its sole member of parliament, Douglas Carswell; critics say he is incapable of sharing the limelight. 'The cult of personality is very strong,' says one Ukipper. 'They'd be better off ditching him,' says a Tory MP.

Illustration by James Ferguson

An easy question to answer is, does Farage want a second pint? A harder one is, might he soon be as outdated as his overcoat?

We head outside, where Farage can smoke. The son of an alcoholic Kent stockbroker, he joined the City aged 18 from London's prestigious Dulwich College, and then became convinced that Britain needed a more Eurosceptic party than the Conservatives. 'I'd been predicting a commodity boom all through the 1990s. Politics took over and I bloody well missed it!' he jokes.

A passer-by intercedes: 'I thought it was a doppelgänger but it's actually you!' Farage is delighted. Voters yearn for a politician they'd like to have a beer with; finally here's a politician who'd take up the offer. 'Every pub's a parliament!' he enthuses.

The Lamb serves food but Farage, 52, has other plans. We walk down Cornhill to Simpson's Tavern – London's oldest surviving chophouse, where he has been a customer for more than 30 years. 'Sadly, most of the waitresses have changed,' he says.

Most of the waitresses have not changed, it seems. 'Haven't seen you here for a while, Nigel,' says one, pouring him a pint before the door has shut behind me. I survey the clientele and conclude that there's unlikely to be a queue for the women's toilets. 'I love it here,' beams Farage.

We take our third pint to the courtyard. An hour gone, and the alcohol we've consumed is already half the recommended weekly limit. 'I know. It's just ludicrous,' says Farage, resting on an old beer barrel, his mood livelier than his grey suit suggests. He reaches for his third cigarette. 'They'll be telling us this is bad for us next. They want to live for ever!'

I ask about his hobby: visiting first world war battlefields. Farage opens up. 'Whenever I go there, I always think, what would I have done? If I was a 19-year-old, fresh out of college . . . would I have been a proper man or not?'

Our table is ready inside. We squeeze alongside each other on a wooden bench with our backs to the window. Farage orders the house speciality – stewed cheese – for both of us, and picks a bottle of wine. For me, this is now entering stag-party territory; for him, it's little more than holy communion. 'The thing we used to drink here was port,' he says. 'We'd all go back to work, all crimson. That's just what we did! No one cared. I don't drink port at all now, ever.'

What happened in the afternoons? 'Chaos. Extraordinary. I remember once there was a really big cock-up . . . I remember the boss saying, "So when did this happen?" "Half past four yesterday afternoon." "Oh well, there we are then." The boss accepted this!'

Farage is quick to depict politics as a sacrifice. 'I'm a loopy optimist, aren't I?' he says. 'I like to think I've changed the centre of gravity on lots of national debates. But there is no life at all – nothing.' It would be even worse, he says, if he'd succeeded in his seventh attempt to enter parliament last year. 'Can you imagine if I'd been elected to Westminster? I'd need to be there every day.'

He has four children, two with his second wife, Kirsten, who is German. In the 2000s, he twice had to remortgage his house in Kent. 'My financial position is slightly better than it was, but for about 10 years it was pretty rough,' he says. How is it better? 'It just is. Slightly better. There we are,' he says, drawing a boundary.

The cheese arrives, and Farage smears his white toast with sauce. 'Yeah, mustard, yeah, lovely, proper job!' he says, reaching for the Lea & Perrins. He is right – it's wonderful. The wine, a fruity Bordeaux, is excellent too. I should visit the 1980s more often.

An old friend of Farage's arrives at a neighbouring table and points at the paper napkin around Farage's collar. 'You must be meeting someone important if you've got that tucked in there!' Farage laughs, carefree. 'Is it a proper lunch, Kevin?' he asks his friend. 'No, we've got a meeting later,' comes the reply. 'They were the days, Kevin,' says Farage, 'they were the days.'

Accused of nostalgia, however, he turns serious. 'The club was lovely, but the club wasn't very efficient. It had to change. The sadness is – this is where I may be nostalgic – the people whose working lives are on computers, they're not as fulfilling as working lives that are actually meeting people doing stuff.'

Farage orders the Edwardian pork chop, well done, with a sausage. 'I can't help it, I love pork chop.' It's my turn. 'Lamb chops? Pork chops?' Farage suggests. 'Mixed grill?' offers the waitress. I order goat's cheese in filo pastry.

There is a pause while Farage's ears relay the news to his brain. 'What? No. They shouldn't serve rubbish like that here. Goat's cheese? I mean . . . Goat's cheese?' He turns to the waitress. 'You can't give him bloody goat's cheese.' I look up at her for sympathy; she looks back with contempt. Farage continues: 'You're not a veggie, are you, or something like that? If you are, fine. But what on earth are you doing here, then?'

And for a brief moment I know how the Romanians must feel.

We move on to less controversial matters, such as the EU. Many of Europe's other populist leaders – Italy's Beppe Grillo, Greece's Alexis Tsipras, even Hungary's Viktor Orbán – are popular among young voters. Farage's success has relied on the old.

I ask if his obsession with past wars informs his combative approach to Europe. He protests: 'If things aren't going swimmingly, there's an argument for radical growth and reform.'

If you don't like that line, he has others – and he delivers them brilliantly. 'I love Europe! France is wonderful. It should be. We've subsidized it for 40 years.' He croaks with laughter, and I find myself joining in.

'For seven years, I had a business relationship in Milan, Milano,' Farage continues. 'Dealing with Italians, just, let me tell you . . . Are we the same? Good lord, no! That's why Europe's fun – it's fun because it's different. A political project that seeks to make it all the same – it's ghastly.'

How would he have voted in Britain's previous European referendum in 1975, had he been old enough? 'I'd have voted "yes",' he says, citing the need to bring down tariff barriers.

What about trade now, I ask? Surely the UK wouldn't be able to negotiate trade deals as easily if it left the EU? 'Iceland managed it!' he shoots back. But on what terms? 'They're happy! Switzerland's happy!'

Still, leaving the EU is hardly likely to answer the UK's problems, I say. 'I've been quite clear: it's not a silver bullet,' he replies, arguing that Brexit will simply give Britain more control of its own affairs. But many of the things that vex Ukip voters are trends beyond the gift of politicians – our future wages will depend more on automation than the EU. 'My friend Jim Mellon has been telling me this for a couple of years,' says Farage. 'That robotics are way more advanced than people think, and that we're going to have a massive social problem.'

I ask if he remembers any particular trades from his City days. He blusters for a while, concluding, 'The great skill of investment is to know when the right time is to get out. Getting in's easy.'

So when does he get out of Ukip? 'Good question. Well asked. Where's my chop? I'm ravenous.' Informed that a well-done chop takes

35 minutes, he decides that he needs a cigarette more than I need an answer.

Eventually the chef taps on the window – the chop is done. But Farage has been dragged away by his Nokia, bringing news of Ukip in-fighting. He returns a few minutes later with a face like a National Front manifesto.

We sit down to our meal, and I gently ask if the party will really suspend Carswell, its only MP. 'I don't care,' he says in a tone that indicates that he probably does. 'The level of support I have within Ukip is phenomenal. The fact that some people don't like it – well, there you are.'

Farage's voice is now a series of bangs, like books falling off a shelf. I ponder the obvious way to lighten the mood: pour him more wine. But when I ask if it's true that he's in favour of legalizing drugs, he still spies a trap. 'This is the wrong time to ask me that question – we've got a referendum to fight. So you're not going to get the answer you want,' he says. 'But if ever there was a subject that needed a genuine royal commission . . . this is the issue.'

Few of his supporters would agree with that, or with his fairly liberal view of gay marriage. 'What you're saying is I'm not a pigeonholed right-wing Tory. No. I'm more of an old liberal in some ways. I think the state should butt out,' he says, his guard still up. 'I'm not as easily pigeonholed as people would like.'

I try to keep pace on the wine, remembering that Farage once took two bottles of gin to an election debate at Methodist Central Hall. In such debates, he excels. Countering him with statistics rarely works. How can opponents beat him? 'Try to make me angry.'

Right now his focus is on touring the country. 'Most people in politics, they view the people as a slight inconvenience,' Farage says. How does he persuade people? 'You actually mustn't try too hard with this stuff. The skill of this is to make people believe they've made their own minds up . . . If they ask you a question, that's their flick switch.' He stresses his reasonableness. 'I'm not this wild-eyed populist that's descended from the hills . . . I pick and choose what I do, what I say.'

Critics say his appeal is limited to those who are already converted. The thought riles him. 'Am I a bit of a blokeish bloke? Yes. Should I change my image? This is what they tell me – these people who come in and want jobs. I should feminize.' He's enjoying himself again. 'I mean, for God's sake. I am what I am.' Fine – but was it really necessary, I ask, to compare the EU to a serial date rapist? 'We can't even tell a joke!' he responds.

Our meals have disappeared and I wonder if I've made it through to coffee. Farage looks at his watch. 'Oooh, gosh,' he exclaims, and I assume the double espresso will have to wait. He turns to a waitress. 'That was amazing. We've got work to do. But we could do with a large port each before we go. Makes sense, doesn't it?' To him, at least.

I ask if he's a fan of that other embodiment of English nostalgia, the poet John Betjeman. His eyes widen with schoolboy enthusiasm. 'Mega. Huge! I love Betjeman, I adore Betjeman, I've visited his grave several times.' He recites a couplet about sportsman C. B. Fry, and eases himself back into tales of Dulwich College and the first world war.

Before the last general election, Farage vowed to resign as Ukip leader if he failed to win a seat in parliament – then reversed course. Was the promise a mistake? 'Of course.' What will he do if he loses the referendum? 'I haven't got a clue,' he says.

Arguably, he loses either way: if Britain votes to leave the EU, Boris Johnson takes the credit; if it remains a member, Ukip crumbles. Farage demurs. 'This is not a greasy pole for me,' he says, before hinting at a broader programme of shaking up Westminster.

The port arrives and we move into the following week's alcohol allowance. I broach the subject of Enoch Powell, the previous bearer of the anti-immigrant flame, who warned of rivers of blood in 1968. Farage once drove him to an event. 'Powell was

The Lamb	
Leadenhall Market, London EC3	
Pint of ale x 4	£16

Simpson's Tavern	
38½ Cornhill, London EC3	
Pint of ale x 2	£9
Stewed cheese x 2	£9
Chump chop and sausage	£16.60
Goat's cheese in filo pastry	£10
Side orders x 2	£8
Bottle of Château de Lugagnac 2012	£36
Large glass of port x 2	£17
Tip	£12
Total (inc. ales at The Lamb) –	£133.60

brilliant in so many ways – militarily, intellectually,' he says. 'I don't want to be Enoch Powell, do I? I don't want to be right, but get the politics of it badly wrong.'

Before we can finish our port, our host brings us a complimentary top-up. Farage is outside for another cigarette. He has a new set of admirers: the old boys' rugby team from Dulwich College are drinking port from a silver ladle. Soon Farage has a ladle of port in one hand and his glass of port in the other.

It has started to rain but Farage isn't quite finished. He leads me round the corner to admire the worn steps of London's oldest coffee house, the Jamaica Wine House. We return to Simpson's to fetch our coats. I reach into my pocket to find the remains of a Marks & Spencer bread roll that I had hoped would line my stomach.

'I hope it was different to most *FT* lunches,' says Farage affectionately, glowing with pride or port. 'I must say goodbye to the bloody girls.' He pops back inside, then strides off towards the City – enchanted by the past, borne back ceaselessly into the present.

Emmerson Mnangagwa

'I'm not a crocodile'

By Alec Russell

A few weeks ago – and less than a month into his new life as an ex-president – Robert Mugabe received a rather awkward telephone call. It was his protégé on the line. Emmerson Mnangagwa, Zimbabwe's new president, aka the Crocodile, had a quibble. He had just been asked to sign off on the passenger list for a state-funded flight the 93-year-old was planning to take to Singapore – the entourage was 38 strong – for the former leader of one of the world's most indebted nations to go for a health check.

Mnangagwa, a careful man with the build of a prizefighter and the conversational precision of a lawyer, has reached the climax of a half-hour account of his 54-year relationship with the founding father of the nation.

'I phoned back and said: "Chef, you are going for a medical check-up. Why do you want 38 people?" He said: "Emmerson, I don't know that list. I know it's myself, my wife and my family." I said: "No. You know the new dispensation . . . it's a leaner cabinet. That can't be understood if you are going to go for a medical check-up with a big number." He says: "Emmerson" –' Mnangagwa pauses for comic effect – 'He never says Mr President. He just calls me Emmerson.'

Mnangagwa sits back and laughs. It echoes around the grand thatched lodge where we are having a late lunch. Aides, security staff, join in enthusiastically. Sycophancy? A touch, maybe. If so, who could blame them? But it seems more than that: Zimbabweans are rather enjoying the freedom to joke in public about their long-time autocratic overlord.

The president recounts how an abashed Mugabe eventually reduced his entourage by nearly half, although he did end up taking a 767 to Singapore and back for just 22 people. Apparently the man whose economic mismanagement fuelled one of the worst cases of hyperinflation since the Weimar Republic rang from Singapore seeking a smaller plane for the

Illustration by James Ferguson

return trip, but the memo never reached Air Zimbabwe. The checkpoints that littered Harare in the late-Mugabe era may have gone, I think, but some things are harder to change. We are an hour into our encounter, late on Tuesday afternoon, in Harare's eastern suburbs. A wood owl whoops from the garden. A rumble of thunder signals a summer storm. I am weighing the question whose answer will decide Zimbabwe's fate. Is the 75-year-old politician sitting beside me a latter-day Gorbachev/de Klerk, apparatchiks who came to power with dyed-in-the-wool reputations but then pushed for reform and accelerated the collapse of the *ancien régime*? Is he a Zimbabwean version of Paul Kagame, the authoritarian leader of Rwanda who prizes economic growth over individual rights? Or, as a veteran functionary of the ruling Zanu-PF party, will he prove unwilling to take on its corrupted ways? Mugabe may be plaintive but he is not penurious. Just before the new year the government approved a swanky pension package including up to 23 staff and four international trips a year. I ask if Mugabe will have amnesty in the event of an investigation into abuses on his watch. Mnangagwa looks surprised. An ex-president loses the immunity he had in office, he concedes. But he adds he doesn't see 'any possibility of us taking him to court or prosecuting him for anything. He's our father figure . . . our founding father. We'll do everything in our power to keep him happy.'

And yet Mnangagwa leaves little doubt he has no time now for his old patron – and no wonder after the drama of late last year. In eight frenetic weeks he narrowly survived an apparent assassination attempt via a supposedly poisoned ice-cream cone; he was denounced by Mugabe's wife, Grace, as the head of a snake that had to be crushed; and he had to flee into exile. Then after 15 days in South Africa and a brief military takeover – coup is a word not officially recognized in Harare these days – Mugabe stepped down, and Mnangagwa returned to be inaugurated as Zimbabwe's new president.

Now he is preparing for his debut on the world stage at next week's Davos meeting of global business leaders, where he will present himself as the man to deliver Zimbabwe from rogue nation status. For my last Lunch with the *FT* in Zimbabwe, seven years ago with Morgan Tsvangirai, the bluff and brave leader of the opposition, I had to enter the country illegally. As Zimbabwe spiralled into disarray, Mugabe abhorred the press. He tended to give one interview a year on his birthday and that was to the state media. He was also a stickler for protocol.

Not so it seems the new president. When I arrived for our rendezvous at his chosen venue, the Amanzi Lodge, I found him on his own by the palm-tree-fringed pool. He had been waiting for 15 minutes, making personal calls. However cosmetic this may ultimately prove – and much is still up for grabs – there is a new zip in the presidency. Mugabe's notoriously elastic timekeeping is at an end.

The waiter arrives to take our order. The president looks up and dead-pans: 'No crocodile meat, please.'

'I'm not a crocodile,' he muses, more, it seems, to set the record straight than out of irritation. I had asked if the moniker irks him. (He says it doesn't.) In Zimbabwean tradition, he explains, his family totem is an even more fearsome predator. 'I'm a lion. It's the former president who has the crocodile totem.' But the Crocodile tag has stuck for decades and spawned very different interpretations. In recent years, with the ruling party divided between his allies and the faction of Grace Mugabe, his cohort was known as the Lacoste grouping, after the designer emblem. Crocodiles, he has said, are known for their strategic patience – all too appropriate given how long he waited in Mugabe's shadow.

For his opponents, however, it is the snapping jaws that are more apt. Zimbabwe's new president is a hard man. He was head of intelligence during the subjugation of Matabeleland in the early 1980s when North Korean-trained forces killed as many as 20,000 people in the southern region. He also oversaw the tainted election campaign in 2008 when the security forces clamped down on the opposition Movement for Democratic Change after it became clear it had defeated Zanu-PF in the parliamentary poll and won the first round of the presidential race. On these two counts alone, the opposition argue, the new guard is no more than old wine in new bottles.

As we move to the restaurant, adorned with hangings, sculptures and furniture from across sub-Saharan Africa, I ask how he reacted when Mugabe turned against him last year. He replies by taking me back to their early encounters in his youth in the liberation movement in the 1960s when he was in charge of a sabotage unit dubbed the Crocodile Group. The president recounts its members and then in some surprise realizes the others are all dead. 'I am the only survivor.'

At this point the wine waiter appears. We agree on a bottle of Steenberg Syrah. The many *FT* readers who abhor 'dry' Lunches are lucky, it seems. It is, the president explains, his 'wet season' – a tradition that dates back 40 years. In 1978 a member of the high command of the liberation army died of cirrhosis of the liver. The overall commander rebuked his subordinates and said they had to vow to limit their alcohol: a week on and a week off or a month on, a month off. 'I chose six months. No wine. No beer. No whisky.' His 'wet season' starts at midnight on New Year's Eve.

Mnangagwa only narrowly survived his time in the Crocodile Group. After blowing up a train he was captured by the white minority regime, tortured by being hung upside down, and then had a stint on death row before a decade in prison. It is a tale well known in Zimbabwe and of course a distraction from the issues at hand, but a reminder of the layers of Zimbabwe's recent history. He only escaped being hanged because of his youth – he was just under the official age of majority of 21. It prompted, he tells me, his only recorded public dispute with Mugabe, over the death penalty. As president he will push for its abolition.

Our starters, picked from the African-American fusion menu, have arrived: Chiang Mai chicken soup for him and spinach koftas with turmeric and mustard for me. I urge him to eat but he moves to the other life-and-death drama of his career – last year's showdown with Grace Mugabe.

The night before the lunch, a public servant with years of experience of the government reflected to me that factionalism was the lifeblood of Zanu-PF. 'Without it, it will die,' he said. Mugabe was certainly a past master of playing off one would-be successor against another. But this game became more complicated last year as Mugabe's wife, Grace – nicknamed Gucci Grace by opposition media for her spending habits – appeared to gain a taste for power herself. As Mugabe became increasingly frailer in public, her faction, known as G40, became locked in a public battle for the succession. Then in August came the most extraordinary episode yet.

George Charamba, the sardonic spokesman of Mugabe, now with the new guard, and the effervescent Zimbabwean novelist Petina Gappah have joined our table. She is one of the former critics who dare to hope their homeland can really change – and badgered the presidency to break with its traditional reserve and agree to an interview. We three barely pick at our food as Mnangagwa tells a story redolent of Nero's court, when every senator with sense had a taster.

Shortly after a rally Mnangagwa was rushed to hospital. He had, he says, been poisoned. 'They kept me going by washing me out.' He had 28 sachets attached to one arm at one stage, he adds. 'The doctors say it [the poison] was hard-metal arsenic toxin. They say it's colourless, it's tasteless and the areas where it could be found are possibly two. Russia and Israel. They were surprised I survived.'

His supporters pointed the finger at Grace Mugabe, saying he was the victim of a poisoned vanilla ice-cream cone. She was also linked to the incident by innuendo because she and her husband co-own one of Zimbabwe's biggest dairies. I ask who was responsible. Mnangagwa havers.

'I suspect who did it. They are still good friends of mine. They now know that I know.' Whatever the truth of this bizarre episode, the G40 faction has been subjected to the full fury of the new order. Members have been arrested and had assets seized. Others have fled into exile and are regularly denounced in the state press. The opposition has long urged a crackdown on corruption but they have a caveat about this move: to date no one in the army – long a player in the predations of the economy – nor in the Lacoste group has been targeted.

There was one last explosive act in the drama. Some weeks later he received an official letter from Mugabe firing him. That evening, 'officials from security services came and said: "Sir, we are part of a group charged with the task to eliminate you. So you must leave now." I said: "Where?" They said: "Just leave because we are going to pick you up tonight and we will poison you, we will kill you, then put a string around your neck and say you hanged yourself."' He fled across the Mozambican border on foot with two of his sons and ended up in South Africa. He was there, in close contact with President Jacob Zuma, an old friend from the liberation struggle, when the army played the pivotal role intervening to stop the G40 takeover of the party and to bring down the curtain on Mugabe's rule.

Mnangagwa insists to me that the generals did not contact him before making their first statement about taking charge. But the suspicion remains that he is in hock to the generals, many of whom have long prospered from Zanu-PF rule. The first to announce the military move was one Major General S. B. Moyo. Now the new minister of foreign affairs, he was named in a UN report as having benefited from Zimbabwe's incursion into the Congo nearly 20 years ago. The new vice-president, Constantino Chiwenga, is another new ex-general, who was head of the army until a month ago.

The sun is setting. Our starters are cleared away. As I embark on my main course, a butter chicken curry, I look across the darkening restaurant to another corner table and reflect on the misfortunes of the last politician I interviewed at the Amanzi.

It was at that table nearly a decade ago, a day or so after the March 2008 election, I had breakfast with Tsvangirai. He was on cloud nine thinking he had won the poll – as indeed he had. But that was the high point of his career. He eventually pulled out of the race in the face of brutal intimidation – overseen by none other than my guest. He is now stricken with cancer, his party riven with splits, and he has lost his greatest campaigning asset – President Robert Mugabe – clearing the way for Zanu-PF to claim the mantle of change.

The president had originally been uncertain about eating anything at all. But an hour of reminiscing about close shaves had clearly piqued his appetite. He is tucking into the chef's special, Thai baked bream with Asian greens and a ginger soy sauce, as he makes his pitch. Zimbabwe is due parliamentary and presidential elections by August. At home they are a critical test of his legitimacy. For the rest of the world the staging of a genuinely free and fair election is a critical test of the elite's commitment to change. For donors familiar with countless failed pledges this would be a key first step to restoring credibility and unlocking a new debt relief agreement. So he tells me, the world and his wife are welcome to monitor them.

'With this new dispensation I don't feel threatened by anything. I would want that the United Nations should come, the EU should come. If the Commonwealth were requesting to come, I am disposed to consider their application.' Mugabe had no interest in allowing potentially critical observers to look at his elections. The acceptance of UN monitors, not just for Election Day, but for the campaign and ideally preceding months, would be a genuine breakthrough – even if the opposition rightly suggest it says as much about Zanu-PF's confidence at the polls as a desire to change.

The president was not finished. Britain, he suggested, was keen to talk about their rejoining the Commonwealth after almost two decades in the cold. He added that he was, too, and that he would seek direct discussions about it after a meeting of the African Union in February. As for the old colonial power, Britain, with which Mugabe had a love-hate relationship: Brexit, he said, could bring the two nations back together.

'Breaking out of . . . Brex. How do you call it? Brexit. Yes, it's a good thing because they will need us. And we will make sure we become very close to them. What they've lost with Brexit they can come and recover from Zimbabwe.' He even predicted that Zimbabwe's Hawk jets would soon be back in the air. They have been grounded after Britain, the only country that can supply spare parts, banned their sale in 2000 in protest at human rights abuses.

In a closing flourish, recalling Margaret Thatcher who was prime minister in Mugabe's first decade in power, he suggested Britain should always have women prime ministers. 'They are more sensible than their male counterparts. The guy we didn't like is that young man Tony Blair [who challenged Zimbabwe over human rights abuse]. I don't know where he is now.'

The message is clear. He wants to open a new chapter, and pretty much without conditions. He cites Germany, France, Britain of course, which has been eagerly pushing itself forward, and Spain as prospective partners. He makes no mention of the US, which has been scrupulously cautious to avoid any endorsement. By now courses and drinks are coming and going as Lunch with the *FT* morphs into a dress rehearsal for a diplomatic summit.

He outlines a new order where Zimbabwe stays close to China – 'a country that has stood by us in difficult times' – while embracing the west. 'We introduced the Look East policy, but let me remind you that was a survival policy.' As he reminds me, he has an old relationship with China, dating back to his youth when he had military training there.

When I raise the concern cited by South Africa's former president Thabo Mbeki a decade ago that China could develop a colonial-style relationship with Africa, he dismisses it. He is heading to Beijing soon after Davos to negotiate 'mega deals in infrastructure and railways'.

Years of profligacy and the ruling party's exploitation of prime economic resources have led to chronic indebtedness, soaring fiscal imbalances and a liquidity crisis. The IMF estimates foreign debt is

$9.4 billion, or 52 per cent of GDP, and is forecast to rise to more than $10 billion this year. He mouths appropriate pledges of being open for business, although investors will want to see him act on his words. The indigenization law which decreed that investors hand a 51 per cent stake to a Zimbabwean partner is, he reiterated, over. 'It's not in the mortuary, it's in the departure lounge,' he says when I ask if it is truly dead. 'The entire economy is open except for two minerals: diamonds and platinum. The rest is open.' (The army is known to have interests in the diamonds, an industry that has been plundered in recent years.) He concedes that the economy is terribly indebted but dismisses the need for scrapping the bond notes, a form of banknote issued in 2016 in theory pegged to the US dollar. Many businesspeople are crying out for them to go in the search for clarity about exchange rates and money supply. He agrees government expenditure is too high before disingenuously blaming it on the west's targeted sanctions against the elite rather than on Zanu-PF's failure to balance a budget. As for land, which sparked the economic and political crises of the past 20 years, he reiterates his pledge to compensate the commercial farmers who lost their titles. When I ask how it will be paid for, he indicates that productivity is improving fast.

By now the head waiter has the dessert menu and is trying to catch the president's eye. There is only one on the menu, fruit salad with, er, ice cream. (The Amanzi only had a couple of hours' notice that the president was on his way.) A boisterous debate ensues around the table as to whether it is right – or safe – to have ice cream. Diplomatically the waiter opts to ignore the president's and Petina's request for vanilla ice cream and serves us just fruit salad.

The recent history of southern Africa has been marked by liberation movements staying on past their sell-by date, blurring the distinction of party and state and immiserating their people. Now, as if in lockstep, Zimbabwe and South Africa are seeking to defy that trend. When I put this declinist thesis to Mnangagwa, he says 'new generations are coming to the helm' – a claim at odds with the reality of his new cabinet.

A theory repeatedly put to me in Harare was that he sees himself as the Deng Xiaoping of Zimbabwe. Another favoured by the opposition is that Britain in particular will settle for stability, if that ensures a growing economy, over true democracy – a trade-off the west has implicitly endorsed in Rwanda. So is he a would-be latter-day Deng? 'I met Deng with President Mugabe I think around 1977 or 1978. Let me assure you I am not Deng.' He concedes though that some are saying he's looking at opening the economy as Deng unleashed China's.

Two hours have passed and his aides signal time is up. What about a sweeping gesture of reconciliation and an apology for the massacres in Matabeleland? The cautious old pro has broken enough ground for one afternoon. He will not be drawn. He refers me to his recent signing of the National Peace and Reconciliation Bill. 'From the past we must take what is good and leave behind what is bad.'

He hands me an apron with the headline 'Crocodile Stew'. Underneath are culinary guidelines such as: 'Beat crocs over the heads with a sledgehammer.' My last sight of the Crocodile is when his official car with the number plate Zimbabwe One roars off into the night.

The only time I spoke to Mugabe in 24 years off and on covering Zimbabwe was at an election rally in 1994 where he gave a sprightly account of his record. Back then Zimbabwe was southern Africa's island of stability rather than the shambles it is today. Since then I have interviewed five liberation movement leaders and all but one have disappointed. Mnangagwa can buck that trend. But that requires two leaps of faith. He will have to shed the crocodile's traditional patience. He will also have to turn his jaws on some of his own kind.

Amanzi Lodge

1 Masasa Lane, Kambanji, Harare

Chicken laksa x 2	$20
Thai-style baked fish x 3	$75
Spinach koftas	$8
Butter chicken x 3	$75
Spicy butternut soup	$8
Mineral water x 15	$30
Stoney ginger beer	$2
Bottle of Steenberg Syrah x 2	$112
Fruit salad x 3	$24
Herbal tea	$2
Melted Mars bars x 2	$16
Total (inc. tax) –	$372

Sheryl Sandberg

'Marry the nerds and good guys'

By Hannah Kuchler

Facebook's chief operating officer is famous for being more open than most executives: about crying in the bathroom at work, or how, as a recent widow, she slept in the same bed as her mother. This is fitting for a company that has redefined the word 'sharing'. As we settle into our lunch, however, it is clear openness does not exactly mean spontaneity. Sandberg has to be one of the most on-message executives. Talking about business, she uses such a set phraseology I can almost recite her lines for her. New products are not only in 'early days' but being introduced in a 'privacy-protected way'. When, at one point, I ask her how she could best describe what it is like to suddenly be a single parent, she confesses it is 'lonely, scary sometimes', then briskly broadens her point to include the plight of poorer single mothers across the US – with statistics.

Then again, a script may be essential. The past two years have shaken Sandberg and Facebook, forcing both to grapple with existential questions. The loss of her husband, Dave Goldberg, who died of a heart attack while exercising when the couple were on holiday in Mexico in 2015, has meant bringing up two children without their father. The company has faced mounting criticism over whether it is doing enough to regulate itself amid the rise of fake news and its own growing power to shape events, including last year's US election. What this means for the biggest social network, which has almost 2 billion users and raked in $10 billion profit last year, is still unclear.

We're at Sol, a Mexican restaurant on Facebook's Menlo Park campus, a Disney-style fake main street complete with a cupcake shop and a nail bar. Sandberg has never eaten here. In fact, she tells me, I am the first person to tempt her away from lunch at her desk in her nine years at

Illustration by James Ferguson

Facebook. When she arrives at the restaurant with a handler I wonder if it is because she needed help finding it.

'This is so exciting,' she claims, once I have explained that no one else can join us for lunch. Usually she has soup or salad at her desk at the centre of Facebook's huge open-plan floor. Enthused by the laminated orange menu, she opts for a 'big salad with chicken on it'. I choose the enchiladas al guajillo, a recipe from the owners' great-grandmother.

Sandberg's personal tragedy followed a series of extraordinary career triumphs. After working as chief of staff for Larry Summers at the US Treasury, she moved to become vice-president of operations at Google. Since arriving at Facebook in 2008 she has been responsible for transforming it into a $432 billion business, earning herself a fortune worth $1.6 billion, according to *Forbes*. The success of her first book, *Lean In* (2013), a bestseller that pushes women to be more ambitious, made her a high-profile advocate for women's rights.

Everything changed when Goldberg died. Grief-stricken, and out of 'desperation' to connect with people, Sandberg eventually sought solace in writing a Facebook post. Connect she did: users shared the post 400,000 times and wrote about dealing with death in the comments.

'I had no desire to share my personal story within that post,' she says now. 'I know why I did it, which is because there is so much silence. It wasn't just the grief. It was the total isolation.'

Her thoughts on how mourners suffer when they are ignored are characteristically can-do: she suggests friends who worry that 'How are you?' is a silly question, should instead ask 'How are you today?' because it accepts the turbulence of grieving.

Encouraged by the reaction to her post, she wrote *Option B*, with her friend Adam Grant, a Wharton professor. Published last month, the book combines her journals with research on resilience after grief and setbacks. Sandberg says she didn't know she was writing a book at first. 'If I didn't journal for a few days, I felt like I was literally going to burst.' Then writing became more than cathartic, a way to honour her husband's life.

Do people still ask her, 'How are you today?' 'Sometimes,' she says. 'A grief expert told me one of the things that the book does is I get to keep talking about Dave. But for a lot of people, year two is a lot of silences. People have moved on. They don't feel like they should bring it up, they don't want to bring it up.'

The second anniversary of Goldberg's death is this month. When I ask what she is planning, her eyes moisten. She says she will defer to her kids. 'I still want to celebrate the day he was born, but if I could close my eyes and not live [for one day] . . . I would,' she says.

One of the surprises of *Option B* is its humour. Was that intentional? 'I don't know. It's that you feel like you lose the right to be happy, and the right to joke, so jokes feel bad. Happiness feels bad. Dating feels bad. Everything that could be joyful. Watching a TV show felt bad.'

She is also on a crusade to get companies to recognize how death can rock employees. She talks admiringly of her own 'boss', Mark Zuckerberg, and how he built her confidence up after it 'crumbled' on her first day back. 'When I called Mark, crying that first night . . . saying, "Maybe I came back too early, I'm not contributing," he said, "You should come back when you want," but didn't leave it at that. He said: "But you made two really good points here today, so I'm really glad you came."'

For her this was the important bit. 'If he had just said, "You should come back whenever you want," I would have heard: "You can't do this."'

A square plate, the size of a side table and covered in lettuce, avocado and chicken, is placed in front of Sandberg. It does not look Mexican. My lunch is extraordinarily orange: enchiladas in orange sauce, with orange rice.

'The chicken's got a yummy . . .' she trails off, perhaps not used to describing food. 'It feels like it's been marinated for a long time, which is always good.'

Few companies have gained such influence, so quickly. Facebook has had its share of growing pains: panics over privacy, fears it could not make money and worries that it was becoming uncool. It overcame many problems with technology: better privacy settings, more sophisticated ad targeting and buying new apps such as Instagram or borrowing new features from Snapchat.

The current questions it faces about its role may be harder to solve. In a letter this year on Facebook, Zuckerberg laid out his hopes that the company would play a role in creating a 'global community'. Despite almost 6,000 words and 82 mentions of 'community', it was short on specific technologies that could help.

I ask Sandberg if Facebook really is a global community that can be imbued with values, or whether it is, as it used to call itself, essentially a utility, like a phone network? She says they moved on from calling it that long ago, which perhaps suggests they now take for granted that people cannot do without Facebook.

'I think we have a very strong sense of values. Even when we were a utility, we had strong content rules: no pornography, no violence, no hate,' she says. The ability to enforce these rules in real time remains problematic: since our interview, a man in Thailand broadcast a video on Facebook's Live service of himself killing his 11-month-old daughter. The video played in people's newsfeeds for approximately 24 hours before it was taken down.

When I ask her what Facebook's biggest challenge is, Sandberg again reveals her skill at swerving questions. It's its biggest opportunity: to connect people around the world. Does she think people could spend too much time on Facebook (the average user spends 50 minutes a day between Facebook, Messenger and Instagram)? Extremes are always bad, some people probably sleep too much. Does she feel the weight of her power when she comes into work? She has a feeling of how much they need to do. Unlike many interviewees, she always knows when to stop, packaging up one- or two-line statements.

I try again on what seems to me the most important question: does she think as an organization Facebook is waking up to the great power it has? But Sandberg does not seem to think Facebook is at a particularly important turning point.

'It's a big responsibility, we've always taken that really seriously,' she says. 'To keep people safe, to make sure they can share with who they want, to ensure terrorists don't use our service.'

Trying to get more specific, I focus on fake news. Zuckerberg initially dismissed as 'pretty crazy' the idea that Facebook posts carrying inaccurate headlines – such as the Pope endorsing Donald Trump – could have influenced the US election. But in the months since, Facebook has begun a project to support journalism, including partnerships with fact-checkers. 'False news hurts everyone. It hurts our community, it hurts us as individuals,' she says. Yet she quickly adds, 'Everyone is going to have to do their part, right? Newsrooms, people who are teaching literacy, and media companies and us. So we're working really hard on the problem.'

As I go to ask another question, my mouth is full. Sandberg smiles.

'I feel that's the hard part of this lunch, it doesn't have the natural, I ask you a question, you ask me a question,' she says, back in sharing mood. She has eaten most of the chicken, left much of the lettuce and appears to be done.

With her smooth manner, it's little wonder that there has been speculation that Sandberg could run for political office, but she says that since her husband's death she feels more tied to Facebook, where people continue to post memories on his page.

When she was young, she thought she would work in government or a non-profit, never a company. What changed? 'I think when technology happened, that Google, Facebook, these companies have as much of a mission as other organizations,' she says. Maybe even as much power and influence as governments, I suggest. 'I don't know if that's right. But they have a mission,' she says.

Zuckerberg too has been the subject of more speculation since his letter. Rumours were fuelled when he embarked on a US tour to meet community groups, churches and businesses that appeared remarkably similar to an election campaign trail. Does she think he might run for president? 'No.'

And you? 'Nope, I've said no.'

The queen of leaning in is still hoping for a female president, even if it will not be her. On election night, Sandberg was ready to wake up her daughter and son so they could see Hillary Clinton become the first woman to accept the presidency. 'But they're nine and 11, so they'll get their chance. Hopefully soon,' she says.

How does she assess the state of the women's movement? There are signs of defiance – such as the Women's March after the inauguration – and of despair, at the rolling back of access to abortion. 'I think we need to review some of the historical context. The women's movement has been going for over 100 years, and we've made a lot of progress, but there are places in the world where women don't have basic civil rights,' she says.

Sandberg gave $1 million to Planned Parenthood recently. She had donated before in private but says it is now 'really important' to show support for the organization which, she adds, does more than provide abortions, offering health services to poorer women.

She worries 'about the lack of public policy on women and families', she says. 'I think the US needs a better safety net . . . If you're a single mum or even a dual-parent working family, what do you do if you've got a sick child?'

Silicon Valley has come in for particular criticism, most recently when a former software engineer at Uber spoke out against the ride-sharing company for ignoring her accusations of sexual harassment. On this she is less expansive. 'I think we have challenges for women in this industry. We have the same biases. We have a problem with women in leadership,' she says.

Lean In the book gave birth to Lean In the organization, a network of 1.5 million working women around the world organized in 'circles' for support, from entrepreneurs in Paris starting businesses to Chinese women quitting state-owned enterprises and saying no to arranged marriages. Sandberg meets them when she travels.

Sandberg was criticized for putting too much emphasis on what the individual can do – with advice such as sitting at the table, not in the corner, at meetings – rather than the importance of institutions. On this point she is animated. 'I think it is a false, false contest that was never . . . It was always both. I said it was both. It's both,' she stresses.

Chief executives complained to her that female staff were asking for pay rises. She declines to name the guilty parties but says that when she said she left work at 5.30pm to see her kids, 'someone told me I couldn't have gotten more headlines if I had murdered someone with an axe . . . I got flowers from an entire Yahoo and Google department saying, "Thank you. We're all leaving at 5.30pm now."'

The book was also held responsible for readers breaking up with their boyfriends. 'You can date whoever you want, but you should marry the nerds and the good guys,' she advised. You dated the bad guys, I ask? 'A little bit.'

I tell her I'm 30 and unmarried: who should I be looking for? 'The

---

Sol Facebook
1601 Willow Road, Menlo Park, CA

....

Enchiladas al	
guajillo	$14.95
Ensalada Sol	$11.95
Diet Coke	$2
Sparkling water	$3.50

....

| Total (inc. tax) – | $35.23 |

guys who want an equal relationship. Guys who want to support your career. You have a great career,' she said. Embracing the idea of Sandberg as agony aunt, I ask how you tell who the good guys are. 'You ask and you ask early and you are not afraid of offending. If they're going to be offended by the answer, you don't want to date them anyway.'

Sandberg often livestreams on Facebook interviews with famous or brave women. At the end she asks a question emblazoned on posters all over Facebook's campus: what would you do if you weren't afraid?

As she reaches for her small Facebook-branded notebook and her smartphone, in a case emblazoned with 'Ban Bossy', I finish by putting her own question to her.

Speaking quietly, she comes in closer. 'I think I wrote this book because it is personal and it is very open,' she says, tears welling. 'I want some good from the tragedy, just something good.'

Then she snaps back to composed, hugs me again and leaves.

Millennials

'Nobody stopped to punch me'

Martin Shkreli

'Nobody stopped to punch me'

By David Crow

O n the way to meet me for lunch, Martin Shkreli is detained by two strangers who want to have their photo taken with 'the drug guy'. That is one name for him – although some have called him far worse. 'Nobody stopped me to punch me, as you can see,' he says.

Shkreli's ability to stroll down a Manhattan sidewalk without provoking an act of violence would be unremarkable but for his status as the personification of US corporate greed, acquired after he bought a life-saving medicine last year before swiftly raising the price from $13.50 to $750 per pill. His decision to inflate the price of Daraprim, a decades-old medicine for Aids and cancer patients, drew a sharp rebuke from Hillary Clinton, who described the 5,000 per cent increase as 'outrageous'. Her remark sent pharma stocks spiralling and catapulted the issue of drug costs to the forefront of the presidential debate.

Despite stopping for selfies, Shkreli is already in situ when I arrive at Felidia, a traditional Italian restaurant in Midtown, sitting at a table in the middle of the dark, empty dining room. An overhead lamp throws shadows across his face, which breaks into his trademark smirk as I approach. The smile became infamous last year during his disastrous tour of TV studios to defend the price of Daraprim, when he alienated viewers with his apparent disregard for the suffering of patients. 'I became a victim of editing,' he says as I take my seat.

Before last year's scandal, the 33-year-old from blue-collar Brooklyn was all but unknown outside pharma circles, where he had a reputation as one of the industry's most promising young entrepreneurs. His business acumen netted him a fortune, which he claims was worth roughly $200 million at one point.

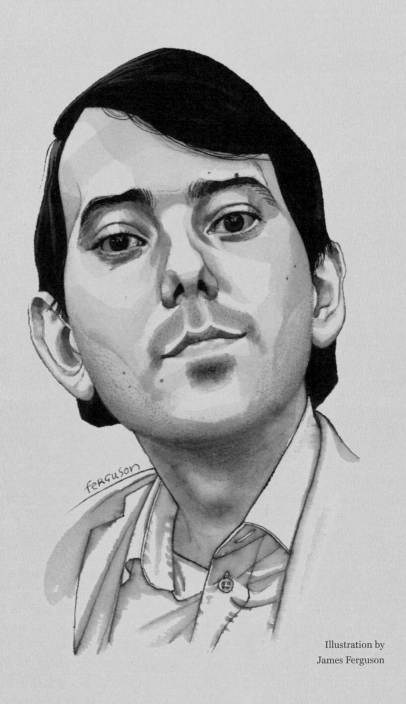

But it all came crashing down. The impression that Shkreli was revelling in his status as a greedy villain did not help. Then the FBI woke him on a rainy December morning in 2015 and frogmarched him to a Brooklyn courthouse to face charges of defrauding investors to the tune of $11 million. He is due to stand trial in June for allegedly running his hedge fund as though it were a 'Ponzi-like scheme'.

If the private Shkreli is any different to the pugnacious public persona, it is not immediately apparent. 'This is my date spot if you will,' he says, gesturing to the dark panelled walls of his favourite haunt as he launches straight into his defence. I should not, he swiftly makes clear, expect any regrets.

'To me the drug was woefully underpriced,' he says. Rather, he thinks he should have charged a higher price still because Daraprim can keep people alive: 'It is not a question of "Is this fair?" or "What did you pay for it?" or "When was it invented?" It should be more expensive in many ways.'

He boasts of other attempts to buy old drugs for fatal diseases with the 'ingenious plan' of inflating their prices as well, and suggests that executives who eschew such tactics are, in effect, defrauding their investors. 'If you have a drug that is $100 for one course of therapy, and you know that you can charge $100,000, what should shareholders think when you say, "I'd rather not take the heat"?' he asks.

When I arranged the lunch, I was told that Shkreli would not want to discuss the impending court case. Yet he appears incapable of speaking about anything else. He confidently predicts that he will prevail, and that his notoriety will help sway the jury. 'I have this fringe theory that I've sort of stress-tested a little bit – the more polarizing and popular a case is, the more likely an acquittal,' he says, citing the cases of OJ Simpson, Casey Anthony, who stood trial for her daughter's murder, and Sean 'P Diddy' Combs, whose attorney now works for Shkreli. 'What's fascinating for all these cases? They were all widely seen to be guilty.'

Despite our having sat down half an hour ago, neither of us has glanced at the menu. The trial is 'all for political show', Shkreli continues, warming to his theme, and the case would never have been pursued were it not for the price-gouging controversy. 'These investigations started years ago and they'd meandered for years. You know that being a public figure is instantly grounds for prosecution.'

Given that Shkreli believes he was targeted for the Daraprim controversy, I ask again whether he wishes he had done anything differently. 'My whole life has been one theme of self-sacrifice for my investors,' he replies, without batting an eyelid. 'I did it for my shareholders' benefit because that's my job. The political risk is being shamed – and shame isn't dilutive to earnings per share.'

A waiter arrives to take our order. Shkreli asks them to choose for him, and I follow suit. Shkreli has already dismissed the sommelier, but I have another stab and suggest that we take a glass of wine. He demurs.

The conversation, like any other in the US these days, soon turns to the presidential election. While not registered to vote, Shkreli instinctively supports Donald Trump despite his flaws. 'The symbolism of his success is in many ways what you're voting for. It's sort of like the Statue of Liberty; he's an icon that represents something.

'I think that his supporters endorse being rash, being American, being polarizing and having this un-PC, unedited attitude. In many ways it's not a surprise that I identify with that.' Later, it occurs to me how often Shkreli himself speaks in Trumpisms, like this: 'I've had my photo taken a lot with people who say, "I support you, you inspire me, you're the American dream."'

Despite her role in his defenestration, Shkreli says he does not hold a 'deep animus' towards Clinton, although he dismisses her as 'a deeply political, bureaucratic creature'.

'If I'm greedy and addicted to money, she's greedy and addicted to power – and apparently a little bit of money too,' he says, referring to the millions of dollars in personal wealth amassed by Clinton, who delivered a series of lucrative paid speeches to Wall Street and Silicon Valley in the years following her tenure as US secretary of state.

'I've built companies I can point to. What can she point to? A career in public service? She made a bunch of money doing that? It makes no freaking sense.'

Our *primi piatti* arrive: two bowls of tajarin, a thin homemade pasta, drizzled in butter and oil with a dusting of freshly grated black truffle, accompanied by steaming cups of butternut squash soup.

I tuck into the spaghetti, which is delicious but would be better still with something from the wine list, and I silently bemoan that daytime drinking is not among Shkreli's flaws. We barely touch the soup, ill-suited as it is to the glorious autumnal day.

Shkreli eats slowly, his progress impeded by constant fidgeting; I lose count of the number of times he twiddles his hair or fastens and unfastens his grey blazer, worn over a white pinstripe shirt and blue jeans. The restaurant is busier now and he strains to be heard.

Despite confidently predicting his acquittal, the prospect of time in prison weighs on him. 'Oh, I've certainly thought about it. Anyone in my position would,' he says. 'The attorney could have a bad day. There could be a surprise witness, surprise evidence. If I go on the stand, there could be a mistake on my own part.'

He thinks any prison sentence would be short – a year or so – and that he would be popular with his cellmates. 'One person told me that the inmates at the white-collar prison are gigantic, huge Shkreli supporters,' he says.

Given that he spends most of his time cooped up in his apartment, where he broadcasts chunks of his day over the internet, he thinks jail would be survivable. 'If you look at my life on a daily basis, it's not very different from a prison-like condition,' he says, 'although I'm going to miss my computer.'

He has no doubt that he will make a comeback regardless, reeling off a list of convicted and disgraced executives who rebuilt their careers after being freed from jail. He is already working on a new venture, a technology company that will soon be announced, although he declines to discuss the details. 'I think it's going to be remarkable and, dare I say, revolutionary.'

Shkreli, who stopped eating around halfway through his *primo piatto*, eventually surrenders the unfinished dish to an impatient server, who replaces it with slices of seared tuna fillet on a caponata of squash and celery root. He looks shocked. 'Oh, I didn't know there was a main course,' he says.

The pharmaceuticals industry was quick to brand Shkreli as an egregious outlier following the Daraprim controversy. In private, many executives blame him for the public outcry over the price of drugs that threatens to crimp their profits and bonuses.

'I heard from a friend that these folks are actually jealous,' he says of those who disavowed him. 'They're 60-something years old and they're saying, "Oh gosh, he outsmarted us." They can feign all the outrage they want but the reality is, I saw an opportunity in pharma, I made a huge fortune, and they didn't.

'They are no different from the maître d' of this restaurant – they are there to look good, manage the place, act important and do absolutely nothing,' he says, gesturing towards the head waiter. 'And unlike the maître d', they get paid a lot of money.'

Perhaps the only people who inspire more venom are former business associates, like the employee who quit his job shortly after receiving a large stock award. Shkreli responded by harassing his family – sending messages to his son on Facebook and posting a letter to his wife that read: 'I hope to see you and your four children homeless and will do whatever I can to assure this.'

At last: something he must regret. Many people have said or done awful things when blinded by rage, but bringing his wife and children into things was surely a mistake. Would he take it back if he could? Not a bit of it: 'I saw him to be a good family man and I wrote a relatively calm letter. I'd had success in the past appealing to the family.'

Shkreli has barely disturbed the thin slices of pink fish on his plate but assures our concerned waiter that everything was fine. Dessert is an 'almost tiramisu' – a concoction of cream, Nutella and hazelnuts – that is too sickly without the traditional coffee kick. He orders an espresso. I ask for a cup of tea.

'I like being an iconoclast,' he tells me, insisting that he is unfazed by how others view him. Yet he often betrays a desperation to know what people think, recently going so far as to hire a professional polling company to survey public opinion: 'It skewed 60/40, like/dislike,' he says.

Shkreli insists the public has him all wrong, and takes offence at the perception that he has lived a privileged life. His parents emigrated from eastern Europe in the 1970s to start anew in the US, where they raised four children. His mother still speaks only broken English. 'My parents were janitors. I went to public high school. I was one of the only white kids in junior high. I don't know why that makes me entitled.'

The family's cramped apartment was a few blocks from the Atlantic Ocean in Sheepshead Bay, a working-class enclave of Brooklyn where Trump's father made a name for himself by building affordable housing. 'When my parents came to America, they began to learn who the Trumps were and in many ways they symbolized the American dream,' he recalls.

The media furore and his trial have brought the 'somewhat dysfunctional' Shkreli family closer, he says, and they recently shared a meal just a few tables away. 'It was our first family dinner in a restaurant – ever.' He admits to having 'what you could call a complex', which he attributes to parents 'whose theories on discipline are very excessive'.

As far as personal friendships go, there are few to speak of. 'There's nobody to just have a beer with and that, in some ways, is sort of sad.' He has had 'an inordinate amount of ex-girlfriends' he claims, but now there is no one of note, his most recent attachment having ended shortly after he was charged. 'Since then the "celebrity and notoriety" have fostered some pretty unhealthy relationships.'

More recently, Shkreli has started to flirt with the alt-right, a loose political collective whose angry concerns are best defined by their gender and the colour of their skin: male and white. But despite his full-throated support for unbridled free markets, I sense he has little interest in the identity politics that fires up this contentious group. 'It's for sympathy, I suppose,' he says. 'People will defend me based on my inclusion.'

Felidia
243 East 58th Street,
New York

....

Prix fixe x 2	$72
Butternut squash soup x 2	
Tajarin pasta with truffle shaving x 2 supplement	$70
Yellowfin tuna x 2 supplement	$16
Tiramisu x 2	
Bottle of still water x 2	$8
Coffee	$5
English breakfast tea	$7

....

Total (inc. service) –	$178

Solace also comes from friends he has made online, and from Trashy, a rescue cat he rehomed. 'She liked to live in garbage cans and near dumpsters and things like that. She was very afraid of everything. She'd hide under the sink for two or three months. Now she sleeps in my bed and she's made this process quite a bit easier; at least one thing loves me in the world.'

After two and a half hours, lunch is over and so, it seems, is the act.

I find myself even enjoying his company. We linger a while and the conversation meanders to some strange places.

He speaks of his love of Shakespeare and magical realist literature, and describes how he is captivated by science and medicine. 'I've never done any art, but I think if you look at X-ray crystallography, it's beautiful,' he says. He is obsessed with chess but was recently beaten in a tournament by a nine-year-old. And then he confesses to mental health problems in the past.

'I see a psychiatrist. I have done since I was 18. I started having panic attacks and they were pretty bad. Then I took this one drug and I've been taking it for 15 years. One of the reasons I love pharma is my experience of that drug.'

The drug in question is a version of Effexor, an antidepressant that was discovered around 30 years after Daraprim. Later I look up the price – as little as 17 cents a pill. The medicine, he says, is a miracle. 'It has made me invincible in some ways.'

Whitney Wolfe

'We're making strides as women'

By Alice Fishburn

Most interviews have something of the date about them. But as I hurry through a heaving London to meet Whitney Wolfe, I'm feeling the pressure to make things go with more of a swing than usual. Wolfe is, after all, the high priestess of dating. In 2012 she was a co-founder of Tinder, the app that revolutionized millennial relationships, before leaving two years later in a swirl of sexual harassment allegations and, in the process, becoming an accidental symbol of the sexism women face in Silicon Valley. She then moved to Texas and launched Bumble, the matchmaking app of choice for 13 million people and counting. Many of them are young hipsters, attracted by its feminist credentials: the woman must make the first move. All this and Wolfe is not yet 28.

Even by normal tech-entrepreneur-on-a-tight-schedule standards, noon seems a little early for lunch, and the Charlotte Street branch of Roka looks completely empty as I walk in. Then I glance up and there is Wolfe, petite, smiling, in a grey jumper and black leather trousers. As we sit, loud chanting erupts from the corner of the restaurant. The Roka team have circled for a motivational send-off before they begin service. Wolfe is delighted: 'I think I need to do this at Bumble. I'm going to ask them to come, spread some of the spirit.'

She's only half joking. When a waiter appears, she quizzes him on the ritual. 'I just thought it was amazing. I love that, I'm going to start doing it.' He looks slightly alarmed and presses us for a drinks order. It's a bit early for alcohol, that traditional lubricant of blind dates, so we settle for a Diet Coke (me) and 'Oooh, mint tea, please' for her.

Unsurprisingly, perhaps, Wolfe is the perfect first date: enthusiastic about everything from the tea to the wide blue skies of our technological

Illustration by James Ferguson

future. Our conversation is punctuated with 'Really?'s and even the odd 'Tell me, tell me, tell me'. When I reveal that my brother and his girl-friend met on Bumble, she gasps. There have been more than 5,000 engagements and marriages from the app so far. 'Bumble babies have started to arrive now,' she says, and they get sent onesies emblazoned with 'My mom made the first move'.

I came of age with the social media revolution but am a chronically late adopter – managing to sleep through the founding of Facebook mere metres from my university dorm. So it's perhaps not surprising that I never joined the third of under-forties that YouGov estimates use online dating services in the UK. Until now, that is. After downloading Bumble – strictly for research purposes – I was feeling somewhat irritated by the lack of interest in my profile until a friend pointed out that all my pictures were of me in a wedding dress. Wolfe finds this hilarious. I feel old.

Rather endearingly, she says she does too. Wolfe's employees may be just a couple of years younger but they often speak a different language. 'I'm so close in age to them, but I feel decades apart sometimes when it comes to digital trends . . . Half a year in tech-app time, it's like a normal-world five years.' What's the solution? 'You just have to run faster than it does.'

Wolfe has surfed an extraordinary sea change in how we approach relationships. Our phones now allow us to identify potential life com-panions through location, ethnic origin or hatred of the same thing and reject them just as quickly. Such opportunities come with a healthy serv-ing of ethical and personal dilemmas. I know of a WhatsApp group of single friends devoted to discussing the profiles, responses and bizarre situations that crop up in digital dating. What photo should you use? And what are the best ways to calibrate your profile?

What is clear is that the digital dating sphere is very lucrative. Match Group, Inc – the parent company for Match.com, OkCupid and Tinder – is valued at $4.3 billion. Bumble's USP – 'truly not a gimmick', Wolfe stresses, and timely for a feminist age – is that the woman has all the power (while both sexes swipe to show interest, only she can start a con-versation). Wolfe may be firmly on-brand but she laughs wickedly at the ambitions of many tech evangelists. 'So many entrepreneurs approach me and say, "I want to start the next big thing," and I say, "Well, what are you solving?" And oftentimes they say, "Oh, I'm not sure. I want to start something big."' Sigh. 'You can never start something big without solving something small, right? And for me, that was not being allowed to text guys first.'

This ingrained social habit is indicative of a much larger issue for women. 'What we're taught growing up has translated into the digital sphere. You must let him be the aggressor . . . you must let him make all the moves . . . and you need to sit pretty and you need to kind of play this same role that you're told to play in real life.' The Bumble team, it seems, has had enough: 'We don't like how it works in real life and we're going to try to change that digitally.'

We're at Roka today because Wolfe doesn't always have the chance to eat sushi in Austin, Texas, where she moved following her exit from Silicon Valley. There's one small problem: my irrational dislike of fish. Wolfe is mortified. Instant, profuse, American apologies ensue along with the suggestion that we relocate. No, no, I state and turn to the vegetarian option.

Ten minutes later, we still haven't made up our minds. If this were Bumble – swipe right for yes, left for no – our inability to commit to any option would be worrying Wolfe's engagement team. Eventually she asks the waiter for the most popular but 'not super-adventurous' dish and goes for the nigiri maguro and a salmon tataki. I panic and order far too many things on the basis that there's not a fin in any of them. Then, in true dating style, I copy her miso soup order.

Warm flannels are brought to us. Mine ends up crumpled on the dish. Wolfe folds hers into symmetrical squares before placing it neatly on top. Her composed look comes with hints of glamour: diamond earrings; a Cartier bracelet jangling on her wrist next to an old elastic hair band. Even in the groomed environs of Roka's clientele, she has a just-back-from-skiing healthy vibe. Later she reveals that this is in fact the case: 'I went off the side of the mountain.' The only casualty was her engagement ring – now in for repairs. (For those wondering, she met her fiancé in real life.)

Wolfe grew up in the conservative surroundings of Salt Lake City, Utah – a traditional background of school, sport and TV. Did she feel engulfed by technology back then? No, but there was endless instant messaging with her friends, allowing for plenty of exposure to early digital mind games. Still, 'there was an escape, I can't think of an escape today. We escape into our phones.'

She then moved to Silicon Valley, where, at 22, she joined the Hatch Labs tech incubator. One of its most famous projects was Tinder. Wolfe ended up working as the vice-president of marketing. She also began to date Justin Mateen, a fellow co-founder. Tinder boomed (it now has an estimated 50 million users) but both the relationship and the job fell apart in spectacular fashion. Wolfe filed a lawsuit against Tinder in 2014 alleging sexual harassment, discrimination and emotional distress. Among her claims was that Mateen called her a 'whore' at a work event. The company settled the case for an undisclosed sum, without admission of liability.

Silicon Valley has long been haunted by reports of behaviour ranging from the frat-boy-esque to the downright sleazy, and the media seized on this saga of real-life dysfunction among the gilded digital youth, while internet snipers took aim at Wolfe. She found herself alternately heralded as a champion of women's rights and vilified as a gold-digger.

She takes a deep breath when our conversation turns to Tinder, sits even more upright and changes the subject. 'I genuinely have nothing but well wishes for them,' she says. 'This is an industry that is not only for one person. Love is universal, and we're trying to do it in a different way.' But the experience clearly left its mark. 'I would read these opinions of complete strangers . . . It hurt my feelings really badly. It shook me up.'

In the middle of all this, Russian entrepreneur Andrey Andreev, founder of Badoo, another dating-focused social-networking site, approached Wolfe about building a new app. Was it a case of once bitten, twice shy? Wolfe insists that, initially, it was the last thing she wanted to do. 'I did not want to go back into the dating industry. But at the end of the day, the world's bigger than just me.' And so Bumble came into being. The site now has users in more than 20 countries.

The issue of sexism in Silicon Valley smoulders on; it recently erupted again when Susan Fowler, an engineer, published a damning blog post exposing alleged sexism by her manager when she worked at Uber. What has Wolfe learnt three years on from the events that led to her departure? 'I want to know if the reaction would have been the same today,' she says. 'I don't know the answer to that. I don't know if it's [just] me that's progressed in my life . . .' She pauses. 'I feel like we're making strides as women.'

Certainly Wolfe doesn't seem to miss life among the tech tribes of California. When I ask about any mentors there, she looks blank. What about the realities of selling a product while maintaining a mission? Some approved start-up-founder soundbites sneak in as she talks about balancing capitalism and conscience. 'There's this funny thing; usually when something tries to be progressive . . . it can sometimes be limited to a small niche, a dot-org or something like that.' But how does this apply to Bumble? 'We want to have millions and millions of views . . . This needs to be viewed as a business but that doesn't mean we can't go beyond that.'

We may be dissecting some of the biggest issues facing young women today but that's not going to stop the food. It's a classic case of over-ordering. My side of the table looks like an organic farm: aubergine, broccoli, asparagus. Food envy sets in as Wolfe embarks on her sweet potato tempura and, in vain, tries to tempt me with some salmon. So, what about feminism? The word itself has become something of a litmus test over the past two years. Every politician and movie star has to opine on whether they identify as one, while the dissections of what women can, can't, should or shouldn't be doing are enough to drive the entire sex slowly mad. 'When I started Bumble, this topic was not really as everywhere as it is now. It goes to show how, when there's a need for something to change, it will find its way to the surface,' says Wolfe.

But is a lot of today's discussion merely lip service? Does wearing a T-shirt with 'feminist' stamped on it really help to change behaviour? 'I hate to use this word but some people have viewed it as a trend, which is unfortunate. It should not be a trend,' says Wolfe. She warms to her theme: 'My biggest pet peeve, if you will, is when I hear men say, "Eww, a feminist app." You have to kind of school people.' Bumble certainly practises what it preaches: male users have been taken to task publicly for their behaviour on the site.

Wolfe says it took her a while to understand what feminism really meant. 'It never touched me personally,' she says. 'I didn't really under-stand the concept of feminism until the media started to talk about it surrounding my name.' Later on, she returns to the theme. 'I had to live through being a woman who thought men always had a one-up . . . I knew I didn't like it. I thought that's how it was.' Her new team consists largely of women.

It's impossible to avoid bringing up gender issues in the time of Trump. Wolfe laughs and deftly steers away from an openly political response, pointing out that Bumble has raised $80,000 for Planned Parenthood. 'We want to be responsive with things that show, "Hey, we've got your back." Even though we are this mainstream product, we will always care about you as if we are the local girl gang, you know?'

Wolfe has finished her sushi – delicious, apparently – while I have been defeated by broccoli. Soon the next round of meetings will start. Do start-up founders ever turn off? 'You know what I will do sometimes? I'll let my phone die . . . and I will say, "You know what, I'm not lying, my phone died,"' she confesses, looking vaguely guilty. Still, compared to the number of people who have entered the restaurant with their eyes glued to screens, she has impeccable techiquette. Her phone stays in her bag until she pulls it out to show me pictures of Bumble's new offices – honeycomb tiles and all. With the energy of someone who has yet to hit that particular hurdle, she tells me about plans for a 'mommy room', grilling me on parenting policy in the UK and work–life balance.

What has all this time with the data taught her about humans? 'You understand when people are the happiest, the most busy, the most detached, most involved.' Sunday nights and Mondays are the busiest times on the site: 'I think that's probably really telling because that's usually people's downtime, when they are relaxing or when they're feeling bummed out . . . a little bit lonely.'

Our view on the idea of technology running our love lives unsurprisingly depends on our culture. One transatlantic dater tells me that, in the US, Bumble is strongly associated with empowered women. In the

Roka	
37 Charlotte St, Fitzrovia, London W1	
Avocado maki	£6.60
Nigiri maguro	£10
Piri piri maki	£8.60
Salmon tataki	£12.60
White miso soup x 2	£9.20
Asparagus	£5.60
Eggplant salad	£6.60
Sweet potato tempura	£8.90
Tenderstem broccoli	£5.60
Diet Coke	£3.10
Sparkling water	£4.10
Mint tea	£3.60
Total (inc. service) – £96.91	

UK, some moan that it just caters to lazy men. Wolfe laughs and counters that they may be looking for someone independent. Nationalities
do matter, though. Apparently French women don't like being told to
make the first move: tell them that it's their choice and they get on
board.

Our mini girl gang is about to disband. And so to the post-date tussle
of who should pay. Wolfe is adamant but I am more so. Forget about
women making the first move, this is an *FT* ruling.

So, can you really hack love? My brother may have met his girlfriend
on Bumble but it turned out she was a friend's sister on whom he had
had a futile teenage crush. At the end of the day, social forces retain their
same old power. Still, without an algorithm, such connections might
never be remade. Wolfe nods. 'It can bring things back around the
second or third time, you never know,' she says. Then she grins. 'I love
that. That's modern love.'

Vitalik Buterin

'I'm basically just floating everywhere'

By Chloe Cornish

U p in San Francisco's Monterey Heights district stands a modest detached house; a house that would be perfectly ordinary were its wide windows not covered in neon green scribbles – half-finished equations, anatomies of computer architecture. They are marks left by the coders who use this place as a hide-out.

The troupe of five or so developers, clad in hoodies and jeans, have an air of Peter Pan's lost boys. They may be young – in their early to mid-twenties – but these programmers are the heart of the most extra-ordinary financial story of recent months: cryptocurrencies, digital tokens with no intrinsic value, suddenly worth billions. I'm here to meet the coders' leader, Vitalik Buterin, the Russian-Canadian creator of Ethereum, arguably the most successful of the hundreds of copycat cryptocurrencies to have emerged in the seven years since bitcoin rose to prominence. On the damp, overcast morning when I take a Lyft car (an Uber equivalent) to his San Francisco headquarters, Ethereum's market value is some $125 billion – second only to bitcoin.

Once I've squeezed past his earnest acolytes, the angular young man I recognize from tech conference stages shakes my hand gingerly, his fingers flattened. With hollow cheeks and downy brown hair, he is more mathematics prodigy than tech magnate.

We had booked a fancy Mexican restaurant in San Francisco's Latin-inflected Mission district, but at the last minute I was told he would prefer a quiet takeaway here at Ethereum's San Francisco home-from-home. He's dressed in a loose canary yellow T-shirt featuring a cartoon character, black tracksuit trousers and a watch with a pink plastic strap.

Illustration by Alex Hedworth

Its face is a cat, whose transparent Cheshire grin exposes the mechanism. I ask for his precise age. He answers without hesitation: '23.96.'

It was his father, Dmitry, also a computer scientist, who first introduced his son to the idea of blockchain and cryptocurrency. He had encouraged his son to build video games from the age of 10. Then in 2011 he told him about bitcoin. Created two years earlier as the world reeled from the failures of the banking system, bitcoin lets people exchange cash online without a bank mediating the transaction. Bitcoin's enigmatic creator remains unidentified, but among its godfathers were cypherpunks: hackers dedicated to privacy, determined to undermine authorities who led us to the financial crisis.

The then 17-year-old Vitalik initially dismissed the idea, but then did his own research into virtual money. Soon he was writing articles – paid for in bitcoins – while studying computer science at Canada's University of Waterloo, eventually leading him to co-found *Bitcoin Magazine*. Back in 2011, bitcoin was considered so radical many believed governments would ban it, pointing to the dark market it supported. Yet it survived, trading at highs of $19,000 at Christmas, although a crash followed.

A blockchain is 'an interesting and new kind of organism' Buterin says after we have slid across floorboards through the open-plan living room to a wooden dining table. That is something of an understatement, I think. Simply put, a blockchain is a ledger stored across thousands of computers. Spreading the record out this way, and securing it with Byzantine mathematics called cryptography, makes it harder to tamper with than traditional information hoards. Centralized data troves, such as your brain, are liable to lose things – and, as Equifax found via the hacking of its customer data files, are vulnerable to attack. By contrast, blockchain ledgers are open for all to read and not controlled by a single entity.

Buterin's particular genius was to see the potential to create a blockchain of his own, Ethereum, that other services could build on, from payments to games. It quickly grew a life of its own, with everyone from scientists to banks and entrepreneurs clamouring to build on it. Aged just 19, Buterin quit university to guide it.

We both make for a bench; after some awkward hovering, he folds his bony frame into a chair. We dither about food. I suggest tacos or pizza.

His collaborator, Thomas Greco, a developer who says he has worked with Buterin for years, suggests Thai. Before I have time to find a menu on my phone, Greco has whizzed through options for nearby Chaiya Thai Restaurant and is ordering with his thumb.

Buterin is the first to admit he had a weird 2017. Entrepreneurs building on Ethereum started using it to mint fresh coins to crowdfund virtual money for their ventures, a novel funding mechanism called initial coin offerings. Bitcoin and ether prices rocketed and ICOs exploded – but fuelled fears of tulip-style mania. 'We've created a culture where some totally random project raising something like $8 million is like, oh yeah, that's peanuts,' he says. 'You know, you're in a bubble!'

The rising ether price has made him a multi-millionaire but unlike bitcoin believers who have tended stubbornly to hold the asset, he was never confident cryptocurrencies would catch on. When prices looked right, he'd cash in – and he has 'financially paid dearly for it', he remarks, cheerfully, estimating his paper wealth would be three to four times higher had he sold less cryptocurrency. After years at $1 to $100, bitcoin jumped from under $1,000 in January 2017 to over $19,000 by December (the ebullience leaked out of the market, however – it's now about $8,000).

Buterin is under pressure to translate breathless blockchain excitement into results. He rapidly explains his efforts to improve Ethereum, which recently jammed under the strain of people swapping virtual cats in a game called CryptoKitties, where players breed and swap digital felines. The scaling initiatives have names such as 'sharding', 'state channels' and 'plasma'. I'm relieved when we switch to simpler stuff – such as his desire for immortality.

Buterin has pondered eternal life since he was a child. Not long after his family emigrated from Russia when he was six, he stumbled on a book by Aubrey de Grey, a controversial British scientist with radical ideas to defeat ageing. Why does he want to live for ever, I ask as we sip green tea made by Greco, while waiting for our food. Buterin is 'kind of puzzle[d] as to why this is even a question'. If you could live for ever, he reasons, choosing not to is 'the equivalent of jumping off a cliff'. He later reassures me that while life extension solutions have been slow coming they could be ready by 2060, which is 'probably enough for you' (I'm 25).

So what would he do with eternal life, I ask, imagining he might yearn to crack unsolved mathematics proofs. Not quite. 'The most important thing is to enjoy it,' he replies. During flights, he practises the languages he's not yet fluent in by watching French, German or Chinese films.

As we talk, cryptocurrency is having something of a cultural shift. The idealistic early coders, who wanted blockchain to transfer power from corporations and governments to individuals, last year started getting overtaken by get-rich-quick schemers. Some ICOs were scams. Buterin watched in dismay as his blockchain was flooded by mercenaries making a fast buck.

'There's projects that never had a soul, that are just like, ra-ra, price go up,' he flaps his long hands, 'Lambo[rghini], vrromm, buybuybuy now!' Then he blurts out a critique of the digital token Tron, breaking the tension by laughing uproariously. Tron's market valuation hit $17 billion without any discernible product.

The outlandish valuations are, he says, 'far ahead of what this space has actually accomplished for the world'.

Even as we wait for delivery, the crypto markets are tanking. By the end of the day, ether will have crashed 30 per cent. This volatility would have traders sweating, but it's nothing to crypto veterans such as Buterin – he doesn't even check his phone.

The boom may disillusion Buterin, but he has welcomed mainstream investment in blockchain. The Ethereum Enterprise Alliance was founded in 2016 to test enterprise uses for the blockchain – members range from BP to JPMorgan. The EEA reflects Buterin's changing mindset. As a teenager, he shared the rebellious crypto community's common attitude: 'the system', i.e. governments, banks and major corporations, 'is basically evil, and we needs [*sic*] to outright resist it and build a new thing' (Buterin has a childlike tic, incorrectly adding 's' to some verbs).

But he came to realize these people 'aren't that different from people anywhere else'. Purists might call this betraying blockchain's roots; Buterin paints it as pragmatism, coloured with anxiety about governments with 'hundreds of billions of dollars of physical weaponry, plenty of prisons . . . increasing amounts of internet surveillance'. Buterin has cause to fret: he watched early bitcoiners who used bitcoin for trafficking get caught. He cites Ross Ulbricht, the impossibly young American libertarian who ran dark web market Silk Road, an illegal online marketplace for illicit substances and goods, largely on bitcoin. Ulbricht's infamous decision to hire hitmen rewrote the narrative of bitcoin, argues Buterin, turning a story about 'possibly a civil disobedient martyr' to 'actual criminal and a public enemy'. Now in his early thirties, Ulbricht last year lost a five-year court battle and faces life in prison.

'Even if your goal is to overthrow parts of the establishment, you want to have and present an image of why this is driving human progress,' he explains. '[*The*] *Lord of the Rings* and *Star Wars* could give people a very, very misleading impression of social conflict.' His reference to hobbits and Jedis invokes a child's morality, righteousness versus evil; Buterin has adjusted to a world without clear-cut villains and heroes.

So who's the most significant person in his life? For once he's silenced. 'Hmmm.' Pause. 'It's hard to think of one single person. Yeah.' We're saved by the delivery's arrival.

Two women on sofas are tapping at sticker-covered laptops and the atmosphere is student house pre-finals exams. Buterin fetches plates and forks (but not knives). We unwrap spiced prawns and vegetable pad pak for him; absinthe green vegetable curry with brown rice for me.

I ask what he remembers about Russia, which he left aged six. Peeling the prawn shells with long, nail-bitten fingers, he recites facts about his hometown, Kolomna: population 140,000; 115km from Moscow. He visited Moscow and St Petersburg last year, meeting Vladimir Putin, and is talking to Russian officials about a crypto-rouble project. He has explained he's establishment-friendly these days, but I have trouble understanding why he'd help an authoritarian government. He paraphrases Frederick Douglass, who was criticized for engaging with slaveholders but said: 'I would unite with anyone to do right; and with nobody to do wrong.'

He later confides he's encouraging the Kremlin to deliver 'crypto-y benefits for the people', but adds, despondently, that he's 'not sure how much of that is actually getting through'.

Willingness to talk has propelled Buterin on a seemingly open-ended diplomacy tour. In the past month, he's visited four countries: Thailand, Singapore, China, America. He has no fixed address. 'Right now I'm basically just floating everywhere,' he says. So, where does he leave his stuff while he's travelling? He races from the room. Baffled, I fork at some aubergine. He returns with a bright pink duffel bag, overflowing with T-shirts. Doesn't he own books? He gestures to his Android phone.

When his fortune grew from $1 million to over $10–$20 million (for once he fudges the numbers), he didn't feel 'yay I get more stuff; it's more certainty that I won't have to worry about money for a long time'. He donates to the Gates Foundation, GiveDirectly and De Grey's anti-ageing SENS Research Foundation.

His most important influence, he says, is the internet, and last June it killed him off: a viral rumour that he was dead knocked $4 billion in market capitalization off ether, revealing how integral cryptocurrency traders see Buterin to Ethereum. 'It's like OK, wow, that's weird,' he recalls. 'My family members were sending me WeChat messages saying, are you OK?' I notice shadows under his piercing blue eyes. For all his public appearances, his celebrity does not sit easily. 'Last year it got to the point where [the fame] got more annoying than good,' he says. He recalls a man trailing him around an aeroplane and through an airport, trying to talk to him.

Was this something he wanted, this leadership position? He doesn't miss a beat. 'No.' So how did it happen? 'Mmmm.

Chaiya Thai Restaurant
Food delivered from 272 Claremont Blvd, San Francisco, CA

....

Tamarind prawns	$14
Pad pak with tofu	$10
Green curry	$10
Brown rice x 2	$6
Green tea x 2 no charge	

....

Total (inc. tax and delivery) –	$50.56

Ethereum got big.' He hangs his head, like I'd scolded him. 'It just so happened that Ethereum evolved without, I guess, other figures quite as large as myself.'

Buterin seems downcast. Attempting to lighten the mood, I ask where he'd like to be in five years' time. 'I have no idea,' he sighs. 'I generally don't plan more than three months ahead, let alone five years.' It's clear that Ethereum started as a project, not a career plan. He ridicules the bitcoin millionaires who've ridden the crypto tsunami to riches, flaunting it as investment prowess.

'It's the luck of the draw, where everyone who won the draw seems to feel like they deserved it for being smarter,' rants Buterin. He impersonates a bitcoin bull: 'I was loyal and I was virtuous and I held through and therefore I deserve to have my five mansions and 23 Lambos!' We laugh.

Having polished off the prawns, he picks up food granules with his index finger and describes walking through a rundown district in China recently. He fixates on the 'scrappy grocery stores, with five-year-old kids helping mommy and daddy rearrange the water bottles'. They reminded him that 'these are the people you're actually serving'. I can sense Buterin itching to get back online. He removes the plates and thanks me for coming. I step into the grey day, a good distance from anywhere and without having called a car. Since the tradition is that the *FT* pays, I left $45 in notes for Greco, but discovered belatedly I was $5 short. Don't worry, Greco tells me later over email. I can pay him the difference in ether.

Zoella

'My dad kept telling me to get out of my bedroom and get a proper job'

By Jonathan Ford

Never before in my career has my daughter begged me to obtain the autograph of anyone I have interviewed. Prime ministers, generals, business chiefs? They've all been greeted with blank stares. But when she heard I was meeting Zoella, my 13-year-old was immediately thrown into a veritable froth of excitement. 'You mustn't forget, Dad,' she texted me firmly as I headed off to Brighton for my lunch with the 24-year-old fashion and beauty blogger.

Before leaving she'd given me the full benefit of her wisdom on the subject of my lunch companion. There were tips on how to handle the interview; even suggestions for questions that I might like to ask – albeit of the favourite music and food variety.

Which is why, when I arrive at Modelo Lounge, a slightly desolate café near the seafront in nearby Hove, I am feeling pretty well briefed. Not only do I know quite a lot about Zoella herself – online big sister, agony aunt, ultimate style guru and key to the hearts and minds of millions of avid, not yet cynical, young shoppers – I am also tolerably well informed about Alfie Deyes, Tanya Burr and the rest of the YouTube vlogging (video blogging) 'Brit crew'.

If you don't have children of a certain age, these names may mean nothing to you. But they are small-screen catnip to teenagers, in much the same way that BBC television stars such as John Noakes and Tom Baker were in my 1970s childhood.

True, the content is rather different to the fare served up on *Blue Peter* or *Doctor Who*: the production values are languid; the subject matter

Illustration by Patrick Morgan

focused principally on video games, pranks and that all-encompassing teen obsession – stuff. But these videos draw vast audiences. Millions of children and young adults devour them every day.

Of this group, perhaps the biggest star to emerge is Zoella herself. The mainstay of her channel features her sitting on her bed dispensing beauty advice, doing her hair or delivering one of her so-called shopping 'hauls' – in which she and her friends show off products they have just bought.

There's also a regular slot called 'ChummyChatter', which involves Zoella and her 'bestie', Louise, exchanging tips about key issues such as friendship, body image, boys and whether to go to university. You can get a flavour of the robust, parent-friendly common sense that's on offer from some recent titles. These include 'Why are you so skinny?' and 'Boundaries and saying no'.

It's hard to explain to the uninitiated the hold she has on the minds of those aged between 13 and 20. But her appeal is undeniable. Since launching her YouTube career in 2009, Zoella has managed to draw 5.3 million subscribers to her channel – 2.3 million since January alone – through a weird osmotic form of public acclamation.

Awards have duly followed. Last year, she was crowned Best British Vlogger at the BBC Radio 1's Teen Awards and this year she has already picked up the Nickelodeon Kids' Choice Award. An offline career is now beckoning. She recently signed a book deal with Penguin and her first novel, *Girl Online*, comes out in November.

Zoella – or Zoe Elizabeth Sugg as she is IRL (in real life) – is the first to admit that hers has been an unexpected rise to fame. 'It's weird because none of us ever intended that this would turn into our jobs,' she says. 'When we started exploring these exciting new things, none of us knew where it would lead.'

A slight, delicate figure with doll-like photogenic features and dip-dyed hair that has been pulled back into a ponytail, Zoella arrives with her manager, Maddie, who is there for reassurance but agrees to be banished to a distant table, where she taps at her laptop.

Our original idea had been to have lunch outside but bad weather has forced a change of plan. Modelo Lounge, selected (slightly ominously) by Zoella for its quietness, is almost deserted. A few business types look up from their burgers or steak and chips and I wonder what they make of this rumpled middle-aged man greeting a petite 20-something, elegantly dressed in a grey shirt dress set off by a tartan scarf. Do they think I'm her godfather? Or someone interviewing an au pair?

Zoella has lived in Brighton since last year. She rents a 'fabulous' penthouse apartment on the seafront where she lives in Ikea-furnished splendour with two guinea pigs – Percy and Pippin – who feature frequently in her videos. A recent one was all about them having a bath.

She moved here mainly because it's where her boyfriend lives. Alfie Deyes also has a successful vlog, called Pointless, in which he and his pals do dares and silly impressions. In fact, Brighton turns out to be YouTube city. It's also home to PewDiePie – a Swedish hipster whose films of himself and friends playing video games draw vast audiences – and video diary maestro Marcus Butler. 'I don't know what it is about this place,' Zoella says with a giggle. 'It's become like the centre of the universe. Whenever I meet anyone who's moving, it's like, "Right, I'm coming to Brighton."'

She grew up in the pretty village of Lacock in Wiltshire, the daughter of a property developer father and a beautician mother. After leaving the local state school with A levels in art, photography and textiles, she considered going to university but rejected the idea, partly because she wasn't sure what she wanted to study but mainly because of anxiety. Afflicted by acute shyness as a child, Zoella still suffers from occasional panic attacks. 'I didn't want to go away from my family, from any comfort that I had.'

Instead, she took a job as an apprentice in an interior design company near home and started a blog. Conceived as a hobby, it was never her intention to do much more than record a few whimsical observations about her life.

'I never had any structure, I never thought this is where I want it to go. It was literally like my little space on the internet, where I just used to write about the things I loved, or things that I thought other people would love as well.'

The formula certainly worked – not least the inspired focus on shopping. Having enjoyed other blogs where writers described their clothing and make-up purchases, Zoella decided to try something similar. 'It started off with me going to car-boot sales with my mum and finding all these little make-up bits for 50p and then writing about them.'

Pretty soon she had moved upmarket, filleting the racks at Topshop, Superdrug and Primark and reviewing the best of what she saw.

There is a brief pause while we order lunch from the bar. Zoella has made no secret of her partiality for junk food so I brace myself for the worst as I scan the menu. But Modelo Lounge, whose proudest boast seems to be that its cuisine is gluten-free, turns out to be inoffensive rather than toxic. Zoella orders a panino filled with halloumi and muhammara dip and a sherbet lemonade. I have the chicken and a beer.

As I munch through my chicken and Zoella picks listlessly at an admittedly uninspiring-looking panino, we return to the story. Her pleasant appearance, quirky manner and shrewd appreciation of teen tastes quickly drew readers, and it wasn't long before her growing band of followers was urging her to make videos. She plucked up the courage – largely because she knew there would be an audience. 'Because I already had people reading my blog that went straight away over to the video, I thought at least someone would be watching.'

By then, thanks to the post-financial-crisis meltdown, she had been made redundant from her interior design job but her nascent vlogging career was nearly derailed by her anxious parents. 'My dad was really confused by it. He kept telling me to get out of my bedroom and go and get a proper job.'

I say I would have been with him on this. But, in fact, sitting in her bedroom with a laptop turned out to be just about the best place for Zoella to be. She may not have been the first teenager to try her hand at vlogging, but she was starting at a fortuitous moment: just as YouTube, bought by Google in 2006, was transmogrifying from an online venue for amusing videos of cats falling off skateboards into something more like a TV network.

Google wanted to encourage 'creators' to produce more professional and appealing content. This would allow the US internet giant to grab a chunk of the estimated $250 billion spent each year on TV advertising.

Google's take would come through a 45 per cent revenue share with creators on advertising in return for hosting and publishing their videos. Though Google does not reveal specific ad revenues, investment banking analysts think it brought in about $5 billion in ad sales last year.

The key thing was to encourage content that would appeal to

hard-to-reach consumers – such as those in their teens and early twenties who are less wedded to conventional TV. (Zoella herself barely watches TV: 'My generation, at least the ones I know, are like 70/30 YouTube.') Thus was the stage set for the current group of YouTubers to emerge.

Zoella's focus on the 13–20 market put her right in the sweet spot of this revolution, although she surprises me by telling me that the age range of her viewers is much wider. 'Nine per cent of my viewers are men, of which the majority is, I think, 45 to 50.' Noticing my eyebrows are rising fast, she adds: 'I like to tell myself it's just my dad watching.'

Zoella and the rest of the 'Brit crew' may be relative novices at stardom, but they have a keen sense of the value of their franchise. It is only a few years since she cashed her first cheque – for £60 – from Google. But Zoella is now a member of YouTube's 'Style Haul' network, which promotes fashion and beauty content for 'millennial women' (roughly those aged between 13 and 30) and connects its content creators with 'big brands and lucrative deals'.

She has also taken on a 'social talent' agency to manage her increasingly complex affairs, in the form of Gleam Futures, an organization that seems to represent almost everyone on the UK YouTubing scene. 'It's just, like, "You sort it", she says, adding, 'If I didn't have them helping me, I'd sort of combust.'

The leading vloggers are a close-knit bunch, often appearing on each other's channels. This cross-promotion helps to pool audiences. Zoella's gang includes her boyfriend, her brother Joe (whose blog, now with 2 million subscribers, started after hers, she insists) and Marcus Butler. There's also Louise (aka Sprinkle of Glitter) and Tanya Burr, a make-up artist who beams advice from her Norwich bedroom, and whose diffusion line of cosmetics Zoella has recently recommended on her own vlog. 'We all want to help each other so we can bring all our channels up together,' she says. 'That's absolutely what social media is all about: sharing.'

I tell Zoella she is known to the advertising world as a 'crowd-sourced people's champion' and she laughs. 'That's cool. I hadn't heard that one before.' But she acknowledges that big brands are lining up to cash in on her popularity. 'They know that there's a way that YouTubers can connect with an audience that they can't, even though they've got all the money in the world.' An example of her reach is that she has a deal with Unilever, marketing their skincare range to younger users.

Advertisers are said to be willing to pay £20,000 a month for banners on well-known vloggers' YouTube channels, while £4,000 can change hands for each mention of their product in the video itself (it costs roughly the same for a shout-out on Twitter). Zoella doesn't like to talk about how much she earns. But, based on the rates commanded by the most successful vloggers, her income from advertising alone could now be running at a rate of several hundred thousand pounds a year.

This opportunity, of course, brings with it conflicts. And it is these that we contemplate over the debris of lunch. I chide Zoella for not finishing her panino, and she promises to take it home in a doggy bag. (In fact, when we leave, it remains on the table, abandoned.)

The essence of Zoella's Vulcan-like grip on her adherents is the existence of a trusting, even intimate, relationship between vlogger and vlogee. How, I ask, can she preserve this while taking money from advertisers to recommend their products?

Basically, she says, it's a question of judgment. She aims to pick 'partners' whose products she respects and thinks would make good content. 'There isn't any amount of money that could tempt me to promote something that I didn't believe in,' she avers. 'I've built this community of people that trust my opinion and I value that far more than a fat cheque.'

She claims to turn down 90 per cent of deals that she is offered. Some products, such as alcohol, are rejected outright. Her anxiety means she's never been much of a drinker – 'I hate the loss of self-control' – and she gave up a few years ago. With cosmetics and clothes, she operates a simple rule of thumb. 'If it's something I wouldn't wear or don't like, I won't

Modelo Lounge
143–145 Church Road,
Hove BN3

....

Halloumi and muhammara dip panino	£6.95
Chicken breast with rocket and parmesan salad	£10.50
Sherbet lemonade	£2.60
Estrella Damm lager	£4.20

....

Total –	£24.25

consider it,' she says. Those she does accept are disclosed to users in a description box on the site.

As the lunch winds to a close, we talk about the opportunities Zoella has to build an offline career.

She is excited about her book, which touches on themes that are important to her such as anxiety, online relationships and cyberbullying, saying that talking about her own anxiety has actually helped her. 'It's good for me to do things outside my comfort zone and push myself.' As to other ideas, Zoella is open to suggestions. But she would quite like to have her own diffusion range of homeware.

What is most striking is her happy-go-lucky attitude to her own new-found celebrity. 'I never expected any of this to happen so I'm just going to go with it and make the most of it,' she says. 'Who knows what will happen in five years' time.'

We rise to leave and I remember my promise. Would Zoella mind sending a message to one of her younger fans? She agrees to record a greeting on my iPhone (signatures being so yesterday) and I leave in a high humour.

It's only when I view the recording on the train going home that I discover I had put my thumb over the microphone at the crucial moment of filming. The face smiles and the hands wave characteristically. But not a word of Zoella's message can be heard.

The Sybarites

'Wait, what happened to our salmon?'

Isabelle Huppert

'I have unlimited self-confidence'

By Anne-Sylvaine Chassany

'This dessert looks so good. It's Tantalus's torture, walking past with it, just under our noses. And they're doing it again.'

We are finishing the tenth course of a meal that has already been going for two-and-a-half hours but Isabelle Huppert is showing no signs of feeling full. What has caught her eye now is a scoop of beige-coloured ice cream in a greyish soup that waiters are bringing to other tables.

'Monsieur, we're going to have that too, right?' she inquires of our waiter. We are not supposed to. Red berries millefeuilles are our scheduled next dish. But the garçon says he will see what he can do. Huppert approves, mischievous, her dark red lipstick long gone. Not for the first time, I find myself laughing, probably the result of two glasses of champagne and a bottle of red wine – but also of relief.

L'Arpège is one of Paris's finest dining institutions. It is run by 'vegetables king' Alain Passard, who is also legendary for his interminable meals. So I was a little nervous beforehand. What if Huppert and I failed to hit it off but had to soldier on through an epic lunch? With more than a hundred films to her name over nearly five decades, including this year's Golden Globe award and Oscar nomination for her performance in the disturbing rape-drama *Elle*, the actress is known for her courtesy towards journalists but she is also guarded and can be blunt. What if the 'Meryl Streep of France', as she is dubbed in the US media, played Hollywood grande dame?

Shortly before 1.30pm, under a heavy shower, I set foot in the Michelin-starred restaurant, just across the street from the Rodin Museum. I am shown to a round table in the middle of the room – not the discreet spot I had requested. Busy and echoing to clinking glasses,

Illustration by Seb Jarnot

with its lacquered wood panels and curved walls, L'Arpège feels like the interior of a cruise ship. Huppert, of course, is quite at home on centre stage. When she shows up 15 minutes later – elegantly assertive in a black blazer over a white-striped silk shirt, skinny black jeans and black stiletto ankle boots underlining her petite figure – the volume in the room dims. 'Such a religious silence,' she says, putting her sunglasses on the table and her red-haired fringe in order. When she asks for a glass of festive rosé champagne, which arrives instantly with six colourful vegetarian amuse-bouches on silver teaspoons, my worries evaporate.

Huppert says she is not an Arpège regular. So I give her a chance to escape the longest option on the menu, a succession of improvised courses based on the morning's harvest from Passard's properties outside Paris. But Huppert is tempted – and she has cleared her schedule. The 'Gardeners' Lunch' it is.

The first dish is a promising broad-and-green-bean hummus, light and slightly acid, with a beetroot purée spiced with crushed hazelnuts, purple basil and sesame oil. The sommelier serves us a rich Saint-Joseph red from the northern Rhône valley, but first Huppert wants a champagne refill. As we eat she tells me a friend invited her here a few years ago. She is, she says, 'very much a vegetables person'.

Passard's radical culinary shift since 2001 has involved growing his own organic vegetables and, for a period, banning meat. He accomplished this while keeping L'Arpège's three stars. We are still raving about the hummus when we are brought a classic: the soft-boiled egg 'chaud-froid' with Xeres vinegar and maple syrup – the contrast is stimulating, the texture soft and melting.

By now we are talking about Emmanuel Macron, France's new president. Huppert is puzzled by how quickly the press has turned on him after he defeated Marine Le Pen in May's presidential elections. Since then the 39-year-old has won a majority in parliamentary elections and introduced a grand presidential style that he has described as 'Jupiterian' and which the left-wing press has denounced as revealing autocratic leanings.

'He was elected with a certain enthusiasm and immediately we grow suspicious,' she says. 'It's strange. We don't even give him the time . . . Since Macron's identity is to have blurred the right and left, criticism comes from the right and left. Now doomsayers will tell you that by blowing up the right and left, everything is in place for the far-right to reach power next time . . . Personally, I want to believe in him, and for a while.'

After such a good start, the mozzarella and strawberry salad feels bland, but we take comfort in the mighty whole salmon – over one metre long, from Scotland, cooked in a crust of salt – to which we are briefly introduced. It has been a momentous year for Huppert on a personal level too. But she is typically insouciant about her Oscar nomination for Best Actress. 'If I had gone through all this in a little country . . . but it's America, it's irrational, it's blown out of proportion. It tells a lot about how people relate to America. When you're there, you're just in a town called Los Angeles.' She seems more overwhelmed by her recent trip to China, where she gave live readings of Marguerite Duras's *The Lover* – a partly autobiographical novel about the author's affair, when she was 15, with an older Chinese man in colonial Vietnam – to huge crowds. 'They knew it so well. The reactions afterwards were insane, so enthusiastic. It was moving.'

Next up is an unexpected mustard sorbet in a cold cucumber soup that brings back memories of the late New Wave director Claude Chabrol, who directed Huppert in seven films. The bespectacled bon vivant used to pick locations according to his love of haute cuisine. Around New Year's Eve 1996 in Savoie, he insisted on driving 40km through a blizzard to get to chef Marc Veyrat's restaurant near Annecy in the Alps. 'We thought we would never make it,' Huppert recalls. When they arrived, the heating was broken and the place was empty, barring a party of Japanese tourists.

Chabrol once said that he saw 'eye to eye' with Huppert and that she would 'never cease to surprise me and perform better than anything I have dreamt of'. Huppert has described her bond with him as 'filial'. She excelled in his Balzac-like depictions of perversion amid the provincial bourgeoisie. In 1978, he chose her to play the title role in *Violette Nozière*, the true story of a 1930s teenager who poisoned her father and was sentenced to the guillotine. Huppert won the Cannes Festival's Best Actress award for the role. Her success in *Nozière* heralded a series of ambiguous female characters and a second Best Actress award in Cannes for Michael Haneke's 2001 *The Piano Teacher*. More recently, she has featured in comedies. But her performance in Paul Verhoeven's *Elle*, as a rape victim who engages in a sexual game with her attacker, is further testimony to her mastery of darker characters.

Before she goes into this there is a more pressing issue: she wants to change the wine. Taken aback, the sommelier brings a lighter bourgogne, but I find it too acid. As he heads back to his cellar, grumbling – he will bring a decent red from Côte Roannaise – a tall figure marches towards us: it is Passard. 'Imagine, people want to eat tomatoes in winter, when all they need is a good parsnip soup!' he exclaims. Huppert promises she will no longer eat tomatoes in winter, but it is summer and we happily tuck into our thin tomato tart, topped with purple basil and anchovies. As she does so, she speculates about a man eating alone and scrutinizes a party of eight, probably an American family. But observation is not the inspiration for her minimalist acting, she insists. 'It's all inside, vertical, not at all panoramic. I can be an actress without getting out of my bedroom. I like watching people, it amuses me, but it has nothing to do with my work. Now, observing people in the street, to see that most have pretty empty gazes, it gives me one clue, essentially that I need to do less. Fiction tends to inflate everything. Observation pushes you to subtract, rather than to add.'

This surely applies to her character in *Elle*. At first, Michèle seems to brush aside her rape and move on to deal with other crises – her unemployed son who is about to become a father, her irritable daughter-in-law, her mother who wants to remarry with a younger man, her video-game company and her sick father, in prison for going on a killing rampage when she was 10. After the rape, she picks up the broken glass on her kitchen floor, takes a bath, orders sushi. She stays alone in her big house, even after realizing that her rapist is the neighbour about whom she fantasizes. 'The many subplots are intended to show she puts the rape at the same level as her many other issues,' says Huppert. 'She wants it to be almost like a non-event, which makes it highly troubling. At the beginning of the film, you could think the rape is minimized. But the end is perfectly clear.'

She says the film raises more questions than it provides answers. Its success, especially in the US, surprised her. She found out later that Verhoeven had envisaged a Hollywood twist and a US actress for the role but that none of those approached accepted it. 'There's a form of provocation,' she says of the director. 'It's a way to send a message to

Hollywood, even if he offends a lot of people in passing. But all ended really well. And he said he could never have directed another actress, so he has admitted his weakness.'

She does not seek in her performances to provoke viewers with 'monsters', she insists. 'My interpretation of these roles is precisely to bring them back to a certain normality. They are so close that everybody can see themselves in them.' Her next film, directed by Neil Jordan and scheduled for later this year, is 'more difficult. My character is evil. People will see what a real pervert is. But I am still going to try to give some clues to understand her . . . It's a way to say that the frontier between evil and normality is thin. Is there such a thing as pure evil? That's the question nowadays, when a guy gets into a Jewish school in Toulouse and kills two children aged five and eight.' She is referring to an attack that took place in 2012, the first of a series of deadly Islamist terrorist assaults in France. 'Verhoeven's film asks the question of good and evil. How to answer it? We can't.'

She breaks off. 'Wait, what happened to our salmon?' Instead, we are presented with a whole roasted lamb, still steaming. 'It looks friendly – I could almost pat it,' she muses. 'Shall we ask the waiter about the salmon? We need to get to the bottom of this. A salmon was presented to us. It looked really nice, we said hello to it.' It is on its way, we are assured, and here it is, half cooked and in green pea mousse and broccoli. Huppert picks up one of the weirdly shaped green tomatoes that decorate our table and gestures over her plate. I realize she thinks it is salt. 'It's a tomato,' I say, giggling. 'Really?' She keeps trying to shake it for a few more seconds.

Huppert's appetite – or rather her determination to experiment – is astonishing. Her hunger for acting seems insatiable too. She has never slowed down, starring in two or three films a year, as well as the occasional play. 'I know this is what people say, but other actresses like Julianne Moore are as busy.' Huppert, who is married to film-maker Ronald Chammah and has three children, has worked with some of the greatest French directors but has no nostalgia. 'The cinema I like is the one I am living now . . . It's more a question of people than a question of genre or script.' As an intriguing hay-whipped cream appears before us, she has a few messages to send across the Atlantic: she would like to work with Stephen Frears, David Cronenberg and Woody Allen. I freeze.

How come she never worked with the Francophile Allen? Huppert would be such an obvious choice. 'Here you go. I find this astonishing too,' she says. 'There's not much time left. He's not that young any more. I know him well. You need a certain context. I heard he's going to make a film in France soon . . .' She pauses: 'Besides, he does so many of them. Frankly, what would it cost him to do one with me, *vite fait, bien fait*? It's really not a big deal. He doesn't know what he is missing. I do. He will when it's too late.'

I am giggling again, but more seriously, I ask her whether she has absolute confidence in herself. 'Yes,' she replies. 'I have absolute confidence in my acting abilities, since the beginning. It may sound arrogant. I never doubt. I have absolutely no fear. I have unlimited self-confidence. There are so many other areas where I am not that, I am not ashamed to say it.' What makes her doubt? 'Crossing the street, meeting people . . . Everything that's vital. But acting, nothing can intimidate me. Acting is never an obstacle. I do it without thinking. It's like eating or drinking. It's a non-event . . . Of course it's an enormous pleasure, but there's no stress.'

Some of her most memorable scenes show her translucent green eyes filling with tears. I cannot help but ask how she makes herself cry. 'Very easily. It's so easy. It's also an enormous amount of concentration. It means I won't say hi to people in the morning. It implies a sort of hyper-concentration. It's demanding. I need silence. But it's not a state I need to be in from 8am, I can easily get into it. I just need to be in my thing.'

Our final savoury dishes come in the shape of three vegetable raviolis in a warm verveine consommé and roasted lamb over courgette flowers. After our millefeuilles, the lunch reaches its resolution with the greyish ice cream that caught her eye: the house's Ile flottante 'moka-verbena',

L'Arpège
84 rue de Varenne, Paris

....

Menu le déjeuner des jardiniers ('Gardeners' Lunch') x 2	€290
Côte Roannaise Clos du Puy Pothiers x 2 glasses	€30
Champagne rosé x 4 glasses	€120
Bottle of Badoit mineral water	€9
Coffee x 2	€14

....

| Total – | €463 (£412) |

a coffee ice cream in a sage and mint sauce – a fabulous, masculine bliss. 'I knew it was divine. Too good. It's delicious,' Huppert says. 'It's not sweet at all! We've lost three kilos.'

It is past 5pm, a ray of sunlight filters through the frosted glass windows. But Huppert is ready for more. When our espressos arrive, she looks disappointed: 'Ah, they're not bringing any sweets with it.'

Carlo Ancelotti

'I don't need to try it, I know this wine'

By Janan Ganesh

'German is the hardest language.' Bavaria-bound Carlo Ancelotti remembers the relative doddle of English, Spanish and French when he grapples with the snaking compound nouns of his new home. 'And the verbs,' he groans, 'sometimes they go in the second position in a sentence, and then again at the end.' He puffs out his cheeks and – there it is – raises the arced left eyebrow that is the most celebrated feature on his Federico Fellini face.

Even in the bland livery of successful men – navy jacket, tieless pale-blue shirt – the 56-year-old Italian football coach is distinctive enough to obviate any need for a caricature. This summer Bayern Munich joins Juventus, Milan, Chelsea, Paris Saint-Germain and Real Madrid as the sixth European super-club to submit to his leadership. He will arrive from Vancouver – where he has a home with his Canadian wife, Mariann – and he will win major prizes. We know this because he always does.

The hand that shakes mine at Babbo, an Italian restaurant of his choosing in Mayfair, has lifted the Champions League trophy three times. It is a record in the modern history of Europe's highest competition. He has prospered in four countries. Steeped in glory, loved by players for his light touch, he is probably the most coveted coach in the world.

He is also the only one you can imagine choosing a club by the local restaurants. Food plays the cameo in most Lunches with the *FT* but Ancelotti, a gourmand, makes it central to this one. My resolve to order lightly – I usually avoid daytime eating altogether – melts in the glare of his keenness. We ask for some starters to share, of which the best judged is a baked aubergine melanzane with a layer of cheese that knocks the

Illustration by James Ferguson

adjacent plate of burrata into apologetic irrelevance. 'You like Italian food?' he checks, and I nod, deciding not to sell him on the superiority of Spanish.

Babbo is technically superb but very Mayfair. Four old women in pearls and taffeta sit near us, two hedgies of indeterminate nationality squint at my guest between mouthfuls from the other side of the room. I give him the name of an edgier trattoria in Islington and he rolls it around his mouth a few times as if committing it to memory. This is a man who titled his autobiography *Preferisco La Coppa*, which declares an ambition for trophies and a taste for ham in one three-word pun.

Italians can be unswervingly faithful to the produce of their region but Ancelotti, who grew up in Emilia-Romagna in the north, veers as far as next-door Tuscany for his wine. He summons a bottle of Guidalberto – 'I don't need to try it, I know this wine' – a blend of Cabernet Sauvignon and Merlot that mimics the strength of claret without zapping you into a thousand-night coma.

For Ancelotti, football clubs are either 'families', such as AC Milan, or 'companies', of which Juventus is a purring example. With his genial style, his cultivation of personal bonds with players and directors, it is clear which he prefers. Silvio Berlusconi ran Milan as a patriarch, involving himself intimately with technical matters. The Agnelli family, which still owns Juve, preferred to put systems in place and keep itself in reserve for strategic judgments. As he raises his glass, I ask him to categorize Bayern. 'I have not had so many meetings with them but I think it is a family,' he says, perhaps sanguinely of an institution that is part-owned by Audi, Adidas and Allianz. 'They have former players on the board. The club is 70 per cent owned by members.'

It is certainly corporate in its ruthless pursuit of players. I wonder who he rates among the nascent talents of world football and that eyebrow vaults up again. 'I cannot tell you on the record because the price will go up,' he says, before naming teenagers from France and Brazil, even taking out his phone to show me the latter. 'Don't tell Arsène Wenger!'

He is more candid about the established greats he has already managed. There is special affection for Cristiano Ronaldo, a self-motivating near-cyborg who took 3am ice baths in Real Madrid's training complex. 'Even though he had Irina Shayk waiting for him at home!' Ancelotti yelps, referring to the Portuguese's former lover. 'He does not care about money, he just wants to be the first' – meaning the best. Other favoured sons include Andrea Pirlo, who played the midfield role Ancelotti himself held down for Milan and Italy in the 1980s, and the country's decorated goalkeeper Gigi Buffon ('I found him at 17 in the Parma academy').

We have both ordered the lobster main course. The dish turns out to be a filleted hunk of the crustacean atop a morass of tagliolini. Like all the best pasta, it is moreish for reasons of texture rather than taste. Having no potent flavour to vie with, Ancelotti's choice of wine suddenly comes into its own. It is as though he does this a lot.

Before our lunch, I tested Ancelotti's name on friends who care little or nought for football but know their José Mourinho from their Pep Guardiola. Most had never heard of him. Two assumed I meant Claudio Ranieri of Leicester City. One knew the name but could not place the face. His lack of cut-through – which, like all things in life, fails to trouble this equable soul – owes everything to the brand of quiet leadership that is also the name of his new management book.

Most elite coaches today are incendiary. There is Diego Simeone at Atlético Madrid, with his bandit chic. Liverpool contains, just about, the white heat of Jürgen Klopp's enthusiasm. Guardiola is bringing his Rasputin intensity from Bayern to Manchester City. Ancelotti has none of this. 'My character is quiet,' he says quietly. 'It is because of my family. My father was quiet. He never shouted. He never kicked me. My mother also. That is the fundamental reason.'

His book describes a manager who nudges more than he pushes, often going along with conclusions reached independently by his players instead of mandating his own. Leaders within a squad are, he believes, 'chosen by the group, not the manager or the president', and the Dutchman Clarence Seedorf was one of these natural characters at Milan. During his time there, Ancelotti had to cram a galaxy of talent into four midfield positions. With gentle shepherding from him, the players thought themselves into the 'diamond' formation – with Pirlo at its base, the Brazilian Kaká at its tip, and Seedorf and Rui Manuel Costa, a lavishly gifted Portuguese, either side – that gleamed on the European stage.

Between sips, I ask whether he feels under-exalted, at least outside the game's cognoscenti. 'You have possibilities to be angry every single day,' he says. 'But the happiness is not in the credit, it is in the work, in the relationship with the players, with the staff. I don't worry what they put in newspapers.'

Lots of people in public life say that last sentence. Ancelotti means it. If anything, obscurity means privacy, especially in Canada. Even after decades in the Italian countryside and Europe's great cities, he is thrown by Vancouver's gorgeous setting. 'The beach, the mountains . . . '

He does not take material comfort for granted. The Ancelotti family worked, but did not own, the farm on which he was raised, turning out slabs of Parmesan cheese to a grateful world. Rural life left him with a discriminating palate (he has a mental map of Italian restaurants worth a damn in London, Paris, Vancouver and Madrid) and a dialect that can stump his own countrymen.

Football-barmy in the Italian way, he launched his career as a tactically astute midfielder at nearby Parma. From there he went to Roma, in the capital, which could have been Saturn for this country boy. A knee injury put him out of the 1982 World Cup that Italy won but no bitterness lingers, just gratitude for a career that survived. 'You are 23 and you don't know if you can play again,' he recalls with a wince. 'The physical therapy was terrible in those days.'

In 1987, Ancelotti made the move that changed his life. A figure of fun called Arrigo Sacchi brought him to Milan. Until then, Italians had favoured a defensive mode of play called *catenaccio*. 'It means this,' he says, tapping the lock on a door next to our table. Sacchi smashed convention by drilling his players to challenge for the ball – or 'press' – high up the field, forcing opponents into errors and exploiting them with a lethal batch of imported forwards such as the Dutch great Marco van Basten. Ancelotti was the point of fixity in this swarm, which dominated Europe and still inspires modern coaches.

Sacchi turned out to be no joke. His pressing game is visible today from Liverpool to Munich. Some of the most in-demand players are midfielders who seldom score or assist but have the sangfroid and close control to retain the ball under intense pressure. Clubs have upgraded their fitness and conditioning regimes to sustain the physical effort Sacchi-ism demands.

As a player at Milan, Ancelotti served as an on-field conduit for these visions. A deep-lying midfielder must think systemic thoughts about the game, like a coach. After a season or two in the position, a future in management is virtually hard-wired. Not coincidentally, Simeone and Guardiola mastered versions of the role as players. Sure enough, after helping Sacchi steer Italy to the 1994 World Cup final, Ancelotti returned to his roots to start his own coaching career: first with Reggiana, then Parma.

Success took him to Juventus and the lofty echelon of clubs from which he has never stooped since. There was Milan, where he clinched two of his Champions Leagues and assembled that luminous midfield. Then Chelsea, where he won the league and cup double in his first season. Then Paris Saint-Germain, where he won the league and imposed professional standards on a club that had more ambition than know-how ('There was no restaurant for the players'). And then, two years ago, *la decima* – a tenth Champions League for Real Madrid, and a hat-trick for Ancelotti.

No tactical revolutions, no psychological ploys, no memorable quotes, just frictionless success in all of Europe's major leagues. There is no record quite like it. Zlatan Ibrahimović, a player who surrenders compliments as though they singe his throat, says Ancelotti is the best coach in the world.

On the subject of galactic egos, how does a quiet man bend them to his will? 'There are things where you can be elastic,' he explains, 'and things where you must be strong. If the players say "Coach, we have a tough week, can we stay in bed one more hour?" that is OK. But when I have a meeting before the game, you must be on time. At Chelsea, we had a meeting at 10.30am and [Didier] Drogba was not there. I don't know if it was traffic or what. He came at 11. He didn't play.'

What Ancelotti lacks in fire, he more than covers with deep, deep

---

Babbo
39–40 Albemarle Street,
London W1

....

Bottle of	
Guidalberto	£82
Roasted octopus	£10.50
Babbo melanzane	£9.75
Burrata	£11
Tagliolini	
lobster x 2	£45.40
Fried zucchini	£4.50
Spinach	£4.50
Petits fours no charge	
Double espresso	£4
Espresso	£3
Grappa Barili x 2	£46

....

Total	
(inc. service) –	£248.23

sanity. Quiet leadership, to judge by the book and his personal manner, is less a technique than a disposition, an aura. By standing still in football's storm of hype and cupidity, he reassures players. He coaches like he played, always providing that fixed point from which others can do spectacular things. The Chelsea squad of 2010 was not so different to the one that fell short in the previous three seasons. The talent was there. Ancelotti got out of its way.

The criticism is that, like a less provocative Mourinho, he is ultimately a hired gun. He slides into great clubs, wins prizes commensurate with their station and moves on without leaving his imprint. He is not associated with a style of play like Guardiola or with a litter of youngsters he nurtured to greatness, like Klopp in his stint at Borussia Dortmund. He is curiously identity-less, like a restaurant in Mayfair.

Maybe that is what it takes to live an itinerant life. He has gone farther, seen more, than his rustic roots ever promised. I press him for his favourite posting. 'France is difficult because football is not always number one. They have rugby and cycling. They also have some violence in PSG. England has the best atmosphere, the best stadiums and no violence,' he says. Despite leaving Italy seven years ago, the disorder and vegetating infrastructure blighting parts of its league, which was Europe's best as recently as the 1990s, still pains him.

'England is different. When I was with Chelsea, we went to play up in Sunderland. The bus could not drive all the way to the entrance. So the security man from the stadium says, "It's OK, get out and walk." I say, "No, I don't go!" There were Sunderland fans all around. After some time, we had to do it.'

And it was OK?

'It was perfect. Some fans took pictures. No trouble. I never received an insult in England, ever.'

We ask for espressos in lieu of dessert but, before the waiter can retreat, Ancelotti has an idea. 'You like grappa?' Yes, Carlo. So what began as an ascetic denial of a sugar rush has turned into a spread of caffeine hits, petits fours and Italy's answer to sherry. I try to pay but Ancelotti has already arranged something with the proprietor. How quiet. How effective.

Wole Soyinka

'I am a closet glutton for tranquillity'

By David Pilling

I t is just as the main course arrives that Wole Soyinka – playwright, poet, novelist, essayist and part-time agitator – reaches into his pocket and brings out a plump green chilli. 'Actually, when I travel I always carry a special paste, which I have made for me – paste which I put in my pocket,' he offers by way of explanation in his plummy baritone. 'This one,' he says, proceeding to dissect the dapple-green pepper, 'I got when I arrived in London. Because I forgot my paste in the fridge in Sochi.'

There's something in the casualness of the gesture that sums up the larger-than-life 83-year-old. Soyinka, one of the great post-colonial literary figures – he won Africa's first Nobel Prize for literature in 1986 – and a fearless denouncer of dictators, is a peripatetic adventurer, seemingly at total ease in his own skin. In the chilli incident is a dash of eccentricity, a deft nod to travels in Russia, and the confidence of a man happy to produce his own fiery condiment in a London fish restaurant. There's the set-in-his-ways gentleman doing things just so and the Bohemian man of letters who doesn't give a damn. His bristly white beard and snow-white Afro, which conjures up a lavish bubble bath, complete the picture.

I am leant in rather close because Soyinka, though mentally as sharp as razor wire, is struggling to hear me over the 1970s soul and hubbub of Friday-afternoon diners. We had asked to have the music turned down at the start of the meal because Soyinka's hearing aid magnifies ambient sounds. The waitress had come back unbudgeable, apologizing but citing 'company rules'. I've been rather tickled ever since by the notion that, as a result, Soyinka has not been responding to my questions, but rather answering inquiries from diners at other tables. His

Illustration by Ciaran Murphy

anecdotes flow in a riverine gush unhindered by my efforts to change their course.

Soyinka chose Pescatori in Fitzrovia, an upscale part of London within eyeshot of the spindly BT Tower, because it has been a Nigerian hangout for decades. He hasn't been for years and there's no sign of recognition from the staff. The moment he sits down, the waitress offers to pour him water, which he rejects as though she were insisting he start with a plate of spinach.

'I'll have a glass of wine,' he says, as if this were self-evident. We opt for a bottle, but when I ask the waitress for a recommendation, Soyinka intervenes. 'Since you're not choosing,' he says, shooting me a slightly contemptuous glance, 'do they have Arneis de Roero?' 'I won't let the waiter choose, on principle,' he says, as she pours us each a generous glass of the Arneis, a white grape variety from Piedmont.

It is the sort of firmly held conviction, about matters great and small, that has so often landed Soyinka into what he calls 'hot water'. Hot water, it transpires, can range from causing a 'hell of a kerfuffle' for diving, under the influence of malarial fever, into the pool of an Atlanta hotel – 'It was the first time any black person had ever immersed his body in that swimming pool' – to spending two years rotting in a Nigerian prison.

Though he writes in English, Soyinka presents an African view of the world and his prose is steeped in Yoruba mythology. Yet he rarely goes easy on African despots – from Omar al-Bashir of Sudan to Zimbabwe's Robert Mugabe. After urging his countrymen to stop paying taxes during the mid-1990s military dictatorship of Sani Abacha and escaping from Nigeria by motorbike, he was sentenced to death in absentia in 1997 and was only able to return when civilian rule was restored in 1999.

Soyinka's adventures, scrapes and brushes with the law – some of which have no doubt improved in the telling – have formed the material for several memoirs, from *The Man Died: Prison Notes* (1971) to *You Must Set Forth at Dawn* (2006). Together with 30 plays, two novels, several collections of poetry and countless thunderous essays, they form a voluminous body of work that makes Soyinka a sort of Samuel Johnson of his age.

He has never been tired of Lagos or London, much less of life. Back in 1965, as factional and ethnic politics began to grip post-independence

Nigeria, he was arrested for holding up a radio station at gunpoint. The idea was to stop a minister from taking to the airwaves. When I inquire about the incident, he mishears me. 'Did you say mimic gun?' he asks. (I didn't.) 'One of the myths, and I have many myths surrounding me, is that I went in with a toy gun, which I find very funny. Let's just say I have never held a toy gun in my life.'

At this point, a different waiter appears with our starters, a plump pinkish octopus tentacle (like a severed arm) for Soyinka and what was supposed to be a prawn and crayfish cocktail for me. I look at the two slices of rolled-up ham and protest that it is not what I ordered. The waiter scowls and thrusts it at me anyway. A moment later the manager appears, whipping both plates away to the evident mystification of Soyinka, who is left with his knife and fork poised above the tablecloth.

A few minutes later, our rightful starters restored, we are discussing Soyinka's childhood in Abeokuta, a city in the fertile wooded savannah of south-west Nigeria. He was born in 1934, the second of six children, his mother a shopkeeper and political activist and his father an Anglican minister and headmaster of St Peter's Primary School. 'I grew up with street theatre of one form or another. The masquerades that many people think are purely sacred have a performance aspect. It was an unbelievable pageant. It awoke my theatrical instincts.' After attending Abeokuta Grammar School, where he won several writing prizes, Soyinka went on to University College Ibadan to study English literature, Greek and western history, and from there, in 1954, to Leeds University. Already prolific, after he graduated he wrote plays including *The Lion and the Jewel*, which attracted the attention of London's Royal Court Theatre. His first work to appear there was a one-act play about apartheid South Africa called *The Invention*. It was preceded by a poetry recital to which Soyinka invited his cousin, a young musician called Fela Kuti, to accompany him on stage. That was a big break for Fela, who went on to become the legendary father of Afrobeat.

The two shared a flat in Bayswater. 'We were impecunious. We shared everything,' he says, polishing off the last sliver of octopus and mopping a dab of sauce from his prodigious beard. 'Everything. I won't say more than that. It was a wild apartment.'

Soyinka returned to Nigeria in 1959 and, when independence arrived in 1960, wrote a play, *A Dance of the Forests*, for the celebrations.

Nigeria's new elite did not like it. Soyinka refused to gloss over Africa's past, including the participation of Africans in the slave trade. The play warned of the dangers of a new corrupt class emerging to occupy the space vacated by the British. Soyinka has been at war with African despots ever since.

The waitress returns with our main course, spaghetti vongole for him and a grilled Dover sole for me. More wine is poured. I've ordered Jersey Royal potatoes, but Soyinka is not tempted to share them. 'I've been ruined by the African yam. I lost all taste for potatoes since I was a student, thanks to mashed potatoes,' he says.

'Excuse me, I am going to bring something out with which I always travel.' It is at this point that he produces the chilli.

Soyinka spent the next several years writing and teaching in Nigeria. In 1967, he met the leader of breakaway Biafra, then embroiled in a ruinous civil war, an encounter that landed him two years in solitary confinement. In his cell, he scratched out protest poetry on toilet paper and cigarette packages.

Despite such hard experiences, I suggest, there is something picaresque about his escapades. 'Fortunately, I have a saving sense of self-deflation. Still, there are certain issues about which I feel very strongly and for which I am prepared to go any lengths,' he says, clattering a clamshell into a side bowl. Even prison? 'That's an occupational risk. You don't really set out to go to jail. It just happens, and you have to accept it as a penalty of taking certain risks. I just like to be at peace with myself,' he says, adding that some things he cannot let lie. 'One is one's own ultimate judge. The view of the rest of the world is trivial.'

Out of jail, Soyinka stepped up his political activity, turning his pen against misrule across the continent. 'With any society coming out of one phase of suppression there's always a contest for the repossession of the space of power,' he says. 'It could be a focused, very purposeful elite or just a demagogue rising from the slums.'

Few leaders – politicians, generals or the religious zealots behind Boko Haram – have escaped his contempt. Of the latter, he says: 'For the first time, I began to accept the existence of the theological concept called "evil". Of course the foot soldiers in any cause are usually obtained from the disenfranchised. But the real initiators of this kind of violence are not. They believe in power.'

When I ask how optimistic he is about Africa, where coups are rarer and governments come and go with more regularity, he is cautious. No sooner is there some positive development in one corner of the continent, he says, than something else – like Boko Haram – sets things back. I ask him to name a good Nigerian leader, but he struggles for an answer.

Soyinka has spent much time in the US, where he has taught at a number of universities. 'My life has been involved with the diaspora on a very personal and visceral level,' he says of his interaction with prominent African-Americans. Donald Trump's election marked an end to his US sojourn. In what has become known among Nigerians as 'Wolexit', he cut up his Green Card. 'To have some redneck ride into power on the steed of racism was for me too much.' Later this month, when he delivers a regular Harvard lecture, 'I'll go in as an alien, an alien from outer space. I love that designation.'

The bottle of Arneis is drained and Soyinka looks mournfully at his empty glass. I suggest another. He brightens, opting for 'a robust Italian red. Montepulciano. Two glasses.'

I ask about the state of writing on the African continent. Nigeria in particular, hardly a stranger to brilliant fiction from the likes of Soyinka, Chinua Achebe and Ben Okri, has recently seen an astonishing flourishing of literary talent. Chimamanda Ngozi Adichie, author of *Half of a Yellow Sun* – which Soyinka describes as 'marvellous' – is but the best known. There are dozens of others from all parts of the country and the diaspora, including Elnathan John, Leye Adenle and Teju Cole, writing in a dazzling range of styles. Many of the brightest talents, including Sarah Ladipo Manyika and Ayobami Adebayo, are women.

'We have a crop of young female writers coming out of Africa these days. It's really very impressive. There is a general unleashing of female energy.' He is reluctant to name names for fear of it being 'taken as some kind of Wole Soyinka endorsement'. (He takes no part even in the literary prize that bears his name.) Many of the writers, he says, reflect a broader female stirring on the continent, from business to politics and even religion – what he calls a 'Here I am, deal with that' attitude. He wonders whether the literary outpouring is some kind of reaction to religious fundamentalism. 'Could it be a kind of subconscious response to the misogynist agenda of extremist religious strains?' The waitress takes away my Dover sole to be re-grilled. I have been so engrossed in conversation it is only half eaten.

I ask about his own work's reputation for difficulty. One reviewer accused him of never writing 'house' when he could write 'habitation'. Short words are so boring, he says, adding that he thinks in Yoruba, whose vocabulary has very precise meaning. 'If it is too difficult, too self-consciously mannered and stylistic, for heaven's sake just throw it in the garbage and read something else.'

Soyinka spends much of his time these days in Abeokuta, where he lives with his much-younger third wife, though he keeps a 'pied-à-terre' in Lagos. 'I am a closet glutton for tranquillity,' he says, despite what he admits are outward appearances to the contrary. But people and events 'keep dragging me back'.

How many children does he have? 'In Yoruba tradition, we say it is unfortunate to count your children. The gods have been unusually generous in my own circumstances, unsolicitedly generous,' he says, emphasizing each syllable. 'I am quite content. I told my children and grandchildren recently that I am changing my title to the Grand Patriarch. That's how I am referred to now by my entire clan.'

How long do you intend to live for, I ask, surprised at my own question. 'By all logic I should not be alive right now because of my lifestyle,' he replies, unfazed. 'I flout everything they teach at medical school, including the fact that I don't drink water.' He looks at his untouched glass. 'I eat only when I want to. I don't obey the rules of cholesterol.'

What about smoking? 'I used to smoke hard cigarettes. Gitanes, Gauloises, cigars and cheroots especially. But I lost interest several years ago,' he says, draining the Montepulciano.

Pescatori

57 Charlotte St, Fitzrovia,
London W1

....

Polpo alla griglia	£11.50
Prawn cocktail	£10.50
Jersey Royals	£3.75
Spaghetti vongole	£18.50
Dover sole	£39
San Pellegrino	£4
Espresso	£2.40
Double espresso	£2.80
Bottle of Arneis	
Langhe	£45
Montepulciano x	
2 glasses	£13.90

....

Total	
(inc. service) –	£170.27

We've been talking for nearly three hours, but he can't resist one last story. 'I had an argument with Fidel Castro about it,' he says, as if this might be a common occurrence. 'By that time Castro had got religion about the perils of smoking and he rounded on a *guerrillero*, saying, "This is bad for you. I have medical evidence." He started bullying him. I said, "Wait a minute. Leave the man alone. Let him find his own time."' Soyinka says this triggered a two-hour discussion. 'Castro loved to argue. But I think that day he met his match.'

The two called it an evening and Soyinka retired to bed. 'The following morning a box of cigars – Cohiba – arrived at my hotel. It just said, "With compliments of the Cuban government". Who did it? To this day, I've no idea. But I still have some of them in Abeokuta.' He pauses. 'That's the story of my smoking career.'

Richard Desmond

'Everyone's having a go at you, so you've got to be the fighter'

By Henry Mance

I n Richard Desmond's hands, simple objects become terrifying. There's the receptionist's bell that he uses to interrupt executives in board meetings, or the cups of tea that occasionally fly over underlings.

For me, the terror begins when he picks up the wine list. This is Coq d'Argent, a rooftop restaurant overlooking the Bank of England. The prices look like cricket scores – and Desmond is on the hunt for an innings victory.

'We'll have that one,' he says, before I can intervene. As the sommelier skips away, the sum of £580 lingers on my retina.

So this, I think, is how it feels to be screwed by Richard Desmond. It took less than 10 minutes.

At least I am not the first. If the media mogul goes down in history for anything, it will be screwing – and not just because of his investments in adult TV, which include the world's most honestly titled channel, Filth.

There was the time when he devised a contractual clause so advantageous that the distributors of his magazines nearly went bankrupt. A judge eventually stepped in; but Desmond nonetheless walked away with £17 million.

Last summer, after employees at his *Express* newspaper titles went a seventh consecutive year without pay rises, the National Union of Journalists described Desmond as 'Britain's greediest billionaire'. 'Worst human being on earth,' opined a Sony executive extravagantly and without any explanation, when mulling a possible bid for his broadcaster Channel 5.

Illustration by James Ferguson

But Desmond usually finds a way to answer his detractors. He sold Channel 5 for £463 million last year – more than four times the amount he paid for it in 2010. Overlooked for a peerage by the Conservative party, he reinvented himself as the biggest donor to Nigel Farage's UK Independence Party.

Arranging this lunch has taken a year, a period in which Desmond has fallen out with two of his closest communications advisers. He usually comes to Coq d'Argent with his bankers. 'You always get a nice table, you can smoke if you want to outside,' he explains. 'Of course I don't smoke because I'm a winner.'

This catches me by surprise; last I heard, cigars were a key part of Desmond's media-mogul shtick. 'The worst thing about giving up smoking is that I've put on 16 fucking pounds,' he says. 'There was one day that I couldn't do up any pair of trousers.'

I lower my gaze, and silently agree that the pinstripes on his blue suit do look unnaturally stretched. Desmond, 63, asks how old I am. Thirty-two, I say. 'Eight years. Then you're fucked.'

The menu features a few dozen French dishes, typed in the kind of dull font that is better suited to reading mortgage terms and conditions. 'What's the fish today?' asks Desmond, who used to be pescatarian, and still rarely eats meat. He settles for the waiter's recommendations – a tuna steak, medium rare, with a tomato salad to start.

I choose from the vegetarian options – a goat's-cheese-based starter, followed by a goat's-cheese-stuffed main. Desmond orders sides of beans and spinach, presumably for us both.

He turns to me, with the question I had hoped to answer after a glass of wine. 'So tell me – what did you think of the book?'

The Real Deal, published this month, is Desmond's autobiography – the story of how a miserable Jewish kid from north London became a billionaire, and clambered on to the ramparts of the British establishment in the process.

In it, Desmond claims to have started selling advertising at the age of five, as an interpreter for his father, Cyril, who had suddenly gone deaf. At 13, he was working in the cloakroom of the Manor House pub, where he quickly realized that if he put two coats on a single hanger he could pocket an extra sixpence. By his early twenties, he had set up his first magazines – *International Musician and Recording World* and

Home Organist. Then, in 1983, he snapped up the licence to publish *Penthouse* in the UK, establishing him as one of the country's porn kings.

Desmond's trick – be it with celebrity magazines, newspapers or telephone sex lines – has been to copy the market leader and to compete with it ruthlessly. In 1993, seeing the leading celebrity magazine *Hello!* was full of obscure European royalty – 'Prince Schnorbitz of Bratislavia' is how he describes it at lunch – Desmond launched *OK!*, a rival which focused on British soap stars.

That, and a tight control over costs. By his own account in the book, Desmond once turned down a prostitute because he calculated her fee was the equivalent to the profit on a page-and-a-half of advertising.

'Did it come across that we weren't in it for the money – but for the craic, for the stirring it up?' he asks. This is how Desmond wants to be seen, and his disarming, jovial persona generally backs it up. But, even at a quiet table overlooking a wisteria-clad patio, his menace is sometimes barely concealed.

His business career? 'There's always some cunt trying to stop me.' The death of *Hello!*'s owner, Eduardo Sánchez Junco, in 2010, with whom Desmond fought a lengthy court battle over photographs of Michael Douglas and Catherine Zeta-Jones's wedding? 'I take full responsibility for that,' he smiles. A decision by ad agency Omnicom to stop buying spots on Channel 5 the day after he sold it? 'I'd have kneecapped them. I'd have gone after the clients directly.'

The food arrives swiftly, along with the wine, a 1983 Bordeaux from the Château Palmer estate. 'This is our last bottle,' the sommelier says, in an act of financial mercy. 'Oh, I bet you tell that to all the boys,' Desmond replies.

The sommelier is worried that the wine has only just emerged from the cooler, and will still be about 11°C. Might this be grounds for a discount, I wonder hopefully? He assures us that it should be fine within five minutes. 'The nose is absolutely fantastic,' he adds.

Desmond picks up his wine glass, and asks if I have any children. No, I reply. 'To your children,' he toasts, undeterred.

We move on to politics. Desmond, who in the *Daily Express* and *Daily Star* owns two tabloids with combined sales of 1 million copies a day, tells me he feels snubbed by the prime minister David Cameron.

'Rude,' says Desmond, who claims Cameron once trod on his foot at a party in a rush to approach that bigger media fish Rupert Murdoch. 'He's very lightweight. But he'd be very good running this restaurant, wouldn't he?'

Desmond fancifully attributes their poor relationship to an encounter years earlier, when Cameron was a PR man whose boss wanted to turn *OK!* into a TV show. He also blames class: 'The non-posh people like me are jealous of the posh people because they have the confidence.'

Despite donating £1.3 million to Ukip so far, Desmond is not sure he agrees with its main policy, leaving the European Union. 'I don't know. I don't think anyone knows,' he says. 'But we need a referendum.'

The main courses arrive, and Desmond greets them with his second favourite f-word. 'Fantastic. They do look after you here, don't they?'

I carve into a courgette tart. Desmond heaps English mustard to the left of his tuna. The cuff of his right sleeve rubs into the pesto. The wine is delicious, especially now that I have stopped seeing the reflection of the *FT* expenses department in my glass.

For decades, Desmond has strived for more. Is he ready to rest yet, I wonder?

In 2012 he married his second wife, Joy Canfield, a former British Airways manager, whom he met in an airport lounge. The two have a four-year-old daughter, and a son, born in January. Robert, Desmond's son from his first marriage, is also expecting a child. 'I'll be a grandfather and a father in the same year,' Desmond says. 'The two boys will be in the same class.'

Why not loosen up, I suggest – starting with a few pay rises for his staff? 'There are two types of people: people who think they're rich and people who think they're poor,' he explains. He puts himself in the latter category. 'All you need is a bad move here, a bad move there, and you're out.'

His father's fate – after losing his hearing at the age of 45, he ran up gambling debts – serves as a lesson. 'Prime of your fucking life, and the phone doesn't go. And if the phone went, you couldn't hear it. So then you do more gambling, more gambling, more gambling.'

Is it paradoxical that Desmond himself now promotes gambling, via his loss-making Health Lottery? 'You can only lose a pound,' he says, referring to the price of a ticket.

Desmond was in his late twenties when his father died. 'The more I talk, the more I feel like my father,' he says at one point. Did he like him, I ask? 'Did I like him?' he repeats. A long pause. 'I didn't know him.'

In his book, Desmond, a liberal Jew, suggests that he finds it easier to do business with fellow Jews. 'Everyone's having a go at you, so you've got to be the fighter,' he says, explaining the camaraderie. 'This weekend the Hasidic rabbi will come round with a cheesecake because it's Shavuot or one of the festivals. It's nice,' he says. 'I mean, I'm not going to eat the cake.' With restraint in mind, we skip dessert, but order espressos.

From outside, it is hard to see where Desmond goes next. His newspapers are past their prime, specializing in dubious headlines such as 'Why watching TV gives you diabetes'. 'BuzzFeeds, SchmuzzFeeds – at the end of the day, you trust the *Daily Express*,' he argues.

The internet is not his game. He once met with some Google managers to discuss putting *OK!* online. 'They're all very smooth, they're all like out of *Thunderbirds*, and they've all got these fantastic sweaters – don't know where they get them,' he says.

'By the time you have the fourth meeting, the whole deal's completely fucking changed. They are the biggest gangsters in the world and they get away with it. One thing I've got to say about the European Union is that they are giving them a good kicking.

'I was always slow to adopt the internet, because I knew what would happen,' he says, adding: 'It's interesting how vinyl's coming back, isn't it?'

So what does happen next? Desmond has to turn round the Health Lottery – which lost £28 million last year, but is a key advertiser for the *Express*. Since it was established in 2011, it has generated £65 million for good causes. He owns property from a former print site on the Thames that he intends to develop. He also holds stakes in an online estate agents, Tepilo, and Lulu, an app for 'girls to review guys'.

At one point, while I am trying to make the most of the wine, Desmond suggests that there may be no more big deals. 'I'm in spend-down. I've got a billion in cash,' he says. 'You can't leave people a billion pounds, can you?' His elder son won't receive more than £100 million, he says.

But when I ask whether the Health Lottery will be his last big project, he doubles back. 'I wouldn't have thought so. Life's not like that. You bumble through. You've got to keep your brain.'

One motivator is his enmity with Camelot, the Canadian-owned company that runs the UK's National Lottery. 'That's why I've got to keep going – so that I can bid for the National Lottery.'

This would give Desmond a public profile that he mostly lacks. He says he was approached to present the UK version of *The Apprentice*, a show now hosted by his former friend Lord Sugar. 'I wanted to be Rupert Murdoch, not Simon Cowell,' he shrugs. (Which is lucky because, according to one person involved in *The Apprentice*, he was 'never close to being a contender'.)

Associates think he is desperate to become a member of the House of Lords. Our espressos drained, I ask if he would accept a Ukip peerage. 'I don't think so. I'm an outsider. I'm like Branson,' he says.

Really? He could be Lord Desmond of Manor House, I say, nodding to the pub where he used to take coats. A mental switch flicks.

'Oh, that is good. I like that, Henry, I like that. That is good, that is good. Oh, that is good. Oh, I like that. Oh, that's funny. I like that. Oh, that's funny. Lord Desmond of Manor House, I like that. Cos then there's a reason, isn't there – there's a story. It's not just another Jew who's made a few bob and wants to be poncey. That's, "Fuck you!"'

I drink the last of my wine, a final jolt of blackcurrant and smoke. Desmond still has half a glass left, but appears to have lost interest. His phone rings, and he listens to his ringtone, a tune by the 1960s US soul duo Sam & Dave, while drumming his fingers on the table.

'Lord Desmond of Manor House,' he says idly, returning to the conversation, before launching into a confusing story about his friend Roger Daltrey, the singer of the Who. 'Pete Townshend liked that story,' he says,

---

Coq d'Argent

No.1 Poultry, London EC2

....

Goat's cheese	£9.75
Tomato salad	£10.50
Courgette flower tart	£21
Grilled tuna	£28
Green beans	£4.50
Wilted leaf spinach	£4.50
Bottle of Château Palmer 1983	£580
Still water x 2	£9
Double espresso	£3.75
Espresso	£3.50

....

Total (inc. service) –	£758.81

disappointed by my reaction. He gets up and goes to the loo while I pay the bill.

The restaurant has emptied. We take the lift down together, to where his driver has been waiting. 'Remember – this is the start, so don't, don't . . .' he tells me. At least it's more subtle than the time he told a hedge fund manager, 'I'm the worst enemy you'll ever have.'

That afternoon Desmond calls three times to clarify various points. Asking about liking his father was a 'very very good fucking question', he says, without elaborating much on his answer.

I take the opportunity to ask what he thought of the wine. 'Fucking nice,' crackles the reply. 'I asked my wife this morning, "Shall I order my usual wine?" And she said, "Yes, you're a billionaire. If you just order a glass of house red, people will think – what's wrong with him?"'

Thinkers and Creators

'You can't walk down the street without thinking about things that men generally don't have to think about'

Rebecca Solnit

'One gets inspired by fury'

By Rana Foroohar

Activist, journalist, writer, authority on everything from empathy to the history of walking – Rebecca Solnit is something of a Renaissance woman. But in this age of gender polarization and short attention spans, it's perhaps no surprise that her breakthrough work was a snack-sized essay titled 'Men Explain Things to Me'. It's the piece that brought us 'mansplaining', a phrase she coined after the host of a fancy party in Aspen tried to explain a 'very important' new book about 19th-century photography to her – without giving her enough conversational airtime to explain that she was, in fact, the book's author. 'Men explain things to me, and other women, whether or not they know what they are talking about,' she wrote in the follow-up bestseller, offering up a small softener: 'Some men.'

Some women, too, I discover during my lunch with Solnit at a small neighbourhood bistro – Chez Maman East – in the low-key San Francisco neighbourhood of Potrero Hill. She has arrived first and waves me over from her window seat. Beautiful (still) at the age of 56 and dressed in California casual chic, she seems appraising rather than friendly, her large blue eyes surveying me, her mouth set in neutral.

Fortunately, we have a shared topic of interest – Silicon Valley. Solnit, whose essays are published in the *New Yorker*, *Harper's* and a spate of other publications, was one of the first people to write about the Google bus, the company-sponsored transport system that whisks paper millionaires from San Francisco to their Valley jobs. She memorably labelled these unmarked vehicles 'the spaceships on which our alien overlords have landed to rule over us'.

I start what I hope will be a data-driven discussion about their

Illustration by James Ferguson

economic power, but she cuts me off. 'The hacking, the leaking, the bots, the trolls, the fake news,' she says. 'This idea that everything is connected was always being sold to us as awesome; these genius wonder boys are making magic things and it's all liberating. And now that means Mueller and loss of privacy and ransomware and revenge porn.'

As she continues with this free-range thread, I nod, listen and peruse the menu, which is the sort of French that Americans love to channel – onion soup, snails, goat's cheese. Unlike in France, nobody is drinking wine or lingering long, even though we are in a residential neighbourhood, far from the digital epicentre of the city. She's part of a San Francisco that I wasn't sure existed any more, I venture, noting the soaring real estate prices in formerly hippie neighbourhoods, bid up to nosebleed levels by the tech legions. She chuckles. 'Yes, but we're a relict species, if you know the term? It's an ecological term for when there are still a few rhinos or spotted owls . . . but there's not a replacement population,' says Solnit, touching on one of her early passions, environmentalism.

'I know a bunch of people in rent-controlled apartments or people like me who managed to buy real estate before it got completely out of hand,' she says. 'My first book [*Secret Exhibition*] was about the visual artists who were part of Beat culture, and a lot of the freedoms seen as heroic virtues of the 1950s and 1960s are really about white flight and the extreme affordability of the city in a boom economy.'

This sort of meditation, covering a lot of cognitive terrain, is typical of Solnit. For any question you might ask, she has an opinion – often multiples of them – strung together in ways that are by turns unexpected, sharp, humorous, nebulous and head-scratching.

Solnit is a hero to many liberal activists, particularly younger women galvanized by the #MeToo movement. Like many of them, she believes that the revelations about Harvey Weinstein are only the tip of an iceberg, and that 'a lot of things in the culture have kind of made masculinity even more destructive to men and to women than it has been [in the past]. Online porn, to mention another wonderful thing brought to us by Silicon Valley. Domestic violence is . . . the leading cause of death for women between 15 and 44 worldwide, etc. The fact that you can't walk down the street without thinking about things that men generally don't have to think about. Men don't generally have to worry about whether they might have a partner who will kill them. And what it meant to be an actress in Hollywood: you're expected, essentially, to be a prostitute, then punished for resisting, and it was a man's industry.'

Solnit also firmly believes that gender discrimination was a deciding factor in the election of Donald Trump. I play devil's advocate and press her on why the American left remains so focused on identity politics, when class – rather than gender or race – is arguably where the real economic and political action is. Solnit immediately chastises me for using that 'horrible, dismissive term "identity politics" that Bernie Sanders and others used, which pretends that we're in a colour-blind, gender-blind society and it's all just economics'.

Wait, I say, pushing back, does she think Sanders did that? 'I think that identity politics is old, and identity politics are about feminists like Mary Wollstonecraft and the French Revolution.' (I am pretty sure the latter was about class, but before I can interject, Solnit is on to her next point.) 'And this whole notion that there's a thing called The Left. All the old arrangements are falling apart. The old right hates Trump. There's a chunk of libertarians who've been mistaken for the left. It's part of the Silicon Valley notion that meritocracy is reality and that there's some mysterious reason why white men own most things, but we don't have to look at it. There are liberals who actually love the country and believe in its institutions and just want to set them right. There is an old Marxist left that looks at class a lot and these other things very little, which is most centrally white guys. It feels like we have these very simple maps for these very complicated things and I feel in a way like I'm an environmentalist and somebody passionately committed to human rights and that aligns me with feminism.'

Ideas such as these, which are squishy and unquantifiable, are anathema to me. But Solnit herself gravitates towards such things. Her writing is deeply psychological; at many points during the course of our interview she refers to how things 'feel', and she rails against the 'tyranny of the quantifiable'. Speaking of the growing wealth gap in America, for example, she says, 'it just feels like you have these warlord empires and people who must faithfully serve them, and then the starving outside the castle gates'. True enough, and yet I find myself wishing that she would pepper her passionately felt arguments with a few sharp Pikettyesque data points, low-hanging fruit that is there for the taking.

Our food arrives. 'Here's your escargots,' says the cheery waitress – 'And my salad,' says Solnit, finishing her sentence in a declarative way. The food is perfectly adequate in a local bistro kind of way. Not the best snails I've ever had, but mopping up loads of garlic butter with crusty bread is never a total loss.

Solnit picks at her simple green salad and asks me to move the bread to a ledge behind me, out of her reach. There are gluten and lactose issues, apparently, which leads to a brief digression about whether Monsanto may be somehow compromising our digestive systems with genetically modified seeds and toxic fertilizers. Solnit orders fries as a treat with her main course of moules marinière ('My doctor said potatoes are OK') and generously shares with me, though I hardly need extra. Our lunch spot may be French, but the portion sizes and garnishes are geared towards Americans. My main, an endive salad, has enough Gorgonzola to feed a small family and the walnuts are candied.

I come back to how Solnit thinks the Democrats will, or won't, come together in the upcoming 2018 midterm elections and the next presidential election in 2020. 'I think there's a classic framework we always hear, that Republicans are totally together and the Democrats are in disarray. And it's crap. The Republicans are in disarray. Trump is the naked, loud version of everything they try to keep clothed and quiet. One of the things we didn't talk about in the last election is disenfranchisement. I constantly hear people, supposedly on the left, talking about how Hillary blew it in the three crucial swing seats, but there was so much disenfranchisement, would Obama have won those places?' Who knows. Still, Solnit is unpersuaded that working-class white men need a disproportionate amount of our sympathy. 'A huge amount of low-end, minimum-wage work is done by people of colour and women, and a lot of the future of work is service work. Part of the crisis for white men is that they don't want to do this stuff.' Fair enough. Solnit is less worried about Democrats' future prospects than I am. She puts her faith in the 'demographics as destiny' argument, noting that 'half the people under 18 in this country are not white, and they are not going to vote Republican'.

Solnit's own destiny as a writer and activist has certainly been shaped by demographics. Her family comes from poor immigrant stock on both sides (Irish and Russian-Jewish), and her father was physically abusive to her when she was young. 'I grew up around a lot of male violence and a deeply misogynistic environment,' she says. 'Some of what motivates me is personal experience.' She's been brilliant at turning it all into prose, though, and has even enjoyed something of her own personal Trump bump over the past year. 'He turned *Hope in the Dark* [her 2004 book about the political landscape in America following George W. Bush's re-election] into a bestseller 13 years after its publication!' she says happily. 'One gets inspired by fury, as I'm sure you know. I joke, sometimes, that if the patriarchy would just stop doing these things, then my books would become obsolete and I would stop talking about these things.'

The truth is that much of Solnit's best (albeit not best-known) writing has less to do with gender and more to do with the world at large. *Wanderlust* (2000), for example, is a combination of history and meditation, a kind of antidote to the soundbite-driven high-speed media of our day. It rambles, like a wonderful walk, across all sorts of terrain, from poetry to history to anthropology. The relaxed pace allows unexpected ideas to bubble up about all sorts of things – time, work, sex, politics, technology – which fuel the work of later years. As she writes in the introduction: 'A new thought often seems like a feature of the landscape that was there all along, as though thinking were travelling rather than making . . . Perhaps this is where walking's peculiar utility for thinkers comes from. The surprises, liberations, and clarifications of travel can sometimes be garnered by going around the block as well as going around the world, and walking travels both near and far.' Says Solnit of the book: 'It was done pre-internet, and I had lots of time to concentrate.'

Our time is nearly up. I ask Solnit about her next project, and though she won't discuss details about books that aren't yet written, she says she's torn between, as she puts it, 'a sense of being a firefighter at the

Chez Maman East

1401 18th St,
San Francisco, CA

....

San Pellegrino x 2	$8
Escargots	$10
Green salad	$8
Endive salad	$13
Moules marinière	$16
Fries	$6
Decaf coffee	$2.50
Café latte	$3.75

....

Total (inc. tax) –	$75.16

conflagration of this political situation, wanting to write about this very moment . . . and wanting to pull back and go to the joys of archival research and bigger, deeper pictures.' There is a way in which the extreme politics of the moment, combined with social media (Solnit has an impressive 124,000 Facebook followers) 'really takes you away from a sense of living in broader spaces, in deeper time'.

As we leave the restaurant, she tells me that she regrets not asking me more about my work. Flattered, I tell her that I'll send her some stories. Then, she surprises me by asking, 'How old are you?' I am suddenly and unusually self-conscious (I showed up sans make-up, with my hair in a ponytail, and in casual clothing, figuring, hey, this is San Francisco and she's a feminist activist). Now I am suddenly unsure of what her question implies. Does she think I'm not professional? Does she not take me seriously? I've never been asked how old I am by any of the numerous male chief executives or billionaires I've interviewed. I'm 47, I tell her. 'Wow,' she says, with very little affect. 'You look a lot younger. Good genes, I guess.'

I ponder for a moment whether I should take offence at her bringing up my appearance; it's a strange question for someone who is so focused on the problems of patriarchy. I decide instead to take it as a compliment. 'My cab is here, here he comes around the corner,' I say, waving. She looks closely and notices what I've missed. 'It's a woman,' she says, with a satisfied smile. The last word, of course, is hers.

Demis Hassabis

'It's massively important to win'

By Murad Ahmed

Before we have a chance to order any food, I ask Demis Hassabis whether his work will lead to the extinction of our species. Hakkasan Hanway Place, an upmarket Cantonese restaurant in the basement of a quiet side street in central London, seems an odd place to be worrying about the apocalypse. But the subject comes to mind because Hassabis is the man who, in the not-too-distant future, could bring about humanity's most powerful creation yet: artificial intelligence.

A modern polymath, the 38-year-old's career has already included spells as a child chess prodigy, master computer programmer, video games designer and neuroscientist. Four years ago, these experiences led him to start DeepMind, an AI company that, he says, has the aim of making 'machines smart'.

For some, this is a utopic idea – a world aided by super-smart digital assistants working to solve humanity's most pressing problems, from disease to climate change. Others warn of a grim Armageddon, with cognizant robots becoming all too aware of human limitations, then moving to crush their dumb creators without emotion.

Hassabis, wearing a figure-hugging black top and dark-rimmed glasses, blends in at Hakkasan, where the decor is mostly black and the lighting minimal. He tells me he knows the place well – it's where he took executives from Google, during a series of meetings that led to the search giant paying £400 million for his fledgling company a year ago. Google is betting Hassabis may be able to unlock the secrets of the mind.

'It's quite possible there are unique things about humans,' he argues. 'But, in terms of intelligence, it doesn't seem likely. With the brain, there isn't anything non-computable.' In other words, the brain is a

Illustration by Patrick Morgan

computer like any other and can, therefore, be recreated. Traits previously considered innate to humans – imagination, creativity, even consciousness – may just be the equivalent of software programs.

Perhaps the best way to understand DeepMind's work is to watch one of Hassabis's entertaining presentations on YouTube. There, you can see him showing off the AI system's technology and how it is able to play retro arcade games such as Space Invaders. At first, the machine pilot is hopeless but, after just a few hours, it is firing missiles to its targets with uncanny accuracy.

As the video illustrates, the machine learns, adapts and then solves problems faster and better than any human. But Hassabis is not interested in creating a computer that's just good at computer games. His ambition is to create 'general' AI systems that use 'unstructured' information from their surroundings to make independent decisions and predictions. Just as humans do.

The uncertainty lies in whether these artificially intelligent beings will be motivated by a desire to guide and assist us or simply to do away with people like old gadgets that have served their purpose. Also on the YouTube video, Hassabis describes his AI computer playing a boxing game in which, after a few seconds of sparring, it corners the opponent and pummels them into submission. The audience laughs as Hassabis explains that the computer 'ruthlessly exploits the weakness in the system it has found'. But perhaps this is an apt analogy. As physicist Stephen Hawking wrote last year, AI would be 'the biggest event in human history . . . unfortunately, it might also be the last'.

Hassabis argues that we're getting ahead of ourselves. 'It's very, very far in the future from the kinds of things we're currently dealing with, which is playing Pong on Atari,' he says. 'I think the next four, five, 10 years, we'll have a lot more information about what these systems do, what kind of computations they're creating, how to specify the right goals. At the moment, these are science-fiction stories. Yes, there's no doubt that AI is going to be a hugely powerful technology. That's why I work on it. It has the power to provide incredible advances for humanity.'

Too soon then, to be worrying about how to wage war with a sentient robot army? 'In our research programme, there isn't anything that says "program consciousness",' he says, as a waitress appears. 'Shall we order?'

Hassabis chooses sweetcorn soup to start, and I opt for vegetarian hot and sour soup. For mains, he recommends the seafood dim sum platter, so I follow suit. He also orders a side of organic barbecue pork ribs; I go for some sesame prawn toast. We both ask for jasmine green tea to accompany the meal.

Born to a Chinese-Singaporean mother and a father of Greek-Cypriot descent, Hassabis grew up in north London, close to where he currently resides with his wife and two children. By the age of 13, he was a chess master. Fascinated by games, he was a regular competitor at the Mind Sports Olympiad, whose organizers described him as 'probably the best games player in history'. When he grew tired of playing, he started to make games too. As a teenager, he helped design Theme Park, a cult video game that simulated the experience of creating an amusement park.

In 1994 he went to Cambridge University to study computer science but he was unconvinced by some of the teaching that focused on 'narrow' AI, which relies on programmers to attach 'labels' to data in order for a computer to make sense of information. 'I remember distinctly one lecture, where I said to my friends around me, "We shouldn't listen to this, they're brainwashing us." I said that slightly too loud and the lecturer called me out and said, "If you think you know everything, you shouldn't come here."' Hassabis walked out of the lecture hall.

It was around this time he decided to create DeepMind, a research-project-cum-tech-start-up. Hassabis says that, even then, he was aware this was a 20-year plan. First, he would need to gather the experience necessary to found such a group and thus, in 1998, he set up a video games company, Elixir Studios, to begin his education in the business world. In 2005, he returned to academia, aged 28, to earn a PhD in cognitive neuroscience at University College London. His research focused on the hippocampus, the brain region crucial for navigation, memory recall and imagining future events.

He took this long route, he explains, because he wanted to learn the lessons of his heroes, such as Charles Babbage (1791–1871), the English genius who first conceptualized a programmable computer. 'Babbage is one of the most tragic examples,' says Hassabis. 'He thought of computers a hundred years before [their time]. His machine worked but he never saw it built.'

With the protection of Google, Hassabis seems likelier to avoid Babbage's fate. DeepMind has expanded to around a hundred employees. Unlike many youthful start-ups, the average age of the group is in the mid-thirties. Typically, most of these workers have one or more PhDs. As a result, DeepMind's London offices are, he says, 'a little more sophisticated' than Google's. There are no coders slumped on colourful beanbags, he says, just 'serious sofas for serious thinking'.

In a reference to Nasa's efforts to put men on the moon, Hassabis says he is trying to create an 'Apollo programme' for AI, by creating an organization stuffed with some of the greatest minds on earth. 'In any normal start-up, just one of our senior researchers is someone you'd build a whole company around,' he says.

But how does Hassabis lead a group of people like this? 'You can't just say, "I'm the CEO, so you do this." You've got to lead by example and respect for your own work. It's not why I did a PhD . . . but to lead a team like this, I need academic qualities . . .' For once, he struggles to explain himself. You need credentials that are unimpeachable, I say? 'Unimpeachable. That's the right word.'

The soup arrives. I wonder aloud whether his mission is more personal than he lets on. How much of it is an effort to understand his own exceptional mind?

He leans down to the bowl, so the steam drifts in front of his face, lifts the spoon to his lips and sips carefully. Then he says: 'If you take a kid who is fairly thoughtful and introspective, then train them professionally from the age of four to 13, playing adults and grandmasters at chess, they can't help but think hard about what their brain is doing when coming up with these moves.

'You're thinking about how to improve that mechanism because you're trying to get better at chess. Chess is an extremely deliberative process. You're consciously planning out everything, which is why it's such a fascinating game. It really encourages me with my type of thinking and brain, to think very hard about what intelligence is.'

But, he says, unlike that of other chess masters, his attention was soon drawn to things away from the board. Aged eight, he bought a Spectrum computer with his winnings from chess tournaments and started programming. 'I realized that this machine was an extension of the mind, in the way that cars allow us to move faster, planes allow us to fly. Computers allow us to enhance our minds in the same way.'

He is also intrigued by how humans interact. For that reason, he likes playing poker and, perhaps unsurprisingly, has won thousands of dollars in professional tournaments. 'A lot of chess players can't handle poker,' he says. 'In chess, if you play the right moves, you win. But life is more like poker than chess, in that there are unforeseen and unknown things in life you can't cater for. We're trying to build something that can expect the unexpected gracefully. That's much more like poker.'

Our next set of dishes arrives. The dim sum are piping hot, gorgeous balls of prawns, scallops and vegetables wrapped in rice flour. I attack them with my chopsticks, drowning them in soy sauce. Hassabis begins by picking up his pork ribs with his fingers and nibbling at the edges. Hakkasan is a Michelin-starred restaurant but he complains that the process of eating is time wasted and would not mind if it involved no more than swallowing tubes of paste. 'I like eating out as an experience,' he says, 'but day-to-day eating? It would be good if there was something more efficient.' Out of politeness, I leave a couple of my dim sum untouched. Not as many, though, as Hassabis leaves behind.

I ask him why he chose to sell his company to Google. DeepMind had plenty of money in the bank, including funding from Peter Thiel, the first major backer of Facebook, and Elon Musk, who leads the commercial space flight group SpaceX. Hassabis says that, before joining Google, he pushed for a number of safeguards to ensure his group was 'semi-autonomous' from its corporate paymasters. DeepMind remains in London, not Silicon Valley. It is also creating an ethics board – he is currently interviewing philosophers and experts, though won't say who – which will govern how its technology can be used. It will, for example, rule out any military uses.

'All these technologies are neutral in themselves,' he says, 'but it depends on how we use them. We need to make sure we understand how we use them and use them in the right way. I don't want it to be neutral. I want it to be good.'

In the end, though, Hassabis has to report to Google's executives. Surely staying independent would have ensured better control of his creation? 'My plan wasn't to sell the company,' he says. 'I wanted to build a Google ourselves. I realized a couple of years ago that trying to build AI while trying to build a multibillion-dollar company at the same time was probably impossible. I'd have to do one or the other. I care much more about the research.'

He continues: 'Larry [Page, Google's chief executive] persuaded me by saying, "Look, I've spent the past 15 years building Google. It was hard. There were a lot of things that had to happen, both lucky and skilful. Why don't you take advantage of all that infrastructure and hard work and short-cut all of that, so you can concentrate on the mission?" I thought about this a lot and didn't have a good argument against that.'

The benefits for Google are clear. DeepMind's technology will become incorporated into its products, says Hassabis, such as making sure it can better predict a person's search results. It's easy, too, to see the more sophisticated uses, from integrating AI into Google's self-driving cars to providing the brains to the robotics under construction at 'Google X', the company's advanced technologies arm.

Waiters whisk away our plates and, after some gentle persuasion, Hassabis agrees to order a dessert. He asks which sorbets are available, choosing pear and passion fruit. I go for the same.

What motivates him? Is it money? The Google deal reportedly netted Hassabis around £80 million. He argues, convincingly, that being rich is of little concern. 'It's important to have money so it frees you to make the correct choices for your goals. But it should never be an end itself.'

Perhaps then, his legacy is what drives him? After all, if he becomes the father of artificial intelligence, Hassabis would be held in the same regard as the likes of Babbage, or another one of his heroes, Alan Turing, the

Hakkasan Hanway Place

8 Hanway Place, London W1

....

Sweetcorn soup	£9
Vegetarian hot and sour soup	£11.50
Dim sum platter x 2	£30
Sesame prawn toast	£13.50
Organic pork ribs	£13.50
Sorbet x 2	£10
Mineral water	£4.60
Jasmine green tea	£3.80

....

Total (inc. service) –	£108.28

British cryptographer who designed the machine that broke the Nazi Enigma code.

He ponders this, a scoop of luminous green sorbet on his spoon. 'You know how you asked me, when I played chess, is it important for me to win? It is massively important, from my own point of view of fulfilling my own potential. Legacy is important in that, one day, I will hope to have done something significant enough with my life, and with the technology, that will have made a profound change to society for good.'

He is late for a meeting, so I ask for the bill. Before he leaves, I ask how long it will take to create general AI. When will Hassabis's lines of computer code, his algorithms, start writing their own lines of code, their own algorithms? He says that, just like humans and all life that came before, his AI is evolving. 'We're building systems that are able to reconfigure themselves in new ways that we haven't pre-programmed. I don't know if you'd call that writing itself. It's more like how the brain works. Even this lunch conversation we're having. It's changing some synapses in both of our brains.' He laughs, before adding: 'Whether we like it or not.'

Jordan Peterson

'One thing I'm not is naive'

By Henry Mance

Some people hear mysticism in Jordan Peterson's voice; others detect anger. But above all he oozes certainty. Airport security is 'creeping fascism'; identity politics is 'murderous'; blaming capitalism for inequality 'is naive beyond belief'. Peterson is to moral judgments what traffic wardens are to parking tickets. He describes his own verbal IQ as 'off the charts'.

'Ingratitude is one of the things that's deeply wrong,' he says at the beginning of our lunch, quickly establishing that small talk will not be served. 'You hear all these radical leftist types in the west complaining about the 1 per cent. By world standards, they're the 1 per cent.'

Oh, sorry – you probably still have no idea who Jordan Peterson is. If social media had never been invented, perhaps none of us would.

In 1999, when he was just a psychology professor at the University of Toronto, Peterson published his first book, *Maps of Meaning*, and almost nobody read it. In 2001, he circulated an open letter to George W. Bush and the US Congress, warning that a vengeful response to the Twin Towers attacks risked producing a 'cycle of terror'. Almost nobody read that either. Peterson seemed destined to remain a well-regarded psychologist with a slot on Ontario public TV. Think Frasier without the humour.

Then came the internet effect. In 2013 Peterson began broadcasting his lectures on YouTube. Three years later he denounced a draft law that he argued could lead to the prosecution of those who refused to call transsexuals by their preferred pronouns. It was theoretical: to this day, no one has asked him to call them 'ze'. But it made Peterson an overnight general in the culture wars. And he likes a fight: 'I'd slap you happily,' he told one critic on Twitter.

Trump supporters have had enough of experts; now they can't get enough of Peterson. YouTube is full of videos with titles such as 'How to

Illustration by James Ferguson

shut up a Marxist (Jordan Peterson speech)' (480,000 views) and 'Jordan Peterson leaves feminist speechless' (878,000 views). His self-help manual, *12 Rules for Life*, has sold more than 1 million copies since its publication in January, but it's an afterthought.

'I have a multimedia empire, you know,' he says, intensely. He feels part of 'an absolute revolution': 'the spoken word now has the reach of the written word . . . Maybe it's easier for people to listen than read, so maybe that increases the market for ideas by 25 per cent or 50 per cent – we don't know, but it's a lot.'

Peterson epitomizes how the internet is reshaping our public debate, and giving a megaphone to the fringes. Even opponents concede that he reaches anxious white males whom the left cannot. He is the anti-#MeToo, the anti-1968, the defender of old-school masculinity. White privilege is a 'Marxist lie'; the glass ceiling is 'a lot more complicated than it looks'. He urges people to set social justice aside, to take personal responsibility, to study the Bible. For anyone who thinks Canada breeds only Justin Trudeaus and Margaret Atwoods, here is a reality check.

It's not just Trumpists. Who isn't occasionally frustrated by identity politics? Who can't see the fractures in our social contract, our liberal ethics? You might recoil from his debating style, but you can't escape the uncomfortable sensation that he is dealing in facts. 'I'm just laying out the empirical evidence,' he insisted in perhaps his most-watched performance, a 30-minute interview with the Channel 4 News journalist Cathy Newman. The most controversial Canadian is righteous. But is he right?

Peterson loathes carbs as much as Marxists. He has 'a very, very, very restricted diet' of meat, fish and some greens – to control severe depression and an auto-immune disorder.

So instead of a restaurant, we meet in a flat in London's Bloomsbury, where his wife, Tammy, prepares the food. (For Peterson, the alternative to the traditional division of household labour is generally 'chaos, conflict and indeterminacy'.) I contribute a bunch of sunflowers and a bottle of wine, which it turns out Peterson can't drink. The flat is small and airless, with a kitchen on one wall and a large TV along another. It is one stop on a promotional tour. 'This really is pretty much life – trying to figure out different stoves,' he says.

He spoons liquid into a bowl for him, and slides a pastry and a Spanish tortilla on to a plate for me. He often uses the longest word possible: he puts down a side plate, and explains, 'This is a subsidiary plate.' Tammy heads out for a walk.

Peterson copied his diet from his daughter, who also suffered from depression; since starting it, he has lost 50lb, stopped snoring and no longer suffers from psoriasis and gum disease. 'I still don't believe it. It just seems too ridiculous.' We sit at a glass-top table, and I ask what he's eating. 'Chicken with chicken broth. It's pretty damn plain.'

Peterson's philosophical starting point is that 'life is suffering', and that happiness is a stupid goal. Has his own life been mostly suffering or joy? 'That's a good question,' the 55-year-old says. On one side of the balance is the 'vicious streak of depression' that has affected him, his daughter, his father and his grandfather; his daughter also had rheumatoid arthritis. On the other are his career and his family; he 'really like[s]' both his children, and his daughter recently gave birth. 'Probably the good has outweighed the bad,' he concludes.

He and Tammy grew up on the same street in Fairview, a frontier town in northern Alberta. The winters were so cold that homeless drunks froze to death; the nearest big city was hundreds of miles away. Peterson's father was a teacher and the local fire chief. He himself was a tearful boy who worked odd jobs from the age of 13. 'I'm a practical person. I'm not too bad a carpenter. I can renovate houses . . . I like working-class people, generally speaking.'

After graduating he had teaching spells at Harvard and Toronto, and developed a personality test for companies based on five traits. (He ranked in the 99th percentile for assertiveness, but only the 30th for politeness.)

When fame came knocking, he couldn't get to the door fast enough. 'I didn't expect this, but it wasn't expectable – this level of notoriety isn't predictable,' he says. He knew he was dealing with 'the most fundamental of psychological ideas'. Carl Jung 'probably accounts for about 40 per cent of what I think', but there's also 'a heavy biological component'.

By now, Peterson has taken off his Ecco sandals, and is sitting barefoot and cross-legged while he eats. But he is not Zen. I mention that critics say he deals in clichés: the seventh rule in his recent book is 'pursue what is meaningful'. That's all it takes to light his fuse. 'Jesus Christ, first of all, one thing I'm not is naive. I've 20,000 hours of clinical practice; you're not naive after the first few thousand. I've helped people deal with things that most people can't imagine.'

The atmosphere is now a few degrees below convivial. I turn to my aubergine pie, which is peppery and filling. Peterson pours himself water, and leaves the bottle out of my reach. I stare at the unopened wine.

Peterson is obsessed by Nazi and communist atrocities; his home in Canada is decorated with Soviet propaganda; his daughter is named Mikhaila, after the last Soviet leader. He sees inequality as 'the norm' in animal life and says he's in a 'theological fight' to put the individual before the collective. But he also wants society to 'stop teaching 19-year-old girls that their primary destiny is career'. Isn't that defining people by a group identity – to say motherhood will shape women's career ambitions? 'Yeah, well, I suppose – I see what you mean. I still think they have the right to make the choice.'

Would this mean fewer women going to university than men? 'I don't know how it should play out practically,' he says. 'The mystery isn't why women bail out of high-powered careers . . . The mystery is why anyone stays. It's a small percentage of people who do the 80-hour-a-week high-powered career thing, and they're almost all men. Why? Well, men are driven by socio-economic status more than women.'

What did he make of Sheryl Sandberg's ideas for women to progress? 'Lean in? I think that, coming from her background, she should be careful of attributing too much of her success to her own endeavours.' Peterson's point is that much IQ is inherited, so Sandberg had a head start. 'Lean in – tell that to the person who's not literate.'

But I'm not sure what this means at a societal level: men and women have the same average IQ. In heterosexual couples where the man has the lower IQ, shouldn't he stay at home with kids? 'It's rare – women won't marry men with lower IQs.' But where they do? 'It might make more economic sense [for the man to stay at home]. Whether it makes more sense, that's a tougher question.'

We're on to the idea that men and women have different preferences. What's the evidence? 'It's absolutely overwhelming. Let me walk you through it.' I decide that wine is now essential, and Peterson pauses briefly to find a glass in a cupboard. We put our plates in the sink.

Last year James Damore, an engineer, was fired from Google after claiming that women are biologically less suited than men to writing software. 'Damore got it right, for sure,' says Peterson. Both men cite David Schmitt, a US psychologist whose research has revealed personality difference between sexes. But Schmitt says the differences are moderate in size, and 'unlikely to be all that relevant to the Google workplace'.

Peterson flips over my notepad and starts drawing bell curves to represent standard deviations of aggressiveness. 'Of course we don't hear calls for 50 per cent gender equality in prison now, do we?' That's fascinating, I say honestly, but I don't get why you like Schmitt, who doesn't agree with you. 'I'd have to look at his analysis. My gut feeling would be because it doesn't fit with his ideological preconceptions,' says Peterson. Bias is other people.

One of my own rules for life is coffee after lunch, but who needs caffeine when you have Peterson? 'Hospitals may do more harm than good', 'solar power kills more people than nuclear' – if you have ears, he can prick them up. His sentences have the arc of well-thrown darts. I have to remind myself to stop admiring his words and to keep interrogating his ideas.

Could *12 Rules for Life* stand up to peer review? 'Have at it, man! Yeah, I was very careful about the claims in the book.' OK, in a chapter on why people don't follow their prescriptions, his arguments centre on the guilt of Adam and Eve. Is that testable? 'The way you would test that is to find out whether people who are harsher on themselves would be less likely to take prescription medication. The probability that's true is pretty high,' he concedes, 'the research hasn't been done'.

Predictably, Peterson doubts climate change is man-made. His book is scathing about environmentalists, whom he accuses of wanting fewer humans on the planet. This, he says, causes students to 'suffer genuine losses in their mental health'. Is there any evidence for that? One second, two seconds – 10 seconds pass. 'No. There's no hard evidence.' He suggests the problem is 'an epidemiological matter': 'the instruments that people used to assess depression in the 1950s aren't the same as the instruments now'. So the point is 'more a hypothesis'.

Peterson may be an academic, but he's dispensing with the academy's constraints. His university salary is around $128,000; that now looks modest beside the $1 million a year he receives in crowdfunding via the site Patreon, in return for YouTube Q&As. Traditional universities charge 'unforgivable' fees, and 'haven't got a hope of surviving in their present form', he says. He has hired three people to work on a proposal for a new online university – 'user-funded at the lowest possible cost, but also crowdsourced in terms of its operation'. He is in touch with Peter Thiel, the venture capitalist who urges undergraduates to drop out. There's a blurred line between the thinker and the salesman, and Peterson has crossed it.

Peterson sees himself as 'more of a traditionalist than a conservative'. Yet he is abandoning traditional institutions. He exalts the meaning found in Bible stories but he no longer goes to church. 'I can't tolerate it. I find the ritualistic presentation of the ideas – I don't know how to say it exactly – I don't feel that the people who are presenting the stories are discussing them as if they believe that they're true.' Does he donate to charity? He gives to a kids' charity in Toronto and to public television, 'but not on a massive scale'.

Tammy has returned from her walk, and is sitting on the sofa reading a book called *Pressing Reset*. Abruptly, she announces we are out of time: Peterson has a call with *Sports Illustrated*. 'That's that then,' he says.

It's a shame, partly because I've only drunk a third of the wine. It's a shame, too, because I had wanted to ask Peterson about his claim that parents should hit their misbehaving children, and not just with 'a swat across the backside'. Peer-reviewed articles suggest it does long-term harm. I'd also like to know more about his eye-catching argument that social inequalities are part of the natural order, reflected in the serotonin levels of lobsters and humans. Interestingly, he never mentions in *12 Rules* that he took antidepressants to increase serotonin levels in his own brain. Perhaps serotonin isn't destiny?

I ask about his influence. He knows that context matters: in 2013, he co-wrote a study that found that a meditation session made people more

---

Meal gratis, except for wine

....

Chicken in chicken broth
Aubergine and pepper pie
Spanish tortilla
San Pellegrino sparkling
  water
Co-op 2016 Chablis £11.99

....

Total –   £11.99

:::

liberal. These days he claims he is stopping angry young men from embracing extremism. But could he be encouraging his admirers to reinforce their prejudices, to build up steam? 'No, I don't think so . . . They never talk about politics to me, when they meet me.'

Peterson jokes that prophets 'tend to meet a pretty dismal end' and is afraid that his outspokenness will go too far – that he will end up 'saying something that would do me in'. But it's hard to imagine what this could be. Peterson has already accused feminists who defend Muslim rights of an 'unconscious wish for brutal male domination', with no apparent ill-effect on book sales. So will people still be talking about him in 20 years? 'I don't know. I don't know what we'll be like in 20 years. There's a lot of things happening in AI and robotics.'

He needn't worry, I think, as I let myself out into the stairwell. How could robots ever replace Jordan B. Peterson? Yes, they would churn out moral judgments. But surely theirs would be constrained by the available data.

Svetlana Alexievich

'I love to sit on my own and think'

By Guy Chazan

S
peaking to Svetlana Alexievich, it can be hard to tell who's interviewing whom. As soon as she discovers I'm English, she wants to know what I think of the Queen and the elaborate rituals of the British monarchy. She would also like to know why I speak Russian, where I studied and when exactly I lived in Moscow.

I tell her I arrived as a reporter in 1991, the year of the attempted putsch against Mikhail Gorbachev and of the Soviet collapse. 'Ah, well then, you know exactly what I'm writing about,' she says.

Cajoling people to tell their life stories is how Alexievich won the Nobel Prize for Literature in 2015. It is the secret behind the 'documentary novels' about Soviet life, published over three decades, which have made her name. These complex collages, woven from hundreds of interviews with ordinary people living in extraordinary times, comprise an oeuvre described by the Nobel committee as a 'monument to suffering and courage in our time'.

The feeling I have under her penetrating gaze is how her subjects must have felt when this unassuming 69-year-old Belarusian interviewed them – why they divulged secrets that had often remained locked up for decades as a burden or a shameful stain.

It's something to do with her soft features, the intimate timbre of her voice and an empathy that is almost palpable. It's also something to do with her ordinariness. Dressed in a brown woollen poncho, Alexievich, who was doing the ironing when the Nobel committee rang, does not look or sound like a literary celebrity. She still lives in the cramped 50-square-metre Soviet-era flat in the Belarusian capital Minsk that has been her home for decades.

Illustration by James Ferguson

Today we are sitting in the breakfast room of the Literaturhotel, a writerly retreat in the genteel Berlin suburb of Friedenau stuffed full of Biedermeier furniture, gold-framed mirrors and oriental rugs. Alexievich, who stays here on her frequent trips to Berlin, initially suggested that we meet at a fish restaurant on the swanky Kurfürstendamm but, after giving readings in Bamberg, Lübeck and Hamburg in less than a week, she is tired.

The Literaturhotel's manager, Christa Moog, pours us green tea and boasts of Friedenau's illustrious literary heritage. Three Nobel Prize-winners have lived here: Günter Grass, the Romanian-born Herta Müller and Alexievich herself, who spent two years in Berlin during a long self-imposed exile in western Europe in the 2000s. Moog then excuses herself to rustle up some supper: meals are not normally provided, but she will make an exception for such a distinguished guest.

From the Queen, we turn to another long-serving ruler, Vladimir Putin, whose brooding presence seems to overshadow the whole evening. Alexievich's magnum opus, *Secondhand Time* (first published in Russian in 2013), is an attempt to understand where Putin came from and why he has such a hold on the Russian people.

Alexievich is reluctant to demonize the president. What worries her more is the 'collective Putin', the sense of wounded national pride and contempt for liberal values that now runs so deep in both Russia and Belarus. She says 60 to 70 per cent of the population hold such views – and that is a challenge for the beleaguered minority of pro-western liberals to which she belongs. 'To be in conflict with the authorities is one thing. We Russian writers have got used to that,' she says. 'But to be in conflict with your own people – that is truly terrible.'

It is particularly hard for Alexievich because these people are the source and wellspring of her work. Each of her books is a dense tapestry woven from encounters with those caught up in epoch-making events, from the second world war to the Chernobyl nuclear disaster of 1986. She is like a doctor probing the scar tissue of a traumatized nation – a hazardous enterprise in a country that is busy consigning memories of the gulag to oblivion, and whose president once described the collapse of the Soviet Union as the 'greatest geopolitical catastrophe' of the 20th century.

In her Nobel lecture of December 2015, Alexievich described Russia as 'a space of total amnesia'. The way she puts it, things now are getting even worse. 'Lawmakers say we should put Gorbachev on trial, a Solzhenitsyn monument has been vandalized and they're putting up more and more statues to Stalin,' she says. 'But it's not Putin telling people to do that – the initiative is coming from the grassroots.'

Alexievich's interest in the lives of ordinary people was sparked in childhood. Born in 1948 to rural schoolteachers in the Ukrainian town of Ivano-Frankivsk, she grew up in a Belarusian village whose men had died in the war. Every evening the women would sit on benches and chat, and the children lapped up their every word. 'They spoke of love, of the war, of terrible things,' she says. 'People talked about death all the time, and this chorus was seared in my consciousness.'

She thought about writing novels, but quickly realized that real, human stories were more powerful. 'Why invent heroes when the things these people say are so much better?' she says.

She cites an example from *Chernobyl Prayer*, her book about the reactor meltdown three decades ago that contaminated large parts of Ukraine and Belarus and rendered hundreds of villages in both countries uninhabitable. In it, she quotes the wife of one of the firemen who helped douse the conflagration at the reactor and was then transferred to a Moscow hospital where he died of radiation poisoning. 'She was told by the doctors not to approach him, kiss him, hug him. They told her: "This is not the man you love, it's a contaminated object."' The line shocked Alexievich. 'I thought – this is pure Dostoevsky.'

Alexievich also wanted to get away from conventional approaches to storytelling. 'There is this tradition, stretching back to Tacitus and Plutarch, that history belongs to the heroes, the emperors,' she says. 'But I grew up among simple people, and their stories just shattered me. It was painful that no one but me was listening to them.'

Our starter arrives – a simple dish of pickled mushrooms and hard-boiled eggs stuffed with prawns. Moog pours us a glass of Pinot Grigio, while bantering with Alexievich in broken Russian – it is clear that the two are close, despite the language barrier. 'Did you know Ms Moog is a writer too?' Alexievich says. I later find two of her novels, both published in the 1980s, on Amazon.

Alexievich's first book, *The Unwomanly Face of War* (1985), an English translation of which is coming out next month, is constructed from interviews with Soviet women survivors of the war. Alexievich says the female perspective was important because women never see war as heroic. 'For them, [it] is always murder,' she says. Her purpose was to get behind the Soviet clichés of the time and find the truth of 'concrete things'. As an example she cites the women soldiers who were only assigned bras, panties and tampons once the Red Army crossed the Soviet Union's western border, 'so they wouldn't show themselves up in front of the foreigners'.

The books exploded Soviet myths – the main one being that 'war is beautiful'. 'It's not, it's horrific,' she says. In *Boys in Zinc* (1991), she punctured one of the biggest myths of all – one enveloping the Soviet intervention in Afghanistan in the 1980s. Alexievich recalls delivering teddy bears to a hospital ward of children in Kabul, and is surprised to see one little boy take the present in his teeth: his mother pulls back the sheet to reveal he has no arms or legs. 'This is what your Soviet Hitlerites did,' the woman shouted at her.

It was a turning point. 'Back in the Soviet Union, everyone said we were heroes helping the Afghan people build a future.' She had been a Soviet patriot, a loyal member of the Young Communist League. Now her faith had gone.

The manager interrupts us to bring the next course: salmon coated in sesame seeds, with rice and a chicory salad, accompanied by 'Sauce de Moog', an eponymous concoction of onions, pear, cranberries and cream, finished with saffron.

Alexievich is delighted. 'It's like you're staying in someone's house, not a hotel.'

As we tuck into the fish, she explains her working method. For each book she interviews more than a thousand people, although only about 300 make the cut. Her purpose, she says, is to write 'the history of the soul'. Reciting a line from the character Shatov in Dostoevsky's *The Possessed*, she says: 'We are two creatures who have met in boundless infinity . . . for the last time in the world. So drop that tone and speak like a human being. For once in your life, speak with a human voice.' It is unsurprising that a portrait of Dostoevsky hangs above her writing desk in Minsk.

Her subjects are often people she encounters by chance in public places – restaurants, buses, airports. 'We start to talk and I take their number,' she says. She says that in their encounters she comes as a journalist, but 'it's not really an interview – it's more like a conversation. You come as a friend – like them, you are a child of your time. And if I weren't their friend, it's highly unlikely they would tell me the things they do.'

Her subjects' bitterness is often suffused with nostalgia for a lost Soviet idyll and deep disappointment with the no-holds-barred capitalism that replaced it when the USSR fell apart in 1991. *Secondhand Time*, her most ambitious work, was informed by a quote from the artist Ilya Kabakov. 'He said, when it was still the Soviet Union, we were fighting a monster, communism, and we defeated it,' she says. 'But we turned round and realized we would have to live with rats.'

This may strike western readers as perverse. How could people feel any affection for a system that created the gulag? Alexievich says this ignores the unique atmosphere of the late Soviet period, a time of equality, deep friendships and love of literature. 'Despite the poverty, life was freer,' she says. 'Friends would gather at each other's houses, play the guitar, sing, talk, read poetry.' When democracy came, they hoped the intellectual freedom they longed for would finally arrive, 'that everyone would be free to read Solzhenitsyn'.

Freedom came and Solzhenitsyn's works were all published – but, by the early 1990s, no one had the time or energy to read them. 'Everyone just ran past them, and headed for the 20 different kinds of biscuit and 10 varieties of sausage,' she says.

I tell her I found it particularly hard to read the testimony of people who defended the White House, the former Russian parliament building that became a symbol of resistance during the 1991 coup attempt by government hardliners. I had been there myself, and recalled conversations with defiant old women who said they would rather lie under a tank than let the Communists come back to power. Their hopes of freedom were shattered in the chaos, hyperinflation and rampant crime of the Yeltsin years that followed, as a new class of rapacious oligarchs took charge.

'I, too, went to those demonstrations in the late 1980s,' Alexievich says. 'No one marching then wanted Abramovich,' she says, referring to the billionaire owner of Chelsea football club.

Not only did many of the intellectuals of her generation lose their jobs, their savings and their ideals: they also experienced no catharsis, since no one from the former regime was ever brought to justice. I ask her if

Russia might have turned out differently if there had been a trial of the Communist party. 'I was convinced there should have been,' she says. But others, including her father, an ardent communist, disagreed. 'He said it would have led to civil war,' she says. As a result there was no reckoning with the Soviet past, no Russian Nuremberg. 'We missed our chance,' she says.

Ms Moog comes in with dessert – slices of mango and bitter chocolate – and we turn to events in Ukraine, the country where Alexievich was born. She condemns the 'occupation' of Crimea, and says the west should give Ukraine weapons to help it fight the Russian-backed separatists in Donbass. 'Those [Ukrainian] boys are just being shot down like partridges,' she says.

Yet she is hopeful about Ukraine's future – it is a country that wants to be part of Europe, unlike her homeland, Belarus. 'Throughout their history, the Belarusians only survived,' she says. Russia always suspected them of collaborating with the enemy, Poland, and submitted them to intermittent slaughter 'because they were in the way'. 'So their philosophy became to keep quiet and hide.'

Literaturhotel
Fregestrasse 68, Berlin

....

Eggs stuffed with
  prawns, with pickled
  mushrooms x 2
Salmon with sauce de
  Moog, rice and chicory
  salad x 2
Mango and chocolate x 2
Pinot Grigio x 2 glasses

....

Total
  (inc. tax and service) – €50

Despite her ambivalence about Belarus, she moved back a couple of years ago, after an 11-year stint abroad. Her parents had died, and she wanted to see her granddaughter grow up. Also, she had left to sit out Putin and Alexander Lukashenko, Belarus's authoritarian president, but realized that 'they're not going anywhere'. Her relations with the Belarusian leader are tense: when she won the Nobel, he accused her of 'pouring buckets of filth over her country'. She also needed to return home for the sake of her work. 'The genre demands that . . . you speak to people every day – you can't do it on Skype.'

With the Nobel Prize money she is buying a new flat, three times larger than the old one, but in the same building. She loves the location, overlooking the Svislach river, and could never move away. The Nobel has in any case made it harder for her to retreat into anonymity. Recently she had an argument with her nine-year-old granddaughter Yanna on a street in Minsk. 'At that moment a woman said to Yanna: "Little girl, you can't talk to your grandmother like that – don't you know who she is?"'

She finds it difficult to be in the public eye. 'I love to sit on my own and think, not to be photographed all the time,' she says. 'I'm not a public person.'

The reticence is of a piece with Alexievich's work, where her authorial voice is rarely heard. There are a couple of exceptions, though. In *Secondhand Time* she tells the story of an old communist who was locked up during Stalin's purges but later rehabilitated. He is summoned after the war and told that his wife, who was arrested with him, has died in the camps. 'They called me into the district party committee. "Unfortunately, we will not be able to return your wife to you. She's dead. But you can have your honour back." And they handed me back my party membership card. And I was so happy! I was so happy.'

In the book, Alexievich says she and the communist argue, and he loses his temper. I ask what happened. 'I couldn't take it, I was just horrified. I said, "I don't understand you – all they gave you was that little crust." And he got aggressive. He said: "You'll never understand, all you care about are clothes and your stomach. But we had noble ideals. We were people of faith."'

The Art of Money

'I was selling this shitty product and it embarrassed me'

Bernie Ecclestone

'I was selling this shitty product and it embarrassed me'

By Murad Ahmed

When Bernie Ecclestone spots me, he raises a hand. I misinterpret the gesture as a hello, then realize that the 87-year-old tycoon is ordering me to abandon my table in the middle of Bar Boulud, a French-style bistro in Mandarin Oriental's luxury hotel in Hyde Park, central London. In his sober grey suit, he shuffles to the back and selects a table away from the crowd. 'Just in case I start swearing,' he says.

Ecclestone is used to calling the shots. Until the start of this year, he was the chief executive of Formula One – ringmaster of the global car-racing series he transformed into one of the world's most-watched sports. His four decades at the helm ended dramatically in January when the US group Liberty Media, controlled by billionaire John Malone, completed an $8 billion takeover of F1's parent company. Ecclestone was shunted into the role of 'chairman emeritus'. What does that involve? 'I'm an adviser to the board,' he says. And what has his advice been? 'They have never asked,' he says with a thin smile. It's an honorary title designed to match his exalted status.

'I've got the highest position there is,' he jokes. 'So high that when I look down, I can't see anything.'

It has been quite a ride for the son of a Suffolk fisherman and housewife who became a used-car salesman as a teenager. The wheeler-dealing provided the capital in 1971 to buy Brabham, an F1 team, at a time when the sport was merely a pastime for motoring enthusiasts. Through the 1970s, he negotiated deals with circuits and television companies on

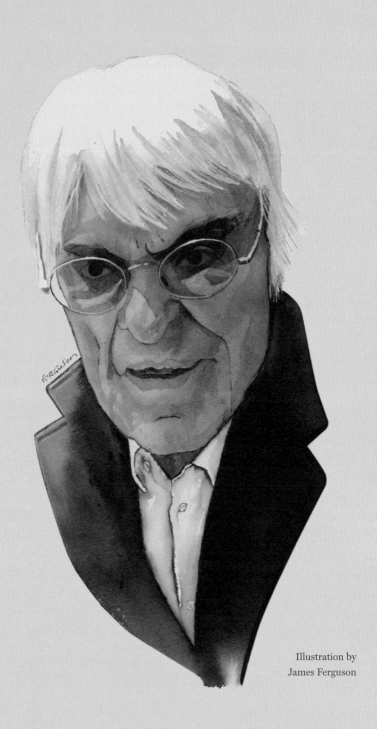

Illustration by
James Ferguson

behalf of teams, selling F1 as a package, rather than race by race. Attracted to the glamour, sponsors opened their chequebooks.

As millions of viewers were drawn to the spectacle, many in the sport became rich. As Ecclestone emerged as F1's legal owner, he steadily sold down his holdings to become a billionaire. The lifestyle changed accordingly. He became friends with Mick Jagger and Juan Carlos I, the former king of Spain. There were women, infidelities and three increasingly expensive divorces. His fourth wife, Fabiana Flosi, is a Brazilian lawyer around a half-century younger than him – and several inches taller.

Ecclestone chose this venue for lunch as it is a few minutes' walk from his home in Princes Gate, a building that once housed F1's offices. The restaurant is in the heart of Knightsbridge, one of London's most exclusive districts.

He is a fun sparring partner; polite, opinionated, sometimes evasive, never dull. His voice barely rises above a whisper, forcing me to lean over the table. The restaurant's other well-heeled diners glance over frequently, as if they sense that secrets are being shared.

People around F1 tell me Ecclestone has spent this season – which concludes this weekend – causing mischief for the new owners, whom he calls 'our American friends'. Stories abound: that at a recent dinner at the Kremlin, he tried to convince Vladimir Putin to allow him to work on the president's behalf to negotiate a lower fee to stage the Russian Grand Prix; that Ecclestone convinced two F1 teams to make a complaint to the European Commission over 'anti-competitive' contracts, even though it was he that brokered the terms; that Ecclestone is behind a corruption investigation by French authorities over the role of the world governing body of motorsports in F1's sale to Liberty Media. Ecclestone denies it all. 'A lot of people say: [the new owners] are doing this and what do you think? Do you think it's good? And I say what I've been saying to you. Wait and see.'

A waiter arrives. 'They know what I like here,' says Ecclestone, who has not even received a menu, let alone looked at one. I select the volaille au curry, which lists artichokes and golden raisins as ingredients, followed by the grilled sea bass. Ecclestone's choice of meal, like the man, remains an enigma.

In recent years, F1 has suffered waning interest from viewers. The decline is partly due to the lucrative deals that Ecclestone struck with satellite TV providers, taking races away from terrestrial TV screens. He bats away the criticism. 'My job was to make sure we built the business so it would sell,' he says. 'Which is what happened. Because we sold at a very good price. So I did what I was supposed to do.'

There's also the fact that races have become increasingly uncompetitive. Some of this is because Ecclestone ensured that more money flowed to the richest teams – Mercedes, Ferrari and Red Bull – allowing them to dominate. Technical changes have also meant that racing has become less risky, more predictable. The lack of overtaking means that after cars exit the first corner the outcome of a race is often settled.

'That's exactly right, that's what I keep saying. I was selling this shitty product and it embarrassed me because I think, without exception, all the [race] promoters are good mates of mine and I feel sorry for them having to try and struggle to sell tickets at such a shitty show. It's like the Stones without Mick.'

I stopped watching F1 regularly many years ago. Ecclestone asks why. In my youth, I say, there were great drivers in the cockpit, such as Ayrton Senna and Nigel Mansell. There were epic duels on the track, like the rivalry between Damon Hill and Michael Schumacher.

Ecclestone agrees: 'Who have we got that's really a character in F1? Just Lewis [Hamilton].' The British driver is certainly one of the sport's current greats and, perhaps, its only recognizable global star. Hamilton sped away with his fourth drivers' championship this year in the dominant Mercedes car. Yet I don't find him an engaging personality.

'No, but he gets to a lot of different people,' says Ecclestone. 'It's very strange. He's not particularly what you would say black [Hamilton is mixed race]. But lots and lots and lots of black people – I mustn't use the word "coloured" on tape, "black" is all right, I can use "black" – speak to me in the street and say, "Well done, Bernie." They're happy and proud of Lewis.'

Ecclestone admits that F1's new paymasters do not tap into his wisdom because his 'experience is outdated'. Perhaps that is understandable. Liberty Media wants to modernize the sport by utilizing social media and digital screening deals that could help reach younger audiences. Ecclestone once said there was no point in targeting teenagers as they aren't rich enough to buy a Rolex, one of F1's key sponsors. 'We used to run a five-star restaurant,' he complains. 'They want to run a

Kentucky Fried Chicken.' He points at his iPhone screen. 'Not much you can see, is there? Not too good for the sponsors. You can't see a sponsor's name.'

I poke my starter with suspicion. It appears to be a brown pâté with no artichokes in sight. I abandon it after a mouthful. (Later, the bill reveals it may have been the rabbit terrine. The restaurant appears to spot the error and does not charge for it.) I'm grateful to skip the dish as Ecclestone's mystery meal does not involve a starter.

Ecclestone has dealt with monarchs and presidents, industrialists and media moguls, winning a reputation for gaining the better terms of any negotiation. My favourite example is a tale from last year, when the octogenarian bet the F1 driver Sebastian Vettel that he could out-pace him in a friendly swimming race, with the proviso that the young German first had to drink a glass of water. When Vettel accepted the wager, Ecclestone ordered a glass of boiling water.

I try to get Ecclestone to reflect on his remarkable career. What's the best deal he's ever done? What is he proud of? He resists the line of questioning.

'Somebody asked me to go and do a lecture at one of the colleges. I said, "About what?" They said, "About business." So I said to the guy that asked me, "I don't need to go to Oxford to talk about this. You can tell them: buy cheap, sell dear and keep the cost down."' Our main courses arrive. Ecclestone's plate contains a meagre burger patty with no bun, draped in melted cheese.

He picks at the accompanying fries, leaves the shredded lettuce on the side and disinterestedly cuts his way through the burger. It is the same meal he's had here for years, he says.

By contrast, my perfectly cooked sea bass is topped off by diced peach, each bite a delicious mixture of sweet and savoury. 'I used to eat a lot more than I eat now,' says Ecclestone, wistfully.

What about regrets? He has a few.

'Maybe the most serious thing I regret was giving my shares to my ex, because when she put them all in a trust for her and the kids, I lost control.'

Ah yes, the 'trust' – the source of many complications. In 1997, Eccle-stone moved his holdings in F1, worth a reported £3 billion, into an offshore trust called Bambino Holdings and registered it in the name of his then wife, Slavica Radic. In 2008, after 24 years of marriage, Radic filed for divorce. At the time, experts thought it would be the most expensive divorce in British history. Subsequent reports suggest the pair reached an unusual arrangement in which the former supermodel pays Ecclestone about $100 million a year from the trust. Clearly, the loss of control over his fortune still rankles.

And the trust almost landed him behind bars. In 2014, he found himself in a German court on bribery charges related to a $44 million payment he made to Gerhard Gribkowsky, former chief risk officer for German bank BayernLB, which was once a major F1 shareholder. Ecclestone was accused of paying Gribkowsky to ensure F1 was sold to a party that would keep him running the sport. Ecclestone maintains the payment was a shakedown, alleging that the German banker threatened to tell the UK tax authorities that the F1 boss was in control of the family trust, a claim that could make him liable for a huge tax bill.

'Dear old Gribkowsky', as Ecclestone calls him, was jailed in 2012 for eight years on corruption charges related to the payments. Ecclestone faced 10 years in prison for bribery, but walked free after paying $100 million under a German law in which criminal cases can be settled with financial penalties with no admission of guilt.

The case could have landed Ecclestone in prison for the remainder of his life. Does he hold a grudge against Gribkowsky? Quite the contrary. 'I don't blame him because I would have probably done the same if I could have done it. He found the weak spot, found some leverage and used it. You can't blame somebody for doing that.'

For Ecclestone, sentiment should never enter the equation. He gives the example of the kidnapping of his wife's mother, Aparecida Schunck, in Brazil last year. The gang demanded £28 million for her release. 'The [kidnappers] phoned Fabiana and said if we didn't pay, her mother would have her head cut off and delivered to her sister . . . I wanted to go and get the people to meet me . . . I [thought] I could do a deal with them.'

I'm stunned at the bravado. Surely he would be too scared to meet the kidnappers? 'No, because why would they kill me?' No ransom was paid and after nine days in captivity, a police operation led to Schunck's release. A number of men have gone on trial over the incident.

If anything, Ecclestone seems impressed by the gang's tactics, saying its elaborate scheme to receive untraced payments was 'quite ingenious'. No anger at the heartache caused? 'If I get upset, how would it help?' The waiter returns with dessert menus. This time, Ecclestone has a recommendation: 'Have the soufflé.' And so we do, along with single shots of espresso.

In the 1990s, Ecclestone was nominated for a knighthood, with character references from Nelson Mandela and Silvio Berlusconi. His stewardship of F1 has helped to create 'motorsport valley' in the south of England where many F1 teams are based, employing thousands. Other British businesspeople have been recognized for less, but civil servants balked at ennobling him. A man who still shocks his country's political establishment – he voted Leave in last year's Brexit referendum and believes that US president Donald Trump has 'done a lot of good things for the world' – has been rejected by it.

'Honestly, I think the guy who should be running Europe, impressed me more than anything, is Mr Putin because he's a guy that says he's going to do something and does it . . . [He's] a first-class person.'

Does Ecclestone approve of Putin's autocratic tendencies, his lack of tolerance for political dissent, his government's homophobic policies? 'When I was at school, if you did something wrong, the teacher used to say, go and get the punishment book and the cane,' he explains. 'Go to your headmistress and get a few whacks or something. That's what he does.'

Ecclestone has got into trouble for views like this before. He once expressed admiration for Adolf Hitler as a man who 'was able to get things done', a remark for which he later apologized.

I suggest that Ecclestone is condoning repression. What if the Russians

---

Bar Boulud

Mandarin Oriental Hyde Park, London SW1

....

Terrine volaille	no charge
Yankee cheese burger	£18
Sea bass	£24
Soufflé x 2	£20
Espresso x 2	£9
Still water	£4
Sparkling water	£4

....

Total (inc. service and tax) –	£88.88

::::::::::::::::::::::::::::::::::::

Tip unknown but enormous

....

on the receiving end of 'a few whacks' have done nothing wrong and just want the right to freely criticize their leader? 'I was with [Putin] after the [2014 Sochi Winter] Olympics on top of the bloody mountain . . . we had a meeting, just the two of us, and we came out and we were walking along and people were coming up to him asking for an autograph . . . that's what people think of him.'

This is Ecclestone's experience of the world, atop a secluded mountain with other men of unquestioned power, bound by their ability to 'get things done'. Born into poverty, he has spent a lifetime constructing the most gilded of cages. You can admire his achievement, without envying it.

Ecclestone clearly has a sweet tooth. The soufflés are superb. A chocolate lid hides gorgeous blackberry filling. The waiter also brings a bowl of warm, mini madeleines dotted with vanilla, telling him they are 'on my behalf, because I know you like them'. Ecclestone grips the waiter's forearm and smiles.

Ecclestone says he is finally out of F1, having recently sold his last shares in the company. He plans to sell the London penthouse and the offices, which have been abandoned by Liberty Media. He wants to relocate to Switzerland, where he owns a hotel in the ski resort of Gstaad – a move that he insists is unrelated to the preferential tax rates. Still, he has more money than he could possibly hope to spend. What will be his final act? Perhaps a charitable foundation? Fat chance. 'I've got a wife, three daughters, five grandkids and one great-grandchild,' he says. 'So I've got enough I can do with my money.'

As if to make the point, he snatches the bill as it arrives. A tussle ensues. I protest that the rules of Lunch with the *FT* mandate that the journalist pays. Ecclestone is sprightly enough to fight me off. He unfurls a wodge of £50 notes from his trouser pocket and stuffs a pile into the leather sleeve. 'I never stopped breaking the rules,' he says.

Richard Branson

'The key to running a company is to be a good listener'

By Andrew Edgecliffe-Johnson

'**C**hicken or beef?'

The call of the Virgin Atlantic trolley-pusher escapes my lips as Sir Richard Branson consults his menu. Without looking up, the philanthropic entrepreneur-adventurer tells me he gave up beef nine months ago, having read what cattle farming was doing to the rainforest. 'I find it hasn't bothered me at all,' he says.

Locanda Verde's carnivorous menu has no such qualms but I surrender thoughts of steak tartare and search for something that might reconcile my appetite and his conscience. The sun-lit restaurant, run by chef Andrew Carmellini in Robert De Niro's Greenwich Hotel, is one of those exposed-brick Tribeca places that somehow remains buzzy five years after it opened. As Branson walks to the table he is accosted by Heidi Klum, the model and TV fashion show judge.

Branson has not eaten here before – he delegated the choice of restaurant – and for a man with a reputation as a sybarite, the pleasures of food seem low on his agenda. 'I'm very lucky I have a wonderful wife who's a fantastic cook,' he says blandly, 'but I'll eat whatever I'm given.'

When the waiter arrives, Branson picks casarecce, a tubular pasta with cauliflower, raisins and ricotta, and a garlic chicken main course with sides of spinach and roast potatoes. Remembering the rainforests, I choose a marinated beet salad for a starter, then my eye jumps to the halibut. In 2011 Branson added saving the seas to his to-do list when he joined the Ocean Elders, a group of dignitaries including Queen Noor and Ted Turner. Is halibut sustainable, I ask him?

'I think halibut's OK,' he reassures me. Instead of wine he asks for just

Illustration by James Ferguson

a splash of orange juice in his water. I order sparkling water without thinking through the environmental impact of bottled bubbles.

Our lunch falls in the middle of a typical Branson week. It began in Montreal with a meeting of his charitable foundation, Virgin Unite, then moved to Toronto for the launch of a Virgin Mobile training programme for homeless Canadians. He is in New York to hold a press conference for the Global Commission on Drug Policy, a group including nine former world leaders that favours decriminalizing drug use.

Next he will be off to Washington for breakfast with Republican senator Rand Paul, before heading for a spin in a 'centrifuge gondola' near Philadelphia to prepare his body for the stresses of a long-awaited suborbital space flight with Virgin Galactic, which he dubs 'the world's first commercial spaceline'. Somewhere between these public appearances, he will also find time to run the eclectic collection of airlines, train operators, gyms, mobile phone businesses, radio stations, music festivals and banks that have built a fortune *Forbes* estimates at $5 billion.

In person, Branson is an almost shy showman. He has barely made eye contact from under his sweep of silver-gold hair. Wearing a dark blazer with two shirt buttons undone and cuffs open at the wrist, he plays with a pen while he talks about his next adventure.

He has performed his fair share of stomach-turning exploits in hot-air balloons, high-speed boats and the like. But, at 64, he knows that going into space will put different strains on his frame. 'There's eight seconds where you go from nought to 3,500mph,' he says. At 4.5 G-force, 'you're going to feel it on your body'.

His dream of experiencing 'the overview effect' that astronauts talk of when they see the planet from afar has been delayed by about seven years, but his best guess now is that in March next year he and his son Sam, 29, will lift off from the 'spaceport' in New Mexico.

Branson is in a space race with Tesla Motor's Elon Musk and Google's Larry Page, his friends and fellow billionaires. (Branson officiated at Page's wedding on Necker, his Virgin Islands home, where Musk is now a neighbour.) He has been dreaming of rockets since watching the first moon landing in 1969, but he insists the competition is more than a rich man's folly.

'The space company will be our flagship company,' he says. 'Because we're the only private company in the world sending people to space, the next few months are obviously something that has a halo effect on every Virgin company.'

His companies span everything from balloon rides and water purifiers to cord blood banking. As our waiter brings a small carafe of orange juice and two slices of focaccia, I ask what Branson – with his seemingly limitless enthusiasms – turns down.

He admits he is not good at saying no. 'I sometimes see it as the university education I never had. We're learning about the train business, the mobile phone business, the space business,' he says, 'and more in our not-for-profit world.'

He only rejects an idea if it 'is not going to transform people's lives or is not going to be fun to do, or it's something we feel uncomfortable about doing,' he explains, nibbling on the focaccia. So there will be no Virgin spliffs, for example, although one of his missions is to urge governments to end what he sees as a failed 50-year war on drugs. 'As a businessman, if one of my companies had failed for 50 years I'd have closed it down 49 years ago,' he says with a flourish.

Our starters arrive – a steaming plate of pasta is placed in front of Branson, and for me a deep bowl of beets, peeled into bright candy-striped cross-sections of purple and yellow, that tastes unashamedly earthy. He spears a piece of cauliflower and declares it delicious.

It's 30 years since he leapt from running an independent record label to competing with British Airways, but Virgin's latest plans are, once again, taking him into businesses he knows little about but reckons he can improve.

He is building two 'very large' cruise ships, 'to see whether we can attract people like myself who've never been on a cruise ship'. He seems unconcerned by the idea of getting into a business he has no feel for, saying: 'The key to running a company is to be a good listener.'

He sees in cruise lines an industry that has been poorly run, just as he did in the 1980s with the airlines. I say that I remember the fun of my first Virgin Atlantic flights, with their cheap tickets, bantering stewardesses and free ice creams. I met my wife on one. But, in the post 9/11 era of plastic knives and high fees, has Virgin Atlantic, I ask, lost what made it distinctive?

'I'm always nervous,' he replies pensively. He maintains that the experience has not deteriorated since the days when Virgin only had one plane, but he concedes that 'other airlines have done their best to catch up'. Virgin Atlantic has also been waiting five years for delivery of a fresh fleet, he says, but it has just flown its first 787 Dreamliner. 'That will transform the perception.'

The airline – unsurprisingly, given its industry's financial record since the days of the Wright brothers – has never been the most profitable part of Branson's group. Last year it halved losses to £51 million and this year executives have said it should turn a profit. Firm numbers about the web of tax-efficient holding companies have always been elusive, but Branson claims Virgin Group 'is in the strongest position it's ever been in' – 'cash rich' with no net borrowings.

The group also has a business model that allows it to spray its cash around more carefully than it does its brand. Delta Air Lines now owns 49 per cent of Virgin Atlantic, Branson has cashed in his small stake in the telecommunications business Virgin Media and many of his businesses are controlled by other investors, with Virgin collecting licensing fees for the use of its name.

It's a model that allows him to embark on seemingly outlandish diversifications while limiting the risk. So while two cruise ships will cost $2 billion, 'We'll bring in outside partners,' he notes. Virgin talks of having 'global branded revenues' of £15 billion in 2012, but it is never quite clear how much of the total flows back to Virgin itself.

Virgin's finances are likely to be bolstered in the coming months by listings of two of its companies. Virgin Money, the UK-based financial services company, plans to raise £150 million in a London flotation, while Virgin America, the low-fare US-based airline in which it has a 22 per cent stake, has filed paperwork for a New York IPO. There is talk of a $1 billion valuation but he has been schooled not to comment.

Though Branson may be a ubiquitous presence in his marketing of Virgin-branded companies, he spends far less time on the business than he does on his philanthropic and personal pursuits. As he pushes his half-finished starter away, reaching again for a pen to keep his hands occupied, he says the trick is that he delegates much more than just restaurant choices.

'I learnt the art of doing that in my early twenties. That enabled me to have a life,' he notes. Branson's life – his Caribbean island home, kitesurfing and periodic attempts at breaking world records (he currently holds four, including the one for oldest person to kite-surf across the English Channel) – is an important part of his carefree brand.

In September, he told staff they could take as much annual leave as they want – with the caveat that they should first 'feel 100 per cent comfortable that they and their team are up to date on every project'. Branson says he has taken extended holidays for years, spending two or three hours a day on business, but delegating enough 'to have time bringing up the children'.

He has just finished building a new home on Necker for his children, Sam and Holly. Both are now expecting children of their own (twins in Holly's case), and are becoming increasingly central figures in Branson's charity work, his adventures and his company.

'They've wanted to prove themselves,' he says, noting Holly's medical school training and Sam's film production company, but both now talk openly about one day following their father into the business.

'I think companies benefit from a face – especially family-run ones – and Sam and Holly are a younger face than myself,' he says. It is 46 years since a 17-year-old Branson started his first business, a youth magazine called *Student*.

'It's been a long time but obviously I'm hoping in 20 years' time . . .' he trails off, implying that succession is far from imminent. He wants Virgin to be, like Apple, 'a global, well-respected brand that will hopefully outlive its founder'.

The unanswered question is whether his children can hold together a group as diverse as Virgin, where the founder has made his own image so central to everything it does, and seems to hold its disparate assets together by force of personality. As if on cue, he asks to be excused – 'I've got to that age!' – and while he is away one of his staff walks up to advise me that we have 10 minutes left. His next meeting is waiting.

We have been talking for an hour but there has been no sign of our main courses. I anxiously call over a waiter, asking for our food and the bill. He blanches and dashes to the kitchen.

Branson is probably Britain's most popular businessman but when he returns I ask him about the hostile headlines he gets for living instead in the tax haven of the British Virgin Islands. Last year he sold his home in Oxfordshire to live there full-time. He defends the decision as an entirely personal one. 'If anybody comes to Necker they'll realize it's a pretty nice place to live,' he says. 'If governments feel the rules should be changed, that's up to governments to change the rules.'

Time is ticking but our main courses arrive at last – a gleaming stack of yellow halibut for me and a heap of crisp-skinned chicken in front of my guest. He groans: 'I hate these American helpings.'

As I take a forkful of creamy mash topped with shavings of fennel, I realize the consummate pitchman has somehow failed to mention his new book, the ostensible reason for our interview. I ask why he wrote *The Virgin Way*, Branson's seventh book.

'If you've had a good life, I do think it's important you capture what you've learnt for future generations,' he says. The dyslexic Branson then admits that he has never been much of a reader of management manuals. 'I still think the best way is getting out there and doing it rather than reading books,' he says, which may not help his sales.

Virgin Books is yet another of the more than 50 companies listed on Virgin's website and I wonder whether the book needs a chapter on trimming dead wood. 'I'm not very good at cutting things back that don't go well,' he admits, his answer belying his earlier comments about how he might have ended the war on drugs in its infancy.

Locanda Verde
377 Greenwich Street, New York

Orange juice	$6
Bottle of sparkling water	$8
Beet salad	$16
Casarecce	$23
Halibut	$32
Garlic chicken	$28
Spinach	$9
Roast potatoes	$8
Total (inc. tax and service) –	$164.54

He cites Virgin Megastores as one business he clung on to for too long. But several splashy Virgin launches – from Virgin Brides to Virgin Cola – have been quietly put to sleep after not working out, and last month he grounded Little Red, a short-haul UK airline.

Branson describes failure as part of being 'a true entrepreneur', saying it doesn't damage the brand, 'as long as you pay the bills'. But after nearly five decades, he has no desire to have to start all over again. So even seemingly bold bets are financed in a way that ensures he is never betting the company. Virgin is investing about $500 million in Virgin Galactic, for example, but 30 per cent of the total cost is coming from Abu Dhabi.

I have polished off my fish but Branson's American-sized chicken has proved too much for him. 'I don't want this wasted,' he tells the waiter, asking if the remains could be bagged up.

Though we have overrun by about half an hour, he seems in no hurry to leave, and when we are offered tea or coffee he chooses English breakfast tea (which the waiter gives us on the house, as I have already paid the bill). 'When I drink too much coffee, I don't like myself,' he explains.

But pretty soon his colleagues are hovering, having decided he can keep his next meeting waiting no longer. He offers them the food, but both will be moving on with Branson before they can find a chance to eat it. So he gets up from the table, his tea unfinished, leaving me with a wave, a smile and a billionaire's lunchtime leftovers.

Ed Thorp

'I have an extraordinary bullshit detector'

By John Authers

As far as Ed Thorp is concerned, Wall Street is no better than a casino – not because it is a gamble, but because it is fixed. 'The invisible hand has become the invisible middle finger. It's a controlled and manipulated marketplace. As Donald Trump would say, "It's rigged".'

Thorp, a sprightly 84-year-old, is uniquely placed to judge. A mathematical prodigy, he worked out how to 'beat the dealer' at blackjack while a post-doctoral student at MIT. After he published a book in 1962 revealing how to count cards, he became so famous that casinos banned him from playing – he says one even resorted to drugging him. Many changed their rules to thwart people using his counting system.

Next came an attempt to beat roulette, using a contraption tied to his foot that is now described as the world's first wearable computer; after that, an expedition into Wall Street that netted hundreds of millions of dollars. His Princeton Newport Partners fund, set up in 1969, is recognized as the first quant hedge fund (one that uses algorithms). Over 18 years it turned $1.4 million into $273 million, compounding at more than double the rate of the S&P 500 without suffering so much as one quarter with a loss. Thorp's then revolutionary use of mathematics, options pricing and computers gave him a huge advantage.

His escapades, as well as his money-making abilities, have made Thorp the 'godfather' of many of today's greatest investors. Warren Buffett, a bridge partner, advised investors in his first hedge fund to move to Thorp; Bill Gross, who founded Pimco and built it into the world's largest bond fund manager, spent time at blackjack tables, then set up as an investor using Thorp's 1967 book *Beat the Market*; Ken Griffin, now the world's highest-paid hedge fund manager, set up his fund

Citadel in 1990 using documents that Thorp gave him from Princeton Newport.

It's an intimidating CV and I am nervous as I meet Thorp at his office in a modern block in Newport Beach, a spectacularly situated town in Orange County to the south of Los Angeles. But in person Thorp, who is wearing a tracksuit and still works out regularly, is not intimidating. A tall man with immaculately clipped designer stubble, he could easily pass for someone 30 years his junior and his face wears a seemingly permanent puckish smile.

After admiring his glorious view of the Pacific, we descend to the ground floor, and he bids me to get into the passenger seat of his red Tesla ('I used to have a Porsche, but this is so much better'). It is a gloriously smooth and quiet ride down the highway to Rothschild's restaurant in Corona del Mar, a family-run Italian place where they are delighted to meet him. It is also, he points out, not too expensive.

This is a key to understanding Thorp, whose success stems in part from the habits he learnt as a child growing up in restricted circumstances in Chicago and then Southern California during the Great Depression and the war. His parents worked and he had to educate himself. He also learnt not to be greedy.

He no longer gambles. 'I enjoyed the process of learning something new and being in a new milieu. Once it became a routine grind, I wasn't interested,' he says. 'Blackjack isn't very interesting because the stakes are so small. If you are used to betting millions in the market, betting a few thousand in the blackjack tables doesn't mean anything.'

These days, quants and hedge fund managers are notorious for their love of poker. 'That's because they can compete with each other. They like doing that a lot,' he says, with tongue in cheek.

We both order specials; he has the salmon and I have the swordfish, which he recommends. We also discover, to our mutual relief, that neither of us drinks at lunch, so this will be washed down by sparkling water and iced tea. I have the minestrone soup, but he abstains as he will need to keep talking.

So, why is he so negative about Wall Street? Without raising his voice, he launches an indictment. 'Adam Smith's market is a whole lot different from our markets. He imagined a market with lots of buyers and sellers of things, nobody had market dominance or could impose things on the market, and there was a lot of competition. The market we have now is nothing like that. The players are so big that they control the levers of financial policy.' There are still plenty of Ponzi schemes on Wall Street, too, he says, and not just Bernard Madoff, whose epic fraud he claims to have spotted more than a decade before it collapsed. In 1991, Thorp did some due diligence for a consultancy that asked him to look through their hedge fund investments. Madoff's returns instantly looked too good to be true, he says.

He tried checking the trades that Madoff had reported making against those reported in the official record. Half of them could not have happened because there was zero volume (the number of shares traded) in those options on the day the trades were supposed to have been made. 'Once you know half of them are fakes, it's pretty hard to believe the other half are real.'

A more detailed check revealed that in half of the remaining trades, 'my client alone had more trading volume than was reported for the entire exchange. This was absolute proof. You didn't need financial theory, no nothing. It was as if I had a video of him pulling a trigger.'

Nobody took any action. 'I waited year after year after year for it all to blow up. One reason it didn't was that he was a pillar of the establishment. And he had all these people steering money to him, charging fees. He wasn't charging fees himself, which was another big red flag.'

As for hedge funds, he says they are now 'a mature asset class, and the risk-adjusted returns for hedge funds are inferior to other asset classes'. So many people are now using quant methods that they are no longer so profitable.

I have had many conversations like this in the 10 years since the financial crisis. So, as we begin to tuck into the fish, lovingly wrapped in home-made pasta, I ask what he suggests we do about it? 'The banks who are too big to fail should have been allowed to fail. Their shareholders should have had to pay the price. Big companies go through organized bankruptcies. Why is it that we couldn't afford for the banks to go bankrupt? It's that they are so influential. They can persuade the government not to let them go bankrupt.'

He also holds that banks' speculative arms should be broken off – essentially a return to the Depression-era Glass–Steagall law that was controversially repealed by President Clinton in 1999. The newly elected

President Trump – we are lunching on the first Monday of his presidency – was elected on a platform of bringing back Glass–Steagall, but now appears intent on deregulation. Thorp winces at the mention of Trump's name, saying he is as negative about him as it is possible to be.

I need to ask Thorp about his own most awkward professional moment. In 1987 his hedge fund's New Jersey office was raided by agents working for the then New York district attorney, Rudy Giuliani. They had had dealings with Michael Milken, the king of junk bonds, and Giuliani was looking at every possible avenue to bring Milken down. Thorp, based in Southern California, was never charged or implicated, but several of his New Jersey colleagues were dragged through years of legal proceedings before establishing their innocence. Rather than fight on, Thorp decided to fold up his fund.

On Milken, who brought bond finance to many smaller companies, he is sympathetic. 'Milken's crime was far greater than any other person on Wall Street because he began unhorsing the old-line white shoe establishment and driving the companies they were running into the ground. He had to be stopped. And unfortunately he gave them some ammunition.'

As for Giuliani, Thorp resists my bait to criticize. 'I don't know how to install an ideal system. First, is there such a thing as an ideal system? And, second, is it politically possible to achieve it? I'm not sure about the first; to the second I'd say absolutely not, because the people with power don't want it to happen.'

By now we have both completed our fish (truly excellent), and are on to postprandial caffeine. I ask about the roulette computer idea he cooked up in 1960 with Claude Shannon, the father of information theory. Thorp had gone to Shannon for advice on his academic paper on blackjack. Shannon asked if he had any other ideas, and leapt with excitement at Thorp's ideas on roulette. That led to experiments in Shannon's basement, full of half-invented contraptions, with strobe lights and tilted roulette wheels.

The idea, Thorp says, was to press a button on the gadget (with his toe) as the ball whizzed around the upper ring of the roulette wheel (or 'rotor'). Pressing again would gauge its speed and rate of deceleration. I can see how this would help predict where it would fall. But what about the separate problem of where the wheel would be? It spins in the opposite direction. Knowing where the ball will drop does not help unless you know the wheel number that will be underneath when it does so.

Thorp explains by whirring his finger around a tea saucer. A roulette wheel has one (or, in the US, two) green pockets. These give the house its advantage, as everyone loses when the ball lands in green. But they also enabled him and Shannon to break the game. By clicking on the contraption when the green passed a certain point, it was possible (by programming the machine with phenomenal mathematics) to work out where the ball would drop and roughly which number would be underneath. Total precision was out of reach, but they could narrow the range to six numbers – good enough odds to give them a crushing edge over the house.

The system worked, but the hardware suffered a fatal weakness. The machine needed an earpiece. They bought the thinnest wire available, and went to elaborate lengths to hide it behind their hair, which they grew longer, but the wire often broke and could not be trusted. These days, they could probably use a Bluetooth earpiece.

Thorp's childhood, lovingly described in his new autobiography, *A Man for All Markets*, was filled with homemade experiments. He loved making things go bang, and built a succession of explosive devices. At school, and university, he specialized in physics and chemistry. In Shannon, he found another overgrown schoolboy who happened to be a maths genius. So why did Thorp become a financier? Should he not have been an engineer up the coast in Silicon Valley?

He grins. 'There are certain times in an industry when something is ready to happen. If you are there at the time, there's a much higher chance that you will be involved.' His roulette gadget came more than a decade before the first Apple computer, and almost four decades before the iPod – wearable computing was not ready to happen.

Instead, he put his insights from blackjack to work on investments, using advanced mathematics to develop strategies based on buying stocks in large numbers, where the odds were in his favour, just like counting cards. Having turned investment into a mathematical problem, he solved it, and programmed computers to help him.

Why was he able to make so much money from this when others do not? 'People aren't good processors of information. Not collectively.

Witness the recent political campaign in America. They can be fooled by fake news easily.'

And there's another point. 'One of the things that's served me very well in life is having an extraordinary bullshit detector.'

Thorp says that whenever he hears a surprising statistic, he tries to test it. Over coffee, I am scribbling fast in shorthand. He is intrigued. How fast can you write with that? I tell him I passed at 120 words per minute. 'And people talk at about 80 words a minute, right?' No, I reply, they generally talk a lot faster – more like 150 – but the tendency to be more considered when talking to a journalist probably saves us. Thorp's eyes narrow as he listens to the conversations at other tables. 'Actually, there's a way I can test that. I recorded an audiobook. So I can listen to that and time it . . .'

As his mind calculates how fast people speak, I tell him *FT Weekend* readers might want some investment advice. Why not copy his friend Buffett and try value investing as advocated by the investment theorist Benjamin Graham – analysing balance sheets to find underpriced companies?

That never appealed, says Thorp. 'The way I sized up the Ben Graham approach was that it would be a total lifetime of effort. It was all I would be doing. Warren demonstrated that. He's the champion of champions. But if I could go back and trade places with Warren, would I do it? No. I didn't find visiting companies something I wanted to do. I never even thought about finance until I was 32.' Buffett was trading bonds aged 11.

Thorp's advice: 'If you aren't going to be a professional investor, just index.' He conducts some more quick calculations in the air. Collectively, those who try to beat the market do 2 per cent worse than those who just buy an index fund, each year, by the time they have paid all their

---

Rothschild's
2407 East Coast Highway,
Corona del Mar, CA

....

Minestrone	$6.90
Salmon with pasta	$24.90
Swordfish with pasta	$26.90
Chocolate mousse	$9.95
Iced tea x 2	$6
Filter coffee	$3.50
Cappuccino	$3.50

....

Total (inc. tax and service) –	$100

fees. That means that you make 'twice as much money if you index as the average guy who doesn't index, after 35 years'. Meanwhile, you can get on with what matters.

This also explains why he did not make more of an effort to keep his hedge fund. 'I realized Princeton would have taken over my life. I would have spent my life just accumulating money.' His secret was to realize that he had enough.

Instead he and Vivian, his wife of more than 50 years, travelled the world and enjoyed their grandchildren. Three of them – triplets – are now at MIT. His book, long in the writing as it was sadly interrupted by Vivian's year-long battle with terminal brain cancer, describes life as an adventure, and ends with advice about work and life balance.

That adventure continues. As I pay the bill – a very reasonable $100 – and we head back along the coast, he tells me about his latest hobby. He has taken up scuba diving with his new girlfriend, a molecular biologist. The Maldives are great. As for what comes next, when he passes on his body will be cryogenically frozen. 'I feel that I have more to contribute and more things to do and enjoy in life than an ordinary lifetime allows.'

He estimates his chances of resurrection at about 2 per cent.

Marian Goodman

'Some are born confident.
I wasn't'

By Jackie Wullschläger

B eneath an ornamental arch which stands out among the honey-coloured 17th-century stone facades lining the Rue du Temple in the Marais, a wooden gate swings open. A few paces ahead of us a burly builder in overalls passes through and, fearing tailgaters, asks what business we have to enter the secret garden of the Hôtel de Montmor.

'Marian Goodman,' whispers my companion so quietly that the builder strains to hear. A diminutive, neat figure who combines sturdiness with delicacy – dark girlish curls, padded navy jacket, large burgundy Prada handbag, tiny pointed blue suede shoes – she looks about half his size as she treads steadily, deliberately, across the cobbles.

'Ah oui, la Galerie Marian Goodman,' he replies, helpfully pointing the way across a manicured courtyard, past lofty arcades and an *escalier d'honneur* to a glass-fronted corner of the immaculately preserved *hôtel particulier.*

Such anonymity is typical of Marian Goodman, who almost by stealth has become a grande dame of American art and one of the world's most powerful and influential dealers.

'I was incredibly shy and timid when I started. I still am,' she says now, speaking so softly that her New York accent is almost muted. Her tone is guarded but warm, her brown eyes gaze out, wary and quizzical. 'Some people are born naturally confident, I wasn't. Everyone has to find their own way, keeping doing what you know how to do, what you want to do. I wasn't part of the daily dialogue. I just felt like I had my own instinct. It's not just about having an eye.'

But a dealer's genius is to shape a cultural landscape out of his or her own instincts, and this Goodman has done more consistently and

Illustration by Sam Kerr

successfully than any living gallerist – and with a self-effacement unique in the screeching contemporary market. She has neither the flashy flagship spaces nor the extensive reach or huge rosters of uber-dealers such as Gagosian or Hauser & Wirth; she never trumpets art-fair sales or reveals revenues. Rather, her Manhattan gallery 'emanates integrity', according to *New Yorker* critic Peter Schjeldahl, and 'gives the art world rare jolts of self-esteem'.

Goodman's taste is high-minded and uncompromising. Without exception her artists – ranging from 80-somethings Gerhard Richter and John Baldessari to the new darling of sculpture, the Argentine Adrián Villar Rojas, whose first gallery show in her Manhattan space opened last month – are deeply serious conceptual thinkers, even when they are pranksters such as Maurizio Cattelan and Tino Sehgal. All boast global reputations.

At 87, Goodman is older than the lot, looks about 60, and is indefatigable. Hours before arriving at the Gare du Nord to meet me for lunch she was in Cologne looking at Richter's latest paintings. Hours later she will be en route to London, where her third gallery launched in 2014, to open an exhibition of South African film-maker William Kentridge.

But 'this is my favourite space', she confides, as she shows me her outpost in the Marais. A twisting glassy pavilion by American conceptual sculptor Dan Graham is on display, disrupting yet reflecting the formal geometry of the Montmor's courtyard and buildings. 'I do love Paris,' she adds. 'London is like New York, very competitive. I like trying a situation where that's not a factor. The French gallery is the smallest, I have a great desire to keep it going. France is having a harder time than before, the government has withdrawn money from museums, collectors have moved away because of the tax burden.'

She has chosen the French capital for lunch to celebrate her gallery's 20th anniversary here. We walk a few minutes down a winding, empty impasse – 'Paris is very discreet,' she murmurs approvingly – to Le Hangar, a small, old-school brasserie. The female maître d' and waitress acknowledge Goodman with friendly smiles, direct us to the quietest table and immediately offer tapenade and toast and mineral water. There are leather banquettes, white tablecloths, handwritten menus and posters of exhibitions of Matisse and Cézanne.

Goodman's first exposure to art was through such posters: her father, Maurice Geller, the son of first-generation immigrants from Hungary, was an accountant who 'was really passionate about art and very widely read and would bring posters home and have these poster shows of French art, so it was definitely in my memory.' In the same Upper West Side block lived Sidney Janis, a distinguished dealer; Goodman recalls playing tigers with his children in front of Rousseau's jungle painting *The Dream* – now at MoMA but then hanging in the Janises' living room. Later she was exposed to American modernism as her father began obsessively collecting Milton Avery; he gave her a canvas by the painter to start her business.

I ask for Goodman's guidance on the menu, mostly traditional French dishes, plus a few Italian offerings. She demurs, insisting it 'changes every day', though I sense that to give advice on personal preferences would for her seem both presumptuous and a step too far towards intimacy. Still, when she chooses tomato and mozzarella salad to start, I follow. She selects chicken with morels as a main; I opt for asparagus risotto.

When she began to get professionally involved in art, she says, 'I really didn't know my way round at all.' She had graduated as a history major from Emerson College in Boston in 1949, married William Goodman, a civil engineer, at 21, and quickly had a son and daughter – 'people today have an easier time being parents, they're older, more mature, more realized as people' – when she found herself on a charity art committee at her children's school. 'I asked if I could have a little room and somehow I met Franz Kline' – a Janis artist – 'and he was a very nice man and gave me a stack of small paintings. It was a sweet friendship, he probably was bemused that I was coming from nowhere and arrived on his doorstep. Everyone was thrilled to get work by Kline and I just was so curious because it was another world. I realized I loved working with artists and I should be serious and get myself an education in art history.'

She went to Columbia in 1963 and 'studied for a year and a half until I got divorced. Then I needed to work, I'd never worked in my life. Women then didn't work. There was more of a mindset against women's competence. A lot has changed . . .'

Towers of crisp tomato and fat slices of buffalo mozzarella heaped with basil appear, accompanied by fresh sliced baguette. Goodman stabs at the salad determinedly and continues, 'There was a sea change in the 1960s in every way – civil rights, women's rights, the world of philosophy, literature. There really was a development in the visual arts, this fantastic collaborative investigation of new ideas. Avant-garde artists had better audiences in Europe. We in America knew very little about Europe then.'

In 1965, when she was in her mid-thirties, Goodman opened her first business, Multiples, publishing prints and introducing early editions by Europeans including Joseph Beuys, Blinky Palermo and Belgian surrealist-conceptualist Marcel Broodthaers to America. She met Broodthaers in Berlin and 'thought it crazy that someone this wonderful was not showing in New York so I went looking for a gallery for him and I thought, with a surge of passion, if no one will do it, I'd love to. He had some wisdom and a very wonderful way of making his critique, with humour. I found him very impressive.'

She opened her first gallery in 1977 with a show by Broodthaers; in the following decade she launched the careers in New York of many Europeans including Richard Deacon, Giuseppe Penone and Lothar Baumgarten – as well as Americans such as the text artist Lawrence Weiner, who work in unconventional or ephemeral materials.

Goodman's taste was forged in the 1960s and 1970s, when 'there was a great deal of idealism; I was very lucky to be there in the years when really it was hard to ignore the world around you'. It defines a distinctive gallery known – as her friend, the Harvard art-history professor Benjamin Buchloh, puts it – for 'a certain subtle social horizon of responsibility'.

When she started out, being a dealer was far less obvious a route to big money, but maintaining ethical credibility while remaining prominent in a 21st-century market dominated by hype, herd mentality, unreal prices and no clear relationship between quality and success is Goodman's signal achievement. How does she do it? Strong instincts and intense nurturing contribute – she is 'a passionate advocate' for her artists, earnestly hand-picked because 'it would be awful to take someone on and realize you've made a mistake' – but it seems to me that something more elusive, to do with belief in art's capacity for transcendence, underpins it.

The mains arrive. Goodman glances at the large portions – 'my stomach isn't strong enough' – and donates half of her chicken breast, smothered in aromatic mushroom sauce and accompanied by wild rice, to me.

'The marketplace is important, too; artists need to live and sell and that's my responsibility,' she continues, then pauses, tapping fingers nervously on the table, because 'it's hard to pick the words. It's how someone can move you. The artists, from my point of view, have the capacity to express their inner selves in a profound way that is certainly enriching. Art can touch the soul – it sounds really corny – but that's the basis of it.'

Eating slowly, Goodman now talks in a rush, focused on the experience that has clearly been on her mind through lunch: seeing a new quartet of Richter's abstractions, which are 'really majestic works of lamentation' for the Holocaust. 'It's so complicated, it's a work of mourning but there's so much beauty in it, areas of painterly magic, incredibly meaningful work. He says it was something he had to do; his life as an artist would not be complete without it. He's a figure of great humanity – and that's something shared by all the artists of the gallery, their art is an expression of that. I'm attracted to that.'

Richter is her bestselling artist – in February an abstract painting fetched £30 million at Sotheby's in London, a price Richter called 'hopelessly excessive' – but that was not always the case. Goodman began representing him in 1985, when 'it was this weird time in New York, all the artists were neo-expressionists and he was outnumbered. It took a long time for people in New York to understand the nature of European art. So I wrote Richter a letter and told him how much I loved his work and that it could make a difference, and my desire to change the dynamic.'

Both are restrained talkers and at their first meeting neither said much, but a close relationship developed. 'It's been an honour for me, that's for sure,' she says. She sees Richter's art as 'a moral reminder; it's also the expression of a full life'.

Our main course finished, the waitress offers dessert. Goodman thaws: will I share a plate of crêpes Suzette with her? Three hot pancakes lavishly coated in Grand Marnier syrup and orange peel come promptly; Goodman gives me the lion's share but consumes hers with relish and also recommends some shortbread thins ('mmm, butter cookies') that follow with coffee. There is also a plate of dark truffles, which she pushes towards me. I am already overfed: would she think it rude if I took them for my son? In a blink, steely dealer turns bustling Jewish grandmother: enthusiastically, she recommends I gather them up in a doily and add the surplus petits fours of sugar-coated almond diamonds.

I ask for the bill – 'Oh, please let me take you for lunch,' she contests – and for her thoughts on painting today: she says Richter is one of only two painters in her stable (the other is Ethiopian-American Julie Mehretu, creator of dense abstractions referencing politicized landscapes).

'The more that is achieved, the more difficult it is for young artists to break loose. Now is a time when there's no great surge of invention,' she says soberly. From the 1990s she largely took on film-makers: Steve McQueen, Yang Fudong, Tacita Dean, Anri Sala, Amar Kanwar. 'I thought they were the most talented artists of their generation, by and large. And I thought to myself: "You must be crazy to do this" – I know the reputation of film.' Yet her countercultural instincts again won out: film is now embraced by museums and, increasingly, by collectors.

The waitress informs me that the gallery has already arranged to pay for lunch. I insist that the *FT* must pay, the maître d' is summoned. She ignores me and defers to Goodman: only with her consent can I have the bill. The gallerist yields graciously, I rummage for euros – Le Hangar is cash only – and try to conclude with talk of the marketplace. Did Goodman expect to be so successful?

'Never! I have been amazed, actually, that it's turned out so well. Luck is a factor for anybody.'

Is she uneasy with today's over-moneyed art world? 'I don't get it,' she says firmly, closing that conversation. Yet she can play the glitzy world with panache: the next evening, in honour of Kentridge, she hosts a banquet for a hundred in the Pompadour suite at Hotel Café Royal.

Le Hangar
12 Impasse Berthaud,
75003 Paris

....

Tomato and mozzarella salad x 2	€18
Chicken with morels	€22
Asparagus risotto	€22
Crêpes Suzette	€10
Decaffeinated coffee	€5
Mineral water	€4

....

Total –	€81

Kentridge, Goodman tells me, 'is an artist with a big heart and soul, the work is so bloody beautiful'.

I wonder if his art of protest – his magnificent new eight-screen *danse macabre* procession, *More Sweetly Play the Dance*, refers to centuries of political struggle and acutely resonates with today's parades of refugees – is somehow tamed by Goodman's gilt-and-Veuve Clicquot reception. But when Kentridge declares her 'optimism and generosity' indispensable to her artists, and I see museum directors from around the world – headed by Tate Modern's Nick Serota – line up to watch his work, it becomes clear that this tiny, shy octogenarian's mix of intellectual, social and hedonistic seduction is an unassailable model for disseminating radical art in the 21st century.

Donald Trump

'I never talk about my bad traits'

By Martin Dickson

'Give him some rice, too!' Donald Trump instructs the server behind the buffet counter. Rice? I haven't asked for rice. I'm more of a potatoes person, and that is what I have just ordered from the display cabinet, to go with my stuffed baked chicken. But if The Donald wants me to try the rice as well, it seems churlish to refuse. This, after all, is his restaurant, the Trump Grill, a wood-panelled, clubby enclave serving American fare in the basement food court of his best-known Manhattan building, Trump Tower.

If truth be told, I would prefer to be ordering from the Grill's set menu – the tourist in me wants the 'Trump Grill Burger' followed by 'Trump's Ice Cream' – but the billionaire real-estate developer has intimated that it would be good to try the buffet, which he tells me is 'the best in New York'.

Business is not exactly brisk at the best buffet in New York. In fact, Trump and I are the only people ordering. But it is a bitter winter's day, not the tourist season when, Trump insists, the queues down here get very long.

Tall, broad and erect, Trump looks good for his 66 years, though his gravity-defying bouffant hair is whiter and not quite as bouncy as I had expected, while wrinkles are invading the bland smoothness of the face beneath. He is wearing his familiar working uniform of grey suit, white shirt and a plain silk tie, today in bright red.

He helps me choose my chicken. 'That piece looks like a winner!' he says, pointing out the plumpest, most golden-brown portion. For himself, he orders a livid beef sandwich and potatoes. As we return to our table, I marvel at his urge to lavish superlatives on the most commonplace

Illustration by
James Ferguson

Trump-related things. Hype seems hard-wired into him. There ought to be an adjective to describe it: trumptastic, perhaps?

But then Trump, or the 'blowhard billionaire' as the New York tabloids call him, has created one of the world's most recognizable brands through relentless self-promotion, using any available medium: he has a shelf-full of books to his name, with uplifting titles such as *Think Like a Billionaire*; he is a TV regular, while his own hit show *The Apprentice*, now rebranded *Celebrity Apprentice*, is about to begin its 13th US series; and he tweets avidly to his 2 million followers on all things from politics (Obama's re-election was 'a total sham and travesty') to business philosophy and golf. 'I've won many club championships,' he tells me – twice.

I am hoping that in the relaxed atmosphere of Lunch with the *FT* I may get beyond the outer showman but the setting is hardly confessional. The buffet means we don't linger over a menu. Sipping Diet Coke as we wait for our dishes to arrive, I open the conversation by asking about his tastes in food ('all types – pastas, steaks . . .' he says) and the fact that alcohol has never passed his lips.

He leans forward and answers carefully with press-conference formality, his voice surprisingly soft. 'I've seen over the years too many people who have destroyed their lives with alcohol . . . I have some good traits and some bad traits. The bad traits I never talk about.' I joke that we can get on to those later but his face does not register amusement.

Far from breaking the ice, I seem to be thickening it. I turn the conversation to the safer subject of property and tell him we have a link: my home is on Riverside Boulevard – a cluster of newish Trump-built apartments that line the Hudson river for 10 prime blocks of the Upper West Side.

He becomes less stiff, more animated. I'm relieved but not surprised: real estate is where he started and, despite his new wrapping of showbiz glitz, is still central to his business.

The son of a self-made millionaire builder in the New York boroughs of Queens and Brooklyn, Trump was sent to a military school to install some discipline in him. He later attended Wharton business school before starting in business with his father – a hard taskmaster and profound influence. Against the elder man's advice, he set his sights on building in glitzy Manhattan. Displaying an eye for location, a genius for self-promoting bull and extraordinary self-confidence for one so young, he had completed Trump Tower by 1983, while still in his mid-thirties.

But then came his comeuppance. The recession and property crash of the early 1990s badly hurt his operations – particularly highly leveraged casinos and hotels in Atlantic City. Businesses there bearing the Trump brand have filed for Chapter 11 bankruptcy protection several times since. But – a vital distinction – Trump himself has never personally been bankrupt, and he has bounced back to create an empire that stretches from property, through an extraordinary array of Trump-branded goods, to entertainment. He co-owns not only *The Apprentice*, now a worldwide franchise, but the Miss Universe beauty pageant.

Trump Tower, where he has chosen to lunch with the *FT*, is still at the heart of his empire. With its bronze curtain glass walls and distinctive sawtooth design, it has worn the years well, and its location, on Fifth Avenue next to Tiffany & Co, is a shopper's dream. Trump works here and lives at the top of the tower with his third wife, Melania, a Slovenian-born former model 24 years his junior, in an apartment of gold-plated rococo luxury with fabulous views over Central Park. It is the fantasy life of any hot-blooded teenage male.

The story of the Upper West Side development is more down to earth: the hundred acres used to be abandoned railway yards. Trump, still only in his twenties, realized that it was among the best undeveloped land on Manhattan. But it took some three decades, with extraordinary financial ups and downs and planning battles, before he finally developed the area, with Chinese backing. And his original vision, to anchor the development with a television studio and the world's tallest building, would be watered down to a line of bland apartment blocks – since sold on.

Trump asks which building I am in. 'Very good,' he says. 'You have to be happy there. It's a great place. You know, I built that whole thing; it's been very successful for me . . . And people love the neighbourhood!'

I point out that it took a very long time to pull off. 'It's the old story. Never give up. But I ended up making a tremendous amount of money and, perhaps more importantly, having built a city within a city . . . People love it. They absolutely love it. So that's great!' He congratulates me on my good taste in real estate and I compliment him on the quality of staff his management company employs in my building. The ice is broken.

Our food arrives. There is chicken and rice on my plate but no potatoes. No matter. Trump points to his potatoes. 'These are great! Do you want the potatoes or the rice?'

'I've got the rice,' I say, keen to avoid further delay.

I ask him what he is working on now, and he turns the conversation to Scotland, and the golf course he has built on the coast near Aberdeen, which opened last summer.

'It is very, very highly rated. Unbelievably rated. Meaning, critically, it's been unbelievable. They are saying it is one of the best golf courses in the world.' The claim may sound trumptastic but the course has, indeed, received stellar reviews from top golfers.

Still, I say, you've had a lot of opposition: the development won backing from politicians and business leaders but was attacked by environmentalists and some local residents, furious that it got planning permission, despite being set amid dunes designated a site of special scientific interest.

'You know,' says Trump, 'there's always opposition when you do something big.' He runs off a list of his developments – in New York, Chicago and Scotland – that have provoked protest. 'I do many things that are controversial. When people see it, they love it!' Indeed, he adds, the Scottish opposition has been tremendously good publicity, making the course an even bigger success.

The conversation pauses as a young man stops by the table and says hello. It's Eric, the third of Trump's five children, who, like his elder siblings Donald Jr and Ivanka, works for the Trump Organization. He has been eating lunch in the Grill.

Eric disappears but, almost immediately, two more faces are there saying hi. It's Donald Jr and Ivanka, and they, too, have been in the Grill, celebrating a 'good deal' their father has just signed for them.

'The best restaurant in Midtown,' volunteers Ivanka, with a winning smile. 'We know, because we eat here all the time!' chimes in Don Jr.

Ivanka is a celebrity in her own right, with jewellery and fragrance products – a living, breathing inter-generational line extension of the Trump brand. There is even a salad in the Grill named after her. Maybe I should have had that?

As they disappear, I am left wondering whether there is a genetic component to trumptastic utterances. 'It's good when you have the kids working with you,' says Trump, 'and they are very capable.' Capable? It suddenly sounds shockingly modest.

Trump has been talking for many minutes now about his construction triumph amid 'these very monumental dunes, the great dunes of Scotland, the very largest dunes in the world' without mentioning a rather substantial problem: he is now in a fight with Alex Salmond's government lest it give the go-ahead to an array of offshore windmills in sight of the Trump course, and a second one he is planning to construct.

I raise the subject. 'I don't think they'll be built,' he says. 'I built a masterpiece. I don't want to see it destroyed by windmills. Windmills are going to be the death of Scotland and even England if they don't do something about them. They are ruining the countryside.'

Warming to his theme, he continues: 'I've done a great favour to Scotland and even Great Britain . . . A lot of people were devastated when their houses were ruined and their values destroyed when they put up a windmill near it. But they had no voice. Now they have a voice: me. I've empowered them to fight. And people are fighting these ugly monstrosities.'

The irony of Donald Trump as the people's champion against monstrous development seems lost on him. And if the windmills get the green light? 'I'll bring a lawsuit and I think it will be tied up for many years in court. How's your chicken?'

'Good,' I venture.

'Great food, isn't it?' he says. 'This place is the hottest place in New York.' I look around for confirmation. Business still seems rather desultory. It must be because it is winter.

A waiter arrives to clear our dishes. 'Look at that empty plate,' Trump exclaims. 'I think he liked it! For a non-heavy guy to wipe out a whole chicken, that's pretty good! OK, good job, fellows!' he says to the staff.

Momentarily, my mind goes all trumptastic. Yes! For a 'non-heavy' (in less euphemistic language, small) guy such as me to wipe out a whole chicken must be testament to my manly appetite and the amazing quality of the food. But the instant passes and I reflect that I did not eat a whole chicken, merely a thigh, and my total calorific intake was probably no more than on any other day. Still, I think, it would be nice to float with such an intoxicating, self-delusory sense of achievement all the time.

I order coffee while Trump sticks with Diet Coke. We move on to politics, where Trump has a record of heavy-handed interventions that provoke derision among Democrats and unease among Republicans. The latest was his promise in October to announce something that would change the course of the presidential election. In the event, he merely resurrected the 'birther' issue – the claim that President Obama was born outside the US – and said he would give $5 million to a charity of the president's choice if Obama released college and passport applications and records. America yawned and moved on.

Did he regret this? 'No, many people love me for it,' he says, and claims that he had even raised the sum at stake to $50 million.

I turn the conversation to ageing: he is known for working extremely hard but is he slowing down? 'No, I feel good . . . I'm in good health – knock on wood!' He strikes a wall panel and praises even it: 'It's nice wood!'

'If you love what you do, if you love going to the office, if you really like it, not just say it, but really like it, it keeps you young and energized. I really love what I do.' There's a touch of real passion about this.

And his legacy? 'You know I've become very successful over the years. I think I own among the greatest properties in the world. I'm worth more than $8 billion.'

Trump Grill	
725 5th Avenue, New York	
Chicken Fresco	$21
Steak sandwich	$21
Diet Coke x 3	$12
Coffee	$3
Total	
(inc. service) –	$74.06

Amid the lunch civilities, this is a tricky moment. The private ownership of his company, along with his deals and extensive licensing of the Trump brand, make it hard for outsiders to gauge his fortune independently. I brace myself and say that, according to *Forbes*, his net worth is closer to $3 billion.

Trump bats away the suggestion. 'I don't know what they say. People don't have access to my numbers but I'm worth more than eight.' He adds that when he was thinking of running for politics, he made a filing that supports this figure. And with such wealth, he says, he doesn't work for money any more. 'I just enjoy creating things.'

Does he see himself handing the business on to his children? 'Yeah, at the right time.' But, he adds, real-estate people never retire. 'They get older ... It's funny, we take out our cosmetic surgery on buildings instead of fixing ourselves, right?'

It is time to pay. He is amused that the *FT* insists on footing the bill for his lunch in his restaurant. 'That's very funny. The first time ever – usually, we just leave, right?'

He escorts me up to the pink marble lobby, lined with stalls selling all manner of Trump-branded goods: books, caps, shirts, ties, teddy bears, cologne, cufflinks. He asks how sales are going. Really well, enthuse the staff, who tell us a particularly strong seller is a tiny book of The Donald's wisdom wrapped together in cellophane with a gold chocolate bar, stamped TRUMP.

Yet business does not seem brisk. In fact, I can see no other customers. It must be because it is winter, I tell myself as I emerge on to Fifth Avenue, my body numbed by cold and my mind by superlatives.

Ali al-Naimi

'Attack emissions, not fossil fuels'

By Roula Khalaf

I am just a few minutes into my lunch with Ali al-Naimi and we are thousands of miles away in another era, racing across the sands of eastern Saudi Arabia on his mother's white camel. It was her dowry in her second marriage and she took it on long trips in the 1950s, just as other Bedouin women now drive trucks and cars on desert tracks; the national ban on women driving, one of the more outrageous aspects of life in Saudi Arabia, is rarely enforced in remote parts of the kingdom. Naimi, Saudi Arabia's legendary former oil minister, laughs. 'In the past you used to see women riding camels, and now you see them driving Toyotas with the camels in the back of the car.'

We are at George, an elegant brasserie and private club in the heart of Mayfair, seated at a small round table beneath a David Hockney print. The diminutive Naimi, 81, is dressed in a three-piece suit, arguably a little too formal for the chic modern setting. For two decades, as the man responsible for the policy of the world's largest oil exporter, Naimi bestrode the energy markets like a colossus. The 'oil king' has never liked reporters. They have chased him relentlessly over the years. At summits of Opec, the cartel of oil exporters, the more determined took to accompanying him on his early-morning runs seeking to dissect his sometimes cryptic words, his mood and even his body language for clues about the direction of oil prices. He could be humorous with them at times and cantankerous at others. Now, six months after retiring, he is in a mellow mood, eager to tell stories.

Having just published a memoir, *Out of the Desert*, Naimi's mind drifts back easily to tales of his childhood growing up in a nomad's tent. I, of course, am keen to press him on the biggest bet of his long career. In November 2014, with the oil price in freefall, he convinced the ruling

Illustration by
James Ferguson

royal family to take an enormous gamble. For decades, the kingdom's role had been as a swing producer, taking its output up or down to balance the oil price. On this occasion, Saudi Arabia abandoned that policy and stunned global markets by opting not to cut its production to bolster prices but instead keep pumping oil to protect its market share. The consequences still overshadow the global economy. After roughly four years at more than $100 a barrel, the price of oil tumbled, hitting a low below $30 earlier this year before staging a recovery to about $50.

We are both starting with the yellowtail sashimi. Naimi orders the Dover sole for a main course, while I choose the miso cod. When the mains are served, Naimi is excited at the sight of the sprouting broccoli. He takes a bite and nods approvingly, telling me he first tasted the lanky vegetable on a trip to Australia. Naimi is a traveller. A geologist by training, he loves hiking – and sometimes indulges in it at curious times. There was, for instance, the notorious disappearing act in the run-up to the 2014 Opec meeting that sent the markets into a frenzy. 'I like to climb, I went to Austria,' he says, as if it was just another trip.

As we settle into our lunch, Naimi explains the logic behind his momentous decision. The era of oil selling at more than $100 a barrel had radically changed the market, encouraging new producers with higher costs to join in, and fuelling the US shale revolution. As oil flooded on to the market, countries outside Opec refused to cut their output. Inside Opec, there was resistance, too. Saudi Arabia was not about to act on its own. 'It would have been stupid of Saudi Arabia to agree to a cut then,' Naimi says. 'More non-Opec production would have come [on the markets]. We had no choice.' As producers pumped more oil after the 2014 decision, however, prices continued to fall, dropping much lower than the range the Saudis had anticipated. The collapse hit Saudi revenues hard and squeezed the state budget. Naimi came in for severe criticism at home. Abroad, many questioned whether his bet would backfire.

Intriguingly, Naimi ends his memoirs just after that fateful Opec meeting two years ago. When I ask why, his eyes twinkle and he smiles. He says, half in jest, that he intends to write another book, and has more to say about people and events. More seriously, he tells me that he knew 'it was going to get worse'.

Naimi is haunted by a period in Saudi oil history that he describes in his book as the mistake that had cost one famous predecessor as oil minister – Zaki Yamani – his job. It was back in the 1980s, amid a surge in non-Opec production from Alaska's North Slope, the North Sea and Mexico. Saudi Arabia became the swing producer. When it sought to regain its share, prices collapsed.

Naimi learnt a lesson and adopted a different tack, but will his own gambit also go down in history as a miscalculation? After all, his successor, Khalid Al-Falih, may move towards reversing it. Meanwhile, predictions in Riyadh that lower prices would inflict lasting damage on the US shale industry underestimated the resilience of that sector: some small producers have gone out of business but, as prices have slowly recovered in recent months, others appear to be weathering the storm.

Naimi is known to be single-minded and stubborn and is not about to show me otherwise. There is no hint of hesitation when he declares that he was 'absolutely correct' in his decision. 'I didn't think or say we want to take [shale] out. I said we don't want to lose more market share. Let the price be decided by the market,' he says. 'Anybody who thinks he or any country is going to influence the price in today's environment is out of his mind.' Going back on the policy he recommended to the king at that time would be inadvisable, he insists. 'I have no idea why they want a reversal because a high price will definitely bring more crude to the market and Opec will further lose [market] share.'

He has put down his knife and fork; the waitress is giving us a worried look. There's nothing wrong with the sole, Naimi reassures her gently. 'I'm a fisherman and I know good fish, and that's good fish.' Then he turns to me and, returning to the past, says that the first time he tasted fish was after he married his wife, who is from Bahrain, the small group of islands east of Saudi Arabia whose name in Arabic means 'the two seas'.

Naimi's extraordinary life story personifies Saudi Arabia's rise to regional powerhouse. Born in 1935, three years after the founding of the modern state, he spent his early years as a poor nomad living in a desert tent. As a child he herded sheep; at 12, he was an office hand, working for Aramco, the oil company then owned by American companies, a post he took on as a result of a family tragedy – he replaced an older brother who had died of pneumonia. Aramco became his home and his family. It sent him to Lebanon for his first formal education and then to US universities; he still speaks with an American accent. He would rise through Aramco's ranks to become the chief executive.

When he was appointed minister of petroleum in 1995 and imposed his authority on Opec the world took greater notice of Naimi. For two decades he was a dominant force at summits when the world's markets moved on just about his every word. He has seen oil as low as $16 a barrel, and oil well over $100 a barrel. He has lived through global financial crises, wars and political earthquakes in the Middle East.

Time and again during our lunch I detect his frustration with Opec. He tells me a story about his first meeting in 1995, which was to begin at 10am. 'Five minutes to 10, I was in the building. I waited, I waited, I waited. At 11am, hardly anyone showed up. Ten minutes before 12, ministers started walking in, and we convened. I raised my hand and said that, if you want us to meet at 12, please tell us to meet at 12. From then on, people started respecting time.' Some ministers in Opec, he also says, 'don't come prepared . . . don't have the facts, don't have the staff or have staff that are not competent'.

Though in his book he reserves his harshest criticism for Russia, which is not a member of Opec, accusing it of failing to follow through on its pledge to reduce oil production during the financial crisis, he tells me that his fellow Opec members also lie. Given the experience of the past two years, maybe Opec has outlived its purpose, I suggest? 'Never,' he insists. 'You don't have another organization that looks after the business. Before 2014 it was successful but in 2014 everybody had excuses.'

Naimi's career came to an end this May, when he took a telephone call from Salman bin Abdulaziz, who ascended to the throne of the absolute monarchy last year. A week later, the retirement that markets had speculated on for years was announced, bringing the curtain down on a long chapter in the history of oil. Although it was more than a decade after he had himself mooted the idea of retiring, the timing was awkward. Naimi departed from the oil scene thinking he had unfinished business: he still did not know if his bet on protecting Saudi Arabia's market share had paid off.

Unsurprisingly, Naimi is a strong believer in the long-term survival of fossil fuels, insisting that technology will find ways of reducing greenhouse emissions, and renewables are too expensive for developing countries. The Saudis signed up to last year's Paris climate change accord, which committed the world to try to limit global warming, but they were also accused during the negotiations of having tried to undermine it.

'Let us attack the emissions, not the fossil fuels; we have brains, we have technology, we can manage the emissions,' he says. Not for the first time he relates a story from a conference packed with people calling for an end to the era of fossil fuels. 'I raised my hand and I said, "Gentlemen, I think I hear you very well, I'm going to go back to my country and shut all our wells,"' Naimi quips. 'There was an uproar – no, no, no.'

I recommend the sticky toffee pudding to Naimi if he's in the mood for something sweet, and order the seasonal fruit plate for myself. Over coffee, we talk about the future of Saudi Arabia. Since King Salman took over, his 31-year-old son and deputy crown prince, Mohammed bin Salman, has been handed responsibility for the economy, and has brought in a younger cabinet with a radical agenda.

With the rise of MBS, as the prince is known in international circles, the replacement of the octogenarian Naimi seemed a matter of time. He was now out of the inner circle of power, and no longer the only voice speaking about oil policy. Before a meeting of producers in Doha in April, MBS and Naimi appeared to contradict each other, confusing the oil markets. Naimi denies any clash and insists that statements had been misinterpreted.

MBS has pledged to end what he calls the 'addiction to oil'. Saudi Aramco is working on a public listing, something that would have been taboo under King Abdullah, the late monarch with whom he has worked most closely. Energy subsidies have been slashed, as have benefits for state employees. I ask Naimi whether this diversification effort will be

George	
87–88 Mount St,	
Mayfair, London W1	
Sashimi x 2	£44
Black cod	£35
Dover sole	£42
Purple sprouting	
broccoli	£6
Sticky toffee pudding	£10
Seasonal fruit	£8
Espresso	£4
Evian water x 2	£10
Americano	£5
Total	
(inc. service) –	£195.50

more credible than previous and largely unsuccessful restructuring attempts over the past 20 years. Watch the oil price, he says. When prices are depressed, Saudi Arabia acts, and when they rise again, it 'relaxes'. This time is more serious, though. 'The best thing is to quit talking and start acting,' he continues. 'I believe that's where we are now. We are beginning to act.'

Nearly two hours have passed and we are back where we started, discussing Saudi women and driving. Will a kingdom that promotes a puritanical Wahhabi Islam, where clerics exert overwhelming influence, ever modernize? Will it ever let its women thrive, and allow them to drive? Naimi takes me back through history one last time, to the 1979 Iranian revolution. Saudi Arabia's reaction to the fall of the Shah was to 'become holier than thou', he says. He believes the contract between the monarchy and the religious establishment, which handed the clerics the authority to impose social norms, is fraying, and senior princes who were the main stumbling block to women driving have passed away in recent years. Naimi has five granddaughters and they all have non-Saudi driving licences. 'I'm a liberal grandfather, I tell them all, "Don't get married until you graduate,"' he says. 'The world is changing, let's change with it.'

Olafur Hauksson

'You have to take the hard times'

By Richard Milne

Visiting Iceland today, it's hard to imagine how a tiny fishing nation without a tradition of big banking became synonymous with the idea of 'Viking capitalism'. About a decade ago corporate raiders embarked on a high-street spending spree funded by the country's largest banks, which built up assets 10 times the size of the country's economy. Among the trophy assets they acquired were the famous toy shop Hamleys and the Premier League football club West Ham United.

The frenzy didn't end there. Across the nation's population of 330,000, even fishermen became full-time traders, while the consumption of luxury goods soared. In his book *Frozen Assets* Armann Thorvaldsson claims that, in 2006, Bang and Olufsen sold more televisions and sound systems in Reykjavik than in any other store outside of Moscow.

Then, in the autumn of 2008, as the world dealt with its biggest financial crisis in 80 years, Iceland went pop more spectacularly than anywhere else, staving off bankruptcy only by letting its big three banks – Glitnir, Kaupthing and Landsbanki – fail.

As protesters streamed on to the streets in their thousands – on one occasion throwing snowballs, eggs and yoghurt at the parliament – the role of special prosecutor was created to look into rumours of epic financial wrongdoing. Nobody applied. When, the following year, a small-town policeman more used to handing out parking fines took the job, conspiracy theorists smelled a rat: clearly, they thought, the problem was being buried.

They were wrong. Olafur Hauksson may not draw recognition from other diners as he strolls into the Hilton hotel just outside the centre of

Illustration by James Ferguson

Reykjavik at noon, but he is responsible for one of the most impressive feats accomplished in the post-crisis world. For Hauksson, 52, now Iceland's district prosecutor in charge of investigating all major crimes on the island, is the only person in the west to have jailed a big bank's chief executive.

And not just one. His first big conviction came just after Christmas in 2012 when Larus Welding, former chief executive of Glitnir, was found guilty of fraud. The verdict was later overturned but soon the floodgates opened. Welding was sentenced to five years in jail for breach of trust in December 2015, and in a separate case last month to one year in jail. Both convictions are likely to be appealed to the supreme court. This was followed by two more chief executives, Hreidar Mar Sigurdsson of Kaupthing and Sigurjon Arnason of Landsbanki, who were each handed two separate convictions and jail terms.

Hauksson has chosen the Hilton's buffet over the trendy city-centre eateries nearer his office because, he says, 'it has a little of everything, so it suits everyone'. A big man – today dressed in a brown suit, white shirt and black-and-brown striped tie – he looks like he is not entirely a stranger to all-you-can-eat lunches.

We get stuck in straight away. The buffet is indeed an impressive spread and good value compared with the prices elsewhere in Iceland, inflated by an extraordinary boom in tourism since the crisis due to a weaker currency and cheap flights. We stock up on sushi, salad and a Chinese takeaway-style box filled with chicken noodles.

At our table, which looks out on a car park and busy main road, Hauksson quickly brings me up to date on his record so far. Of his financial cases, 14 have reached the supreme court for judgment, bringing 11 convictions, two acquittals and a retrial.

I ask how it was to start with what was essentially a blank sheet of paper and no roadmap from elsewhere on how to proceed. Picking up a piece of sushi, Hauksson answers: 'That's the question that is a bit compelling today. It's why others didn't do the same when there was the same situation there as there was in Iceland.'

He pauses to dip his sushi in soy sauce. 'The worst thing is that these questions will not be answered ever. You will always have this obstacle in gaining trust in the financial sector again,' he adds.

In other countries, there have been convictions for financial crisis misdemeanours. Tom Hayes, a former UBS banker, was jailed for 11 years in 2015 for manipulating Libor, the benchmark interest rate, despite arguing that his bosses knew what he was doing. Jérôme Kerviel was sentenced to three years in prison in France in 2010 after amassing € 50 billion in hidden trades at Société Générale.

But such cases targeted, in Hauksson's words, 'the keyboard person' – the underling who performed the trade, rather than someone up the food chain.

Hauksson, by contrast, has concentrated on the big fish. Many of the cases have been highly complex, alleging market manipulation or breach of fiduciary duty through the use of shell companies to prop up the banks' share prices or loans where the lenders bore all the risk.

So how did he go about pursuing the people at the very top? He says it was mostly about following the document trail very carefully – particularly in times of stress and crisis, emails can be especially revealing.

It was also, he tells me, about keeping going to the logical conclusion rather than stopping. 'It's finding out who is responsible. That's a totally different thing. In some ways, it was clear where this all came from. It was important to make the employees aware that if they cannot point to someone else, they will be the one to blame,' he says.

It is a simple point but it makes me stop. I spent several months at the end of 2015 reporting on Volkswagen's emissions scandal. So far at the German carmaker – just like at the big US and European banks – there has been plenty of talk of big fines but only relatively junior employees have been fingered for potential criminal responsibility.

Getting people at the top is essential to restoring trust in the system, I suggest. 'Yes, it is. And it has maybe come out on other countries too that this was a mistake not to try.'

I mention some of the cases from other countries, such as VW and Wells Fargo, where bank employees opened accounts without customers' authorization. Hauksson pushes aside his plate. 'This is one of the problems,' he starts, 'you have some kind of culture, everything has been done this way for long periods of time. And that's why it's a bit difficult sometimes to point at some specific order from the top.'

Returning to his Icelandic cases, which have, for instance, shown that the banks themselves accounted for up to 80 per cent of the trade in their own shares on some days, he says: 'The executives, they have some tools to control things. They have reports: for example, how much the bank itself was actually buying up its own shares, so they couldn't deny what had actually been happening . . . They were obligated to react on that.'

Some have argued that it was easier for Iceland to be aggressive because of its small size, whereas the big US and European banks were more systemically important. Eric Holder, the former US attorney general, said in 2013 that it was difficult to prosecute large banks 'when we are hit with indications that if you do prosecute . . . it will have a negative impact on the national economy, perhaps even the world economy.' He later backtracked but no chief executive at a big US bank has yet been prosecuted.

Iceland's rapid rise and sudden crash was certainly devastating. Stefan Olafsson, an Icelandic professor, has called it 'probably the most rapid expansion of a banking system in the history of mankind'.

Its collapse caused Iceland's currency to plummet, which in turn led to inflation and loan repayments soaring. Many Icelanders who had taken out loans in yen or Swiss francs at a lower rate of interest found they were now facing penury.

'Almost everyone was affected by the crisis one way or another,' Hauksson reflects now, yet he is clear about the imperative to investigate. 'It's a bad thing, whether a society is small or big, to have these matters unsolved. These are the most serious economic crimes that have ever been committed in Iceland. Taking into account how many people it touches, how it affects the economy, if this behaviour had not been dealt with, it would have been a fault for the system,' he says.

'Let's have some more,' he says eagerly and, minutes later, we return from the buffet with our small plates laden with lamb, chicken, salmon, potatoes and mushrooms. Hauksson has taken some more sushi as well. 'One time is never enough.'

He was brought up in Reykjavik, the fourth of five children in a middle-class family. Hauksson's eldest brother was handicapped from birth so he and his sisters helped look after him.

'In a way my whole life I have been working,' he explains. 'During some prosecutions we are more at work than home. It is bad, working late hours and weekends, and it wears people out. We have had incidents at work where we have actually had our employees very badly ill. I have four times seen one of my employees going into an ambulance. That's not an easy thing, so you actually feel a little bit the pressure that comes with the job.'

After law school he rose through the ranks to become head of police in Akranes, a sleepy town of 6,500 people across the bay from Reykjavik. His biggest investigations were 'attempted murder or a drug case', he says. His main tasks included collecting taxes and dealing with family affairs. He also issued parking fines and broke up drunken brawls. He had no financial experience.

The role of special prosecutor must have seemed a thankless task on an island where the elite is small and interconnected? 'No one wanted it,' he says, recalling his decision to belatedly throw his hat into the ring. 'Maybe I was too narrow-minded when I decided to apply. Maybe everyone else knew that this would be horrific. I don't know. But I found it appealing,' he says.

Hauksson was provided with advice on how to set up the special prosecutor's office by Eva Joly, a Norwegian-born, French investigating judge known for her cases against Elf Aquitaine and Crédit Lyonnais. He was also aided by the Icelandic parliament's special investigation commission – a kind of 'truth and reconciliation' report on the crisis published in 2010.

Hauksson started off with a staff of three and 'no computers, no phones, nothing'. By 2013, under a centre-left government that came to power after the popular uprising known as the 'pots and pans revolt', the special prosecutor had 109 people working for him. Two years later, with the party that was in power before the crisis back in office, his budget and staff were slashed again. Yet he ploughed on, securing conviction after conviction and even securing a retrial in one case due to a lack of impartiality from one judge, who then proceeded to attack him in no uncertain terms.

As we tuck into the chicken, I ask Hauksson about where he gets the personality to withstand the pressure. 'The stubbornness?' he asks with a smile. 'Of course, I have been in this system for a long period of time and in a way you know your way around, you know what's proper, what's decent . . . You have to be persistent and you have to be very much self-driven because there is no one else driving the case to the court.'

He argues the crimes themselves are simple matters such as

embezzlement, merely with a complicated 'wrapping' of financial jargon around them. Is it like gang crime, I ask, where you know one of a group did the crime but you can't work out who? 'It's maybe more that you are almost looking into some well-organized criminality,' he replies.

There's time for one more trip to the buffet, this time to collect a selection of desserts, and in my case some cheese. Hauksson orders a coffee and immediately sets off on a long anecdote about a fishing trip the previous week, his first for a long time. 'I found myself a bit rusty. I was doing poorly at the beginning of the day. It's always interesting to know how nature can teach us lessons, because in the last hour I got a bite.

'I fought with that fish for 40 minutes and it went up and down. And I thought that it was either me or the fish,' he says, pausing to eat some dessert. 'It ended that the fish won. It broke the line. Most often I would have been raging but this time I felt humbled . . . I will be in better shape next time.'

Hauksson may have been clearing up financial wrongdoing, but Iceland is still struggling on the political side. Its prime minister was forced to resign in April after appearing in the Panama Papers' revelations about offshore companies. The anti-establishment Pirate party were the big gainers in early elections held in October and may still end up in government. Still, trust in Iceland's parliament is one of the very lowest in Europe. Did the politicians miss a chance to rebuild trust? 'Maybe the work of our politicians should be more transparent, there should have been fewer scandals, and more focus on re-establishing the trust,' Hauksson says.

With the restaurant thinning out of the few tourists who have been eating alongside us, I ask Hauksson about the recent extraordinary boom in foreigners visiting Iceland. The number of tourists has jumped from

Vox Restaurant

Hilton Reykjavik Nordica,
Sudurlandsbraut 2,
108 Reykjavik

....

Lunch buffet x 2	IKr7,700
Coke	IKr490
Pepsi	IKr490
Coffee	IKr500
Tea	IKr500

....

Total –	IKr9,680
	(US$87.24)

about 500,000 in 2010 to an expected 2.4 million next year, raising fears of another bust to come like the financial one.

Hauksson says such booms and busts have long been in Iceland's nature as a nation depending on the vicissitudes of the sea. 'The fish is coming and going, and if it is coming you try everything possible to get it, and when it's going it's not out there any more and you have to take the hard times. It's always tops and bottoms.'

Aliko Dangote

'Only the toughest of the tough survive here'

By David Pilling

As a rule, I don't get worked up over oil refineries. But the one gradually taking form on 2,500 hectares of swampland outside Lagos, Nigeria's Mad Max commercial capital, is so big, so audacious and so potentially transformative that it is like Africa's moon landing and its Panama Canal – a Pyramids of Giza for the industrial age.

If Aliko Dangote, the billionaire businessman behind what even he calls his 'crazy' $12 billion project, can pull it off, he will go down as the continent's John D. Rockefeller, Andrew Carnegie and Andrew Mellon combined. And once he's built it, he intends to treat himself to a small indulgence: he'll buy Arsenal, his favourite football club.

'When we finish this project, for the first time in history Nigeria will be the largest exporter of petroleum products in Africa,' he tells me, summoning the drabbest of platitudes for a project of pharaonic ambition. I am sitting with Africa's richest man discussing his life of superlatives over Thai food on his 108-foot yacht, moored in Lagos Lagoon. Yet the image he projects is more like a modestly successful encyclopaedia salesman. When I arrive at the dock, Dangote, a Muslim, is praying in his quarters. He soon comes out to greet me and turns out to be the most solicitous of hosts. 'Feel at home,' he says. 'We can hang that for you,' he adds, when I place my crumpled jacket on the yacht's white leather couch. 'Can we offer you something to drink?' Dangote goes through the options arranged before us: 'There's vegetable spring rolls, chicken wings in a barbecue sauce, green Thai curry, some kind of seafood salad, noodles,' he says. 'You are my guest, so what do you want? You want rice? Plain jasmine or with egg?' I plump for the jasmine. 'You

Illustration by James Ferguson

don't eat egg?' he asks. You asked me to pick one, I protest. 'That looks like satay,' I say, pointing to one of the plates.

'It is satay, actually.' He spoons me out several of the dishes – it's always fun to be served by a billionaire – and we dig in. It's tasty, and there's a plate of green chilli sauce to liven up proceedings. Dangote crunches into a spring roll and ignores the gently buzzing phone on the table.

A few numbers on the refinery will help illuminate the scale of his 'craziness'. When it is up and running – if it gets up and running – it will process 650,000 barrels of oil a day, a third of every drop Nigeria produces and approaching 1 per cent of planetary production. That will make it the biggest oil refinery of its type in the world. As a sort of side concern, it will pump out all the plastic Nigeria's 190 million people need (or imagine they need), plus 3 million tonnes of fertilizer a year, more than all its farmers currently sprinkle on their fields. To make things more interesting, Dangote is building the whole thing on a swamp. (It's a tax-friendly swamp, at least.) That requires sinking 120,000 piles, on average 25 metres in length. No port in Nigeria is big enough to take delivery of the massive equipment, which includes a distillation tower the height of a 30-storey building, and no road is strong enough to bear its weight. Dangote has had to build both, including a jetty for which he has dredged the seabed for 65 million cubic metres of sand.

There is not enough industrial gas in the whole country to weld everything together, so Dangote will build his own industrial gas plant. There aren't enough trucks, so he's producing those in a joint venture with a Chinese company. The plant will need 480 megawatts of power, about one-tenth of the total that electricity-starved Nigeria can muster. You guessed it. Dangote is building his own power plant too.

For years – and absurdly – Nigeria has exported all its oil as crude and then reimported refined petroleum, such as petrol and benzene. That has been a lucrative racket for the middlemen who scheme over import contracts and who concoct ways to scam a system distorted by subsidies. 'I'm sure you know about this game,' Dangote says.

Because of its reputation for skulduggery, he says, he has shunned the oil trade. 'It is very simple to destroy a name,' he adds, referring to a family business that stretches back to his great-grandfather on his mother's side, Alhassan Dantata, a prodigiously wealthy merchant who imported kola nuts from Ghana and exported groundnuts from Nigeria. 'But it's very difficult to build it.'

He tries to fast at least once a week, he says, looking guiltily at our feast. 'It helps to clean your system. More peanut sauce?'

Many of today's billionaires spin their fortunes from intangibles: the internet, the media, banking or hedge funds. Dangote has made his money from more prosaic things: salt, sugar, flour and, above all, cement. An awful lot of cement.

He was born in Kano, an ancient trading town in northern Nigeria, where he was brought up by his grandparents after his father died when Dangote was eight. After studying business at Al-Azhar University in Cairo, he moved to Lagos to strike out on his own. He too became a trader, but unlike the other businessmen whose fortunes were built on import licences available to the friends of politicians, Dangote had a hankering to make things.

Now 61, building his refinery is the culmination of that ambition. It will produce every litre of refined petroleum Nigeria needs, which could end the import business at a stroke, saving the country billions of dollars in foreign exchange. Won't he make enemies of those he is depriving of easy money? 'You can't just come and remove food from their table and think they're just going to watch you doing it,' he says. 'They will try all sorts of tricks. This is a very, very tough society. Only the toughest of the tough survive here.'

Most Nigerians assume that Dangote is tougher than the next guy. While to many he is a hero who builds factories, employs thousands and reinvests his money at home, to others he is a villain: a ruthless monopolist who squeezes favours from the government of the day and crushes competition like limestone in a cement mixer. Some accuse him of avoiding taxes by invoking an investment incentive known as 'pioneer status'. Others say he is more of a rentier than an entrepreneur, gouging the country with high prices and raking in ludicrous profits. 'People throw a lot of mud at you and you have to see how you can clean it up,' he says of his detractors.

In person, he is charm itself, a soft-spoken man with a pleasantly round face, close-cropped hair and a greying moustache so delicately trimmed that it is almost not there. He projects integrity and humility, even piety. I've met mere millionaires with more swagger than him. Yet

Dangote is a billionaire 14 times over and the 100th richest person in the world, according to *Forbes*.

He is a networker extraordinaire. To watch him work a room is to witness a kind of genius. He irradiates a Dickensian bonhomie as he glides from table to table, picking up goodwill – and intelligence – with each pressing of the flesh. If there are competing obligations – the wedding reception of the daughter of a Big Man, a dinner for the vice-president, a foreign investors' post-conference gala – he manages to be at all three events at once, an apparition moving unhurriedly through the room as though he has all the time in the world. Like Bill Clinton, he remembers your name; like Al Capone, he's got your number.

Even Dangote's yacht – named *Mariya*, after his mother – manages to be understated, if such a thing is possible in a 108-foot vessel with a price tag, according to Lagos's gossipy tabloids, of $43 million. It was styled after a boat owned by fellow Nigerian billionaire Femi Otedola, though intriguingly Dangote had his built a few feet shorter.

He makes no secret of how he got his big break, one that transformed him from a wealthy man – and by all accounts a bit of a dilettante – into a business colossus whose interests straddle the continent. It happened one day not long after the election in 1999 of Olusegun Obasanjo, the former military leader who had embraced the country's lurch to democracy by running for the presidency. Dangote contributed both to that campaign and to his subsequent re-election in 2003.

'Obasanjo called me very early in the morning and said, "Can we meet today?"' says Dangote, recalling the presidential summons. He wanted to know why Nigeria couldn't produce cement, instead importing it by the boatload. Dangote told him it was more profitable to trade than to produce. Only if imports were restricted would it be worthwhile. Obasanjo agreed. Dangote has never looked back.

Now Africa's undisputed King of Cement, he produces in 14 countries. I hear that the business makes 60 per cent margins, I say. He waves the number away. 'We have a margin of 47 per cent,' he says, as if that were a mere bagatelle. No one else can compete on efficiency, he says.

Critics say Nigeria pays more for cement than it ought to, slowing investment in construction and housing. When I put that to him, he immediately reaches for his phone, checking out today's prices in Ghana,

Benin and Ivory Coast. His own price is competitive, he says, adding that people often forget the high transport costs of importation.

Muhammadu Buhari, the current president, despairs of a manufacturing base that has shrivelled as a consequence of oil addiction, bemoaning that Nigeria even imports toothpicks.

'What Nigeria needs is to produce locally what we can produce locally,' Dangote says, nibbling at a skewered satay, and defending the thinking that has made him rich. 'Nigeria still imports vegetable oil, which makes no sense. Nigeria still imports 4.9 million tonnes of wheat, which does not make sense. Nigeria still imports 97 or 98 per cent of the milk that we consume.' Of the latter (astonishing, considering the country's roughly 20 million cows), he says, 'The government needs to bring out a draconian policy to stop people importing milk, just like they did with cement.'

His phone is still vibrating. This time he takes it. He's flying to India the following morning on his private jet and is making final arrangements. While he's talking, I take a second helping of the seafood salad, a ceviche-like dish of calamari and succulent prawns marinated in a wincing sauce.

'It has been very, very, very hectic,' he says of his recent schedule. Only that morning, his doctor warned him to slow down and get more sleep. He reckons he rarely gets five hours a night. 'The heart, it keeps pushing and pushing and pushing, but there must be a limit.'

Often he's firefighting. Problems erupt in one country or another and he is constantly criss-crossing the continent by jet. In Tanzania, where he's built a $650 million cement plant, he's battled with the president over a threat to seize assets. Not long after I met Dangote, his country manager in Ethiopia was murdered.

When he's not dealing with crises, he's fending off friends and relatives, who are often seeking help of a pecuniary nature. 'People call me in the middle of the night to tell me about their problems,' he smiles wryly.

Tony Blair, the former British prime minister and a friend of Dangote's, told him he needed to screen his calls. 'Tony said he only makes three phone calls a day,' Dangote says incredulously, helping himself to noodles. Each day scores of emails come rat-tat-tatting in. 'You try to be polite and reply but they come back to you with a longer email, not minding that here is a very, very busy person,' he says mournfully. He reckons that he takes more than a hundred calls a day. 'Look, Aliko,' he says Blair told him, 'the world is not going to fall apart if you don't answer your phone.' Dangote's schedule is also inhibiting romance. Twice divorced and with three grown-up daughters, he's on the lookout for a new bride. 'I'm not getting younger. Sixty years is no joke,' he says, 'but it doesn't make sense to go out and get somebody if you don't have the time.

'Right now, things are really, really very busy, because we have the refinery, we have the petrochemicals, we have the fertilizer, we have the gas pipeline.' With sweet talk like that, I think to myself, it can't be long before he wins some lucky woman's heart. 'I need to calm down a bit.'

His ambitions are changing. He is talking about pulling back from the business, concentrating on strategy and letting others run things day-to-day. 'I'm trying to step back from some of the boards.' He will float the cement business in London, perhaps by the end of this year, and has already appointed independent directors – including Blair's wife, Cherie – to help satisfy London's pesky governance requirements. He remains Nigeria's strongest advocate, though he consistently denies political ambition. If he ran for president, you wouldn't bet against him. 'Nigeria has always had a lack of visionary leadership,' is the closest he'll come to declaring political intent. 'There's no country in Africa that has the energy of here. Nowhere, I'm telling you.'

He is less coy about another ambition: his designs on Arsenal, a Premier League football team he has long supported. 'I love Arsenal and I will definitely go for it,' he says matter-of-factly, as though discussing the

---

On board *Mariya*

Lagos Lagoon

....

Satay chicken with peanut
  chilli sauce
Vegetable spring rolls
Chicken strips with
  sesame-seed coating
Chicken wings with
  barbecue sauce
Noodles with mixed
  vegetables and shrimps
Oriental salad with
  calamari and king prawns
Chicken with fresh ginger
  and vegetables
Plain jasmine rice
Fried rice with egg
Thai green curry with
  chicken and vegetables

latest model of iPhone. He reckons it's worth about $2 billion. Long frustrated with the club's decline under Arsène Wenger, the recently replaced manager, he says that as owner, he would involve himself in rebuilding the team – 'chipping in my own advice', as he puts it. 'When I buy it, I have to bring it up to the expectations of our supporters.'

But first he has a refinery to build. 'When you visit, you'll see what a headache I am talking about,' he says of a project into which he has sunk more than $6 billion of his own money. 'Once I have finished with that headache, I will take on football.'

Sandra Davis

'I'm a very expensive shoulder to cry on'

By Barney Thompson

A few years ago Debrett's, the ultimate authority on British etiquette, branched out into the world of marital break-down and collaborated with the London law firm Mishcon de Reya to produce a *Guide to Civilised Separation*. 'Throwing your husband's vintage wine collection down the loo or cutting his suits to shreds might seem like a therapeutic gesture when you're in the throes of rage and despair,' it advised, 'but it can rebound on you and undermine your case.'

As we unfurl our napkins at an outdoor table at the Chiltern Firehouse, the celebrity hang-out hotel just off Baker Street, I raise this with my guest. She if anyone will understand. Sandra Davis is one of London's top divorce lawyers. Head of Mishcon's family law division, she has handled the break-ups of a string of celebrities: Jerry Hall, the Texan supermodel, in her split from Mick Jagger; Thierry Henry, the Arsenal footballer; Tamara Mellon, co-founder of British fashion brand Jimmy Choo.

There are many more we do not know about – and, she makes it pretty clear, it's going to stay that way. But as we wait – in vain, as it happens – for a waiter to take our order, she does at least confirm the wine story actually happened.

'Yes. Every bottle – Château Lafite, et cetera,' she says. 'It was becoming an issue in relation to how the assets were being divided and the wife just thought, "Sod it," and poured the whole lot down the toilet.'

How many bottles?

'Hundreds.'

Ever since the landmark case of White v White in 2000, London has earned a reputation as the divorce capital of the world. Before then, the

Illustration by Ciaran Murphy

main earner in a relationship – usually the man – was required to meet only the 'reasonable needs and requirements' of the ex-partner. But when the case of Martin and Pamela White, farmers who were divorcing after 33 years of marriage and business partnership, came before the House of Lords, the ruling transformed the law. 'If, in their different spheres, each contributed equally to the family, then in principle it matters not which of them earned the money and built up the assets,' declared Lord Nicholls of Birkenhead. 'There should be no bias in favour of the money earner and against the homemaker and child carer.'

The battle for equality in dividing up the assets of the matrimonial home had begun. Instead of being catapulted into a life of reduced circumstances, the financially weaker spouse could fight back.

The Whites were arguing over roughly £4.5 million, a modest sum in comparison to the sort of settlements in which Davis is often involved. In 2014, she was on the legal team that helped Jamie Cooper-Hohn, estranged wife of hedge fund manager Sir Chris Hohn, to secure what was at the time believed to be a record settlement – £337 million, about a third of Hohn's fortune. Two years later, Davis found herself on the other side, representing the late Saudi billionaire Sheikh Walid Juffali in his battle with his ex-wife Christina Estrada. In the end Estrada won a £53 million cash settlement – less than the £196 million she had been seeking but more than the £17 million her former husband had initially offered. The case raised eyebrows largely because of what she claimed as her 'needs'. These, on an annual basis, included £83,000 for cocktail dresses, £138,000 on beauty care and £250,000 for the presidential suite at the Ritz in Paris for October half-term.

Our immediate needs are marginally more modest. A black-and-white clad waiter appears with our cocktails – mine a £16 concoction I have chosen because it has 'Beelzebub' in the name and bee pollen syrup in the ingredients. We marvel at the two tiny flowers placed on top. Davis has a freshly squeezed grapefruit juice – but only because there is no freshly squeezed watermelon juice.

Not everyone is comfortable with this jurisdictional shopping. Some judges have argued that the 2000 ruling is encouraging opportunistic marriages because the money involved – lump sums and maintenance orders – mean the recipients will never again have to lift a finger to support themselves.

Such has been the swirl of debate that Lord Wilson, a member of the Supreme Court, intervened in March to defend the legislation. It was, he argued, 'unrealistic to tell a wife, left on her own perhaps at age 60 after a long marriage, that, following payments for say three years, she must fend for herself'.

The problem has become more acute since White *v* White because of London's attraction to the global super-rich as a place to live and work. Given that such people often have more complicated financial arrangements than most, the court battles are often ferocious, unedifying and astoundingly expensive.

This indubitably keeps Davis busy. But hasn't it all got out of control?

'Well, it depends which sex you are,' she says wryly. 'If you are an international executive who has moved here for work for a couple of years and your marriage fails while you are here, you might not necessarily think there is jurisdiction to petition here because you didn't get married here and you're not a national. But [your spouse] can issue a petition and the whole of your financial landscape can change.' That is a euphemism to savour along with my cocktail.

After half an hour, the heavens open and the battering of raindrops on the awning above makes conversation impossible. We flee indoors. Amid the confusion Davis spots a free table and bags it before anyone can object.

When the hotel opened in early 2014 it was frequented by the paparazzi, hosting regular celebrity parties. But shorn of its celebs as it is on our Friday afternoon, it is visually disconcerting. The bar is a riot of clashing colour – swirling carpets, golden sofas, marble-topped tables, waitresses in all-enveloping, cultish robes.

We finally order. I choose the lamb but the lamb is off the menu (though they bill me for it anyway, as I discover later) so I ask for the torched mackerel with roasted heritage beetroots and wasabi, followed by the Galician beef bavette with spiced runner bean salad and fragrant herbs. Davis opts for the Sutton Farm courgettes with spiced goat's curd and courgette flowers, plus the hot-smoked salmon. I have a glass of

Sancerre; to my delight, since I hope this may loosen her lawyerly tongue, Davis calls for a glass of pink champagne. She ends up drinking only half of it.

Davis started out at Mishcon as a trainee in 1979, even as divorce was on a relentless march. When the Divorce Reform Act came into effect in England and Wales in 1971, making it easier for couples to divorce once they had separated, rates rocketed. The high-water mark was 1993, with 165,000 divorces recorded; that year, marriage dipped below the 300,000 mark. Today, the Office for National Statistics says that 34 per cent of marriages will end before a couple's 20th anniversary, and 42 per cent will break down overall. (The 'danger zone', statistically speaking, is between the fourth and eighth anniversaries, which strikes me as information more couples should know.)

Early on, Davis had the idea that she might like to become a barrister: 'I think I watched too much Perry Mason when I was a kid,' she says, 'because I always liked the idea of performing in court.' But a junior barrister, then as now, didn't earn much. She headed instead to the small firm of solicitors founded and run by Victor Mishcon – a leading light of London's Jewish community and Labour peer. (In recent years, as the *FT* knows too well, the firm has become a frequent adversary of the press on behalf of their varied clients.)

'It was very much sink or swim,' she says. She clearly swam. Towards the end of her training contract, Mishcon's head of divorce fell ill and Davis took over, moving into the second-largest office in the entire practice – only Lord Mishcon's was bigger. Within two years she was a partner. 'I just learnt on the job.'

In the early part of her career, family work was seen as 'a bit grubby'. But that reputation soon changed as big-money clients started rolling in. A *Tatler* guide to the best divorce lawyers in London puts her fees at £610 an hour, a figure she does not dispute. 'Correct at time of going to press,' she says (so probably higher now). For someone whose specialism demands discretion, aren't those lists a nuisance? 'Well, I wouldn't want to be off – to be left out of the count would be a bit of a slight.'

Unusually for the top of the legal profession, women dominate those lists. To Davis, this is not surprising. 'Clients are emotional, they're under stress, they need support,' she says. 'So the skills you require are not just strategic legal skills, they're softer skills as well – how to communicate difficult messages, how to support people when they're breaking down.'

But she makes no pretence at being a full-time confidante. 'I'm a very expensive shoulder to cry on. I'm not trained to be a therapist and I shouldn't act as one. I'm a strategist – someone who will help them navigate the process and enable them at the end of it to be independent.' It must help that she is a blend of the sympathetic and businesslike: soberly dressed (only an ornate ring hints at her elevated fees), with an earnest gaze and a habit of picking her words very carefully.

Without doubt, the most famous divorce Mishcon de Reya has been involved in was that of Diana, Princess of Wales – a case led by Anthony Julius, with Davis as part of the team. The terms were never made public but it was rumoured that Diana won £17.5 million, sealing the reputation of Mishcon's family division. 'She took him to the cleaners,' was how Geoffrey Bignell, Charles's former financial adviser, expressed it to the *Daily Telegraph* in 2004.

Davis is reluctant to expound on the Diana case and makes clear she is all too aware of her clients' distress. Before we part she asks me to stress this point. 'There may be a whole raft of objectively amusing anecdotes that I've experienced over the years, but divorce is miserable. Nobody should go through it thinking it's anything but miserable.'

Most accounts of the divorces of the super-rich focus on the money. Davis comes back time and again to the children. As we sat down, she presented me with a copy of *Splitting Up: A Child's Guide to a Grown Up Problem*. It is a collection of heartbreaking observations from children on their parents' separation.

'I ask [my clients] to show me a picture of their children and I put that on the table – that's very tangible because it has meaning . . . I try and do what is right for the family as a whole because those people have to co-parent for many years to come.'

'Children replicate what they see,' she points out. 'They're just going to make the same mistakes in their own relationships if they see their parents behaving badly. Using children as little spies, interrogating, using them as mouthpieces is all totally toxic.'

At last, the food arrives.

'Very green,' says Davis, inspecting it, and she is right. My mackerel and beetroot are the standard hue but the salmon and the bavette are semi-submerged under a green sauce, while the courgettes perch above a veritable soup of the stuff.

I wonder what the effect of seeing so many relationships fall to pieces has had on Davis's own family. She has said before, albeit half joking, that she hopes she hasn't entirely put off her two sons from getting married. Now she comes to one of her big solutions to the whole problem: it's time, she thinks, for Brits to get over their disdain for the pre-nup.

'To consider "what if" at the best of times rather than the worst of times has to be sensible,' she says.

But who wants to talk about pre-nups while they are in love's first bloom?

'It's de rigueur in mainland Europe and the English aren't in theory as romantic a nation as the French or the Italians. And it's commonplace in America. So why do we English think it's so unattractive to talk about money? It's the most important contract of your life – it makes sense to think about the possibilities of failure when you're in your first glow.'

There is time for a quick coffee before her next appointment – an espresso for her and a cortado for me. The picture of disorganization at the Chiltern Firehouse is complete when a waiter marches up with a starter we didn't order.

I ask a last question. What does one of London's top divorce lawyers say is the secret of a successful marriage?

This gets a hoot of laughter. 'All I can say is: plants always need a bit of water. Relationships change over the years and you need to be alive to those changes.' She sips her coffee and adds: 'Communication is key.'

Chiltern Firehouse

1 Chiltern St, Marylebone, London W1

Courgette	£14
Torched mackerel	£15
Lamb	£26
Salmon	£28
Grapefruit juice	£7
Beelzebub, With Love cocktail	£16
Still water	£5.50
Glass of Chapitre rosé	£21
Glass of Sancerre	£13
Beef bavette	£28
Espresso	£3
Cortado	£4
Total (inc. service and donation to charity) –	£208.58

A client awaits. With a last smile, Davis recalls a newspaper diary item that said the 13 most bone-chilling words in English were: 'Oh shit, I've just had a letter from Mishcon de Reya's family department.' She hands me her card, which immediately feels talismanic, and goes in search of a taxi. Who is the client, I wonder – and does the other side know what's coming?

Stars of Page, Stage and Screen

'I'm becoming a bit of a recluse. I like solitude. I like silence'

Chimamanda Ngozi Adichie

'The Englishman doesn't have to be the superhero'

By David Pilling

I'm excited and nervous to be meeting Chimamanda Ngozi Adichie. Excited, because she is one of the world's best writers. *Half of a Yellow Sun*, her novel about Nigeria's Biafran war, remains one of the most enthralling pieces of fiction of the past decade. Nervous, because Adichie – at least the one who jumps out of the pages of *Americanah*, her follow-up novel about the experiences of an African woman living in the US – has a controlled, but cutting, anger.

Ifemelu, the book's heroine and, one suspects, an alter ego for the author herself, is a master of put-downs on matters of race and gender. Worryingly for me, bumbling white male liberals get particularly short shrift throughout Adichie's work. In *Half of a Yellow Sun*, Richard, an Englishman, embraces Biafra, learns Igbo and stays throughout the escalating horrors of war. Adichie rewards him by making him unable to perform sexually.

I am thinking about all this in the Yellow Chilli Restaurant & Bar, an airy two-storey building painted in canary yellow, in Ikeja, a less chaotic part of frenetically high-pressured Lagos. Waiters are drifting around in snazzy yellow waistcoats, like backing singers in a Motown band. The air is sticky, despite the efforts of the fridge-sized air conditioner. One of the staff is killing flies with a tennis-racket-shaped device, which crackles with electricity every time it zaps a buzzing insect.

The lunch, which has taken months to arrange – not least because of the difficulty of obtaining a Nigerian visa – has been set for the late hour of 2.30pm I left early to allow for the Lagos traffic and arrived at 2pm, occupying a table on the second floor. For an hour, I've been studying the unfamiliar menu – ogbono soup, obe dindin, yam pottage. By

Illustration by James Ferguson

3.30pm, I wonder if Adichie will show. By 4pm, I'm convinced she's not coming.

Finally, she appears, looking slightly sheepish, and slides into the opposite side of our booth table. 'You may actually enjoy the interview,' I offer, and am treated to a sceptical look. Has she read Lunch with the *FT* before? Yes, she says, softening. She has even read one I'd done a few weeks earlier with Liberia's president, Ellen Johnson Sirleaf, the first female elected head of state in Africa. It read like a short story, she says. 'I also thought you were a bit unfair. A part of me wonders, were she male, whether you would be as . . .' I would have been equally tough, I jump in. 'I'm sure you would. You probably would have been. No, I don't mean you,' she says, executing a charming retreat. 'And it's not just you.'

She turns to the waiter, flashing him a smile. There's something mischievous and challenging about the way she interacts. 'Yes, Mr Chima,' she says, reading his name from a lapel badge. 'Do you have Chapman?' The waiter nods enthusiastically, and Adichie explains that Chapman is a non-alcoholic cocktail popular in Nigeria. I ask if they have white wine. 'Yes. We have Drostdy-Hof,' beams the waiter, leaving me none the wiser.

While he's fetching the drinks, I ask her whether it's appropriate to write about what she's wearing. Readers have objected that men's clothes are rarely described. 'A lot of these things are about the how, right? I was raised by my mother to care about my appearance, so I have no trouble with it.' She pauses. 'Like, I'm wearing red shoes, and you need to notice,' she announces. I check under the table and am confronted by *Wizard of Oz* dazzle.

Our drinks appear. Drostdy-Hof turns out to be a mouth-puckering South African chardonnay. The colour of her Chapman matches her shoes. 'This is just very sugary, very sweet. I would probably have a glass of wine, but I'm breastfeeding, I'm happy to announce.'

It takes me a moment to process. Adichie, 38, is famously protective of her private life. I had no idea she had a baby. Is this my world scoop, I ask? 'This is the first time I'm saying it publicly. I have a lovely little girl so I feel like I haven't slept . . . but it's also just really lovely and strange.' Her voice has a wonderfully rich timbre. When she says 'lovely' – soft and round as a peach – it feels like a gift.

'I have some friends who probably don't know I was pregnant or that

I had a baby. I just feel like we live in an age when women are supposed to perform pregnancy. We don't expect fathers to perform fatherhood. I went into hiding. I wanted it to be as personal as possible.

'In this country of mine that I love,' she goes on, sliding to a halt on the word 'love', 'people think that you're incomplete unless you're married.' Her husband, also a bit of a secret, is a Nigerian doctor who works in the US, where Adichie spends time when she's not in Lagos. Can I ask the baby's name? 'No, I won't say,' she says with a disarming smile.

We turn to the matter of food. I tell her I had been thinking of ordering jollof rice – although I'm not sure exactly what it is – because characters in her novels often crave it. She recalls a sentence in my most recent Lunch interview where I had talked about dark meat lurking underneath the greens. 'So I was hoping that today you would have something with things lurking underneath things,' she says, dissolving into laughter at the thought of torturing a poor Englishman.

She scans the menu: egusi, oha, otong, afia efere. 'To be fair, I don't actually like any of these things,' she says finally. 'Why don't you do jollof rice and goat curry?' Then, with a twinkle, 'Goat meat: that hopefully will be a strong taste that might not appeal.'

Then she confesses she has notified the restaurant in advance about her particular dietary requirements. 'I called them to make sure I could have my steamed greens.'

Food features prominently in her writing. 'It's probably the best way to get into time, place, class, culture. It's a breathing detail that lives on the page.' In *Americanah*, she describes Nigerian food, approvingly, as 'sweaty and spicy'. Nigerian characters who have spent too long in the US, like Adichie, develop effete tastes. She admits to sneaking off to a 'bougie' (bourgeois) Lagos establishment for her smoothie fix.

These days, though, she rarely ventures out. 'I'm becoming a bit of a recluse. I like solitude. I like silence,' she says, stirring the Chapman with her straw. Is she working on something new, I ask, knowing that this is a taboo topic. 'It's a very bad question. It's a question that puts you in a panic,' she says, making clear the subject is closed.

Her three plates arrive: white disks of boiled yam, a chicken stew and some kale-like 'ugu vegetable', not exactly what she had ordered, although she doesn't object. I try some at her invitation. It's crunchy, salty and delicious. My jollof rice is bright orange and peppery hot. It comes with a bowl of dark-yellow soupy curry in which three pieces of goat meat are partially submerged, like hippos in a river.

There is, I say, a hard edge to her heroines, particularly the formidable Ifemelu, who lets no foible go unrebuked. 'I've had to spend a lot of time convincing people that she's not me, but in some ways she is,' Adichie says, taking a bite of chicken. 'She's almost an act of defiance, because I really find myself questioning the idea of the likeable character, especially the likeable female character.'

Ifemelu is bright, outspoken and restless. 'I liked her. I didn't always like her. She can be soft or prickly. I wanted her to be all of those things, because I just think that we need more women to be all of those things – and for it to be OK.' Too often, strong female characters are judged, she says, referring to a theme she explored in a phenomenally successful TED talk in 2013. 'Before the book came out, some people in publishing said "maybe we could make her more likeable". And I thought, "Lord no".'

Like Ifemelu, Adichie says she 'enjoys a good argument'. I decide to take her up on it. Why, for example, does Ifemelu appear to believe that only black people – not Asians or Latin Americans or even black people with lighter skin – understand real discrimination?

'I don't think she thinks that. I do think she thinks that other people don't know what it's like to be discriminated against for being black,' she corrects me.

'There is no united league of the oppressed,' she adds. 'Even within the African-American communities, there are differences, so that the lighter-skin African-Americans have a certain kind of privilege. It's a tainted privilege because it's a privilege within a racist system, but still. And obviously it has its history in slavery. The so-called house slave was lighter-skinned and the field slave was darker,' she says.

Americanah provoked strong reactions in the US, both positive and negative. Critics accused Adichie of everything from being overly obsessed with race to belittling the African-American experience. 'I don't want to sound self-righteous but in the American "left left", there isn't room for asking questions,' she says.

What about prejudice among Africans – say, of Nigerians towards Ghanaians? 'You know about that,' she says, exploding into laughter. 'We in Nigeria have an unearned and funny sense of superiority. Nigerians are the Americans of Africa.'

I order another wine and ask if I can share her water. 'I like drinking from the bottle, so as long as you're fine with my having sipped from it. Generally my hygiene is good,' she teases.

The inter-ethnic rivalries that have plagued post-independence Africa, she says, are different from racism, the origins of which she traces to transatlantic slavery. 'How do we justify treating people like . . . like monkeys? We do that by claiming they are not quite like us. You read about these plantation owners in the south who had children with black women. A part of me thinks, surely just that thing in us that makes us human, surely it would overcome? But no. They just sold their kids.'

She only learnt about race in America, she says. 'In Nigeria, growing up, I never thought about appearance. I knew I was Igbo and I grew up in an Igbo place.'

Half of a Yellow Sun tells the story of the Igbos' struggle for an independent Biafra in the late 1960s. After two years of defiance, they were bombed and starved into submission by Nigeria's military. 'I just felt so moved by my father's generation. I adore my father. I am such a daddy's girl. He's just such a lovely man,' she says, lingering again over the word 'lovely'. In the war, he 'lost something, a kind of innocence', she says prodding at the *ugu* greens. 'I think they really did believe in big and grand things and the war just sucked those things out of them.'

In one of the novel's most difficult scenes, the hero, a servant called Ugwu, rapes a woman after being press-ganged into the army. 'It was very difficult to write because I love him,' she says, staring at the bottom of her glass. 'That's what war does, dehumanizes people. I read things that people did that I was horrified by, but I also remember asking myself: "What would I have done?"'

'I knew that was the point where I was risking having my reader . . . suspend love for him. But it was a risk I felt was worth taking, because I hoped that, I don't mean to say I hoped that they would forgive him, because that seems a bit simple, but that they would see it for what it was.'

She asks if I'm enjoying the rice. I am very much, I say. It's like comfort food. The goat is also tasty, although, for all her pride in the fieriness of Nigerian food, I'd have liked it spicier.

We've been talking for more than two hours and I realize I'll never make it to a dinner scheduled for 7.30pm. Besides, the conversation is flowing so well. I order a third glass of wine.

We touch briefly on American politics, including her continuing admiration for Barack Obama, whose presidency she says was sabotaged by Republicans. 'I adore him.' Bernie Sanders is 'your dishevelled, like-able uncle', but not a realistic candidate. She'd vote for Hillary Clinton.

I wonder about Nigeria. With its huge population, entrepreneurial drive and ample oil reserves, it has been the perennial hope of Africa – and the perennial disappointment. Things are better than they were, she says, recalling the days when even getting through the notoriously corrupt international airport was a test of endurance. 'Nigeria is way too young to expect the kind of thing that I would ideally want for Nigeria, but the idea of holding people accountable is slowly happening.'

Technology and a stronger middle class are helping. These days, if a policeman asks for a bribe, she says, you whip out your mobile phone and threaten to post his photo on the internet. 'I don't know if it's a delusional kind of hope, I don't know if it's a hope that is hoping because there's nothing left to do but hope. But I'm still hopeful that I will see a better Nigeria.'

There's a sudden zap-zap-zap behind us. 'My friend, what are you doing?' she quizzes the waiter, who is swiping his racket through the air again. 'I'm playing with flies,' comes his straight-faced reply. 'How many flies are there that you're playing like that?' she retorts, brow furrowed in mock irritation.

We've finished lunch, but people are already drifting in for dinner. I want to broach a last subject: how should people engage with Africa? Some characters in *Americanah* are ridiculed because, although they show interest in Africa, they also display ignorance, viewing it through a prism of pity and horror.

The Yellow Chilli Restaurant & Bar

35 Joel Ogunaike Street, Ikeja, Lagos

....

House white wine x 3 glasses	N2,550
Medium water x 2	N500
Edikang Ikong soup with chicken	N2,300
Jollof rice and goat curry	N3,000
Ugu greens	no charge
Boiled yam	no charge
Chapman	N750

....

Total (inc. tax and service) –	N11,000 (£29.25)

....

'I think I'd rather you not engage than engage in a way that is patronizing,' she says. 'It comes from a sense of superiority; it comes from an ignorance that refuses to acknowledge itself. So Africa becomes this vague mass of wars', even if the country under discussion – and Africa has 54 countries – has been peaceful for decades.

What about poor Richard? An Englishman who devotes his life to the Biafran cause comes across as a bit of a wet rag. Adichie smiles knowingly. 'You know what's interesting to me. I've been asked by many, many white British men about Richard. You see, this is the white male expectation of being at the centre,' she says, draining her mocktail.

'He's kind of meek and he's kind of uncertain, but in a way that I find quite sweet. He learns Igbo, his friends accept him, this interesting woman loves him. Isn't that enough?' That's an excellent point, I concede. But Adichie hasn't finished with me yet. 'The Englishman,' she says, scolding and laughing simultaneously, 'doesn't have to be the superhero all the time.'

Leïla Slimani

'Knowing how to talk is a great power'

By Simon Kuper

O f course the restaurant doesn't have my reservation, but a table is found on the enclosed veranda. Mere minutes after the agreed time – early for Paris – Leïla Slimani strides into the Marco Polo restaurant. Everyone had warned me she was beautiful. She is also supremely, Parisianly elegant, her scarf wound so precisely it looks like a catalogue photograph. She kisses the Italian restaurateur and shakes my hand. We're sitting downwind from a smoking couple, but Slimani is unbothered. 'I adore Italian cuisine,' she sighs.

This is Paris's sixth arrondissement, so around us the French publishing industry is at the trough. Slimani, 36, is its new star. Her first novel, about a nymphomaniac, did well. Her second, *Chanson douce* (*Lullaby* in English), about a murderous nanny, won the Prix Goncourt in 2016, has sold more than 600,000 copies in France, and has been translated into about 40 languages. Its opening sentence, 'The baby is dead', is already famous. Last year Slimani published a non-fiction book about sexual repression in her native Morocco. Meanwhile President Emmanuel Macron has made her his personal representative for promoting the French language. And she's become a global feminist voice.

Slimani takes the briefest glance at the *formule*, the day menu, then remarks, '*Et voilà*, I have chosen': tomato mozzarella salad, followed by spaghetti vongole. I opt for prosciutto, then the vongole. The waiter initially accepts this, but soon returns to suggest I change to the cheaper day menu. He doesn't even bother explaining why. It's simply the way you should always order in Paris: the *formule* is cheap, fresh and easy on the kitchen. I copy Slimani's choices. Meanwhile, the textbook *FT* Lunch opening gambit has failed: Slimani rejects my suggestion of wine. 'I'm looking after my children this afternoon,' she smiles.

Illustration by Vanessa Dell

She grew up in a big house in the Moroccan countryside. One grand-mother was a French Alsatian who had met her Moroccan husband when (clad in magnificent north African costume) he liberated her village from the Nazis. The other grandmother was an illiterate peasant. Slimani's mother was one of Morocco's first women doctors, and her father a banker who served two years as economics minister. But a financial scandal landed him in jail and broke him, although he was posthumously exonerated. Slimani also had an illiterate nanny, who (along with the British nanny Louise Woodward and New York nanny Yoselyn Ortega, who killed two children in her care) inspired *Lullaby*.

The household was mostly francophone. 'I feel I belong to many cultures,' says Slimani. 'My grandmother spoke German, my parents spoke Arabic and French, I heard a lot of Spanish. I don't feel I was raised in French culture. I feel I was raised in *la culture*, the world of culture. I read Russian novels, English novels, French novels.' Now that she represents *la Francophonie*, she's practically legally obliged to have lunch in French, but her English is near perfect.

'*Francophonie* shouldn't place itself at war with English. I find that ridiculous, tacky. English is necessary. Above all it's a beautiful language, which opens up to a marvellous literature, culture. One should speak French and English.'

The waiter brings the *tomate mozza*, and she thanks him with a flurry of grazies and mercis. A publisher and his guest have taken the next table, barely a metre away, and are delighted to find themselves beside Slimani.

She arrived in Paris after high school knowing nobody, to attend a *classe préparatoire*, a crammer for France's *grandes écoles*. One day she saw a photograph of a beautiful Simone de Beauvoir drinking coffee in Café de Flore – an unthinkable act for a woman in Morocco. Slimani went to a library and with great embarrassment asked for De Beauvoir's *The Second Sex*, thinking it was an erotic text. When she discovered it was feminist instead, she was initially disappointed, then captivated.

Did Parisians treat Slimani as a north African immigrant? 'No, because I did my *prépa* over there [she points right], then studied at Sciences Po [she points left], then I worked in central Paris. I never encountered anyone who insulted me. I've never been a victim of racism.

Or [it was] of such a ridiculous kind that I don't even remember it.' Is that because she's from a high social class? 'Obviously. I know the codes.'

But she insists that her parents gave her 'codes that work everywhere. I am friendly with grocers, I can spend my afternoon smoking fags with them, or I can spend it with the boss of a big French publishing house. I don't enclose people in a social class.' Or rather, she explains, it's as if she can film people using two cameras: with one, she sees the person, and with the other, class. Hence the acutely observed nanny–employer class struggle in *Lullaby*. Slimani entered the battle that is Parisian life with another social asset: mastery of language. She speaks as she writes, in complete pellucid sentences, with a very French precision about emotions. When I say she exudes certainty, she nods: 'I was like that even when I was small. I've never been shy. I always knew how to talk. I realized that just by speaking you can do many things: you can transform something, move someone from one idea to another, seduce, teach, transmit. Knowing how to talk is a great power.'

In 2008 she started covering Morocco and Tunisia for news magazine *Jeune Afrique*. In 2011, she witnessed the Arab spring in Tunisia. 'It was beautiful. Tunisians are adorable people. Tunisia is a guiding light for the Arab world.'

And Morocco? 'Unfortunately, the Islamists are in power. People vote Islamist, *voilà*.' Has her international literary fame given her any influence in her native country? 'Not at all. Intellectuals don't have anything like the power in Morocco that they had in France. People there read very little.'

She quit journalism to write novels. Her first unpublished attempt was, she says, awful. In 2013 her mother and husband gave her a Christmas present: a place in an amateur writing workshop at the publishing house Gallimard. Her teacher, the editor and novelist Jean-Marie Laclavetine, provided a blinding insight: 'He said the problem was that I asked lots of questions about the psychology of characters – what they think. But a novel is above all actions. It's characters who do something. And I was also influenced by existentialism, by De Beauvoir, by the idea: we are above all what we do. I have never been interested in who I am. Identity, for instance, doesn't interest me.'

Disappointingly for those who read her nymphomaniac novel as autobiographical, Slimani doesn't write about herself. Some of her main characters are Parisian women of north African origin, but that's almost incidental. The novels go elsewhere. She says, 'I think you need to have been a writer a long time to be able to write about yourself. It's the most difficult subject.' In this sense, the lunch companion is like the novelist: Slimani, armoured by her perfect style, doesn't do self-revelation. Normally when you eat with someone, barriers fall, but not today. We address each other throughout with the formal *vous*.

Did she foresee *Lullaby*'s success? 'Not at all. I thought it was a book that would pass fairly unnoticed . . . I thought it was a staging post towards my next book. I've found an enormous number of flaws in it, which I hope to eradicate in my next books.'

But it's such a confident novel, I say: with every sentence you seem to know where you're heading. 'When I was writing I didn't know. I knew the start, and the end. There had to be a murder. Because it was hard to construct a novel about the relationship between a couple and a nanny without something at stake. I wanted to mix the thriller, tragedy, fairy tale, the *contemporary* novel.' I say *Lullaby* has traces of Georges Simenon. I earn the briefest smile: 'He's a great writer of detail, of atmosphere. His descriptions of Paris influenced me.'

Simenon wrote about the mostly working-class eastern Paris of the 20th century. Today those same buildings are inhabited by the well-off urban caste known here as bobos: bourgeois bohemians. *Lullaby* captures the tribe marvellously. On a dinner party: 'They talk about their jobs, terrorism, real estate. Patrick describes his plans for a Sri Lankan holiday.'

Does Slimani identify as bobo? 'Read Stefan Zweig on Vienna, when he writes about cafés. A lot of the people he describes are the bobos of their time: open, attached to culture, travel, cosmopolitanism.

'And they were Nazism's first victims. I mock bobos a lot, because there are some slightly ridiculous things, but what they represent as a way of life is largely positive. For Trump and Marine Le Pen, their enemies are the "shit bobos". Because bobos incarnate everything the identitarians, xenophobes, populists detest. And it's what I am.'

Lullaby also captures the tedium of modern parenting: long freezing afternoons in desolate playgrounds, the ceaseless tasks, incomprehension between parents and children. I mention a passage in which the mother reflects that freedom is freeing yourself from others.

Slimani nods: 'There's a sentence of Proust's: "I am true only when alone." That's why I adore Chekhov. He describes that constantly: that human relations are false almost in their essence. We can't express our solitude.'

Family routine is the reality for most people in mid-life. So why is it so often boring to read about in novels? 'Because it is very boring! It's a repetitive banal life. Yet these are also the greatest pleasures: being with people you love, Sunday lunch in a beautiful place.'

Is it hard to toggle between a Chinese book tour, advising Macron, then coming home to a boring evening *en famille*? 'Personally, I don't get bored with my family. I laugh a lot with my children. What I like most is being at home, seeing nobody, watching films, [TV] series, telling my children stories.' Even as a mother she reveals no imperfection.

Our spaghettis are perfectly OK, but Slimani leaves half of hers uneaten. She pre-empts the waiter's dessert suggestions by going straight to coffee.

Actually, she reflects, despite her fondness for the private sphere, there is one public cause that inspires her. 'Feminism could be a great collective adventure. Maybe it already is.'

I ask her about the French version of #MeToo, #BalanceTonPorc, or 'Betray your pig', a social-media campaign in which women publicly named their sexual harassers. 'I experienced it as very good. OK, *balance ton porc* isn't a very elegant formula, but sexual harassment isn't very elegant either. Rape isn't elegant. I think women are living in an extraordinary moment of liberation of speech, of collective feeling.'

Then: 'Would you permit me to smoke?' Our neighbouring publisher lights her cigarette, and reminds her he noticed her when she was 'young and talented'. 'That's true,' she replies.

The waiter brings us complimentary biscuits and chocolates. She thanks him but doesn't touch them. By now it's nearly 3pm. Marco Polo

---

Marco Polo
8, Rue de Condé, Paris

....

Tomato mozzarella
  salad x 2
Spaghetti vongole x 2
Day menu x 2   €41
Coffee x 2   €7

....

Total –   €48

:::::::::::::::::::::::::::::::::::::

is still packed with digesting publishers, but Slimani has to go. She rewraps her scarf just so, produces a leather-bound smartphone and orders an Uber. Her life is currently a whirl of interviews and public talks. 'I think France is fairly exceptional in its relationship to literature. You go to a small village and there are 300 people come to hear you talk about literature.'

But she says fame hasn't changed her.

Her father's demise taught her (and *Lullaby* reaffirms) that everything earthly can be snatched away in an instant.

Hilary Mantel

'I do a lot of work when I'm asleep'

By Henry Mance

In her *Who's Who* entry, Dame Hilary Mantel lists just one recreation: sleeping. It turns out even that is stretching it.

'I have a sense of doing a lot of work when I'm asleep. Of leaving a problem overnight, waking up with some image or stray word that is probably the solution,' she says, when we meet. 'So it's a way to get extra work in. I think of it as a very active process.' For good measure, she also records her dreams in her diaries, of which there are now 106 handwritten volumes. 'It's just like having a separate life.'

If this is her secret, we should probably all copy it. Mantel is the greatest English prose writer of our time, in the eyes of the judges who gave her the Booker Prize for a second time in 2012 and of many others.

With *Wolf Hall* and *Bring Up the Bodies*, her books on Thomas Cromwell, she did for historical novels what Robert Caro did for political biography and *The Simpsons* did for cartoons: she elevated the genre. She enthralled Britain again in the reign of Henry VIII – an odd achievement for a former Marxist who thinks the current royal family should be released from captivity. 'I suppose what one would like to see is a cut-off point that they themselves impose or a kind of chosen, elective dwindling of their role,' she says, co-opting the Queen's own pronoun to advocate her abolition.

We are sitting in a grandiose hotel on the south Devon coast. It has the kind of impossibly plush seating you might dare to purchase one day, only to ruin with red wine the next. 'Provincial pretentious,' says Mantel, with a chuckle that becomes familiar. 'Provides its own form of entertainment.'

Five years ago a *New Yorker* journalist interpreted Mantel's move to the south-west as a sign that she had 'discharged her public duties as an author'. Cue another chuckle: if Mantel was trying to avoid publicity, she

Illustration by Luke Waller

has done a terrible job. In 2013 she described Kate Middleton as appearing 'designed by a committee'; in 2014 she published a short story imagining the assassination of Margaret Thatcher. The furores were immediate – and to her, utterly inconsequential. 'It depends whether you value people's opinions. And I don't value the opinion of the *Daily Mail*, so.'

This month BBC Radio 4 will broadcast Mantel's Reith lectures. It is 'a kind of manifesto' on historical fiction, 'saying, this is how I do it,' she explains. Her arguments prepare the ground for the final part of her Cromwell trilogy, *The Mirror and the Light*, which is half written and will 'hopefully' be published next year. They have greater resonance, too. In Tudor times, news and rumour were barely distinguishable. Today Mantel sees the world again 'at the mercy of a rumour system', this time online news. Can she help us to tell history from myth, truth from fiction?

Appropriately, the woman who once compared the royal family to mollycoddled pandas has a black-and-white dress and bountiful, round eyes. She reaches into a lime-green handbag for her glasses, and decides on the vegetarian set lunch and still water. I choose the same – noting that, like the Conservative manifesto, the menu is light on pound signs. We are placed in the reception room and are brought canapés.

Mantel's own story is arguably more striking than her fiction. She grew up 'female, northern and poor' in a household into which a lodger arrived and gradually supplanted her father. She married aged 20 in 1973, divorced and remarried the same man, a geologist named Gerald McEwen. She suffered years of pain, was horrifically mistreated by doctors and prescribed steroids that marked her appearance. After she had correctly diagnosed herself as having endometriosis in 1979, doctors removed her womb and ovaries. She had never seriously considered having children, and now she never could.

This pushed Mantel into writing. Her earliest ambition – to be a knight of the round table and a railway guard, simultaneously – was too masculine, too unattainable. She started to train to be a barrister, but lacked the funds. She thought of politics, but lacked the health. So she chose to be all those things and more, on the page and on her own schedule. 'A lot of fiction is about living out sides of your personality that you didn't get to live in real life. It's just creating multiple CVs for yourself,' she says.

That is where her critics leap in. For them, a line must be drawn between history and historical fiction. When Mantel writes about Henry VIII's chronic pain, his wives' childlessness and Cromwell's ambition, is she really not just writing about herself? When she imagines Cromwell's grief for his late wife, is she not fabricating? David Starkey, a historian, bombastically accused Mantel of a 'deliberate perversion of fact'. Her response is a whisper: 'I think he may have been outraged by my sales.'

'The historian will tell you what happened. The novelist will tell you what it felt like,' the novelist E. L. Doctorow once said. Mantel sees her work as separate to a historian's, but no less true. She is subjective, but so is a historian. Each narrative is a 'proposal' to the reader: 'It's just a version, it can be questioned. It's like a painting with the brushstrokes in . . . You wouldn't mistake it for the living person.'

Isn't that disingenuous, I ask? Your books are bestsellers, adapted by the BBC and the Royal Shakespeare Company – they are many people's sole view of Tudor history, even though many of their scenes are imagined. She brushes off any risk. 'To take that to its logical conclusion would be saying art is corrupting.'

We are shown to a dining table next to the window, which affords us an excellent view of the oversized curtains and little else. An appetizer arrives – mushroom fricassee – soon followed by starters of goat's cheese for Mantel and wild garlic velouté for me.

How does Mantel feel about those novels and TV shows that do cut corners? 'I think, why bother? If you're going to set your fiction in the past, you owe the reader a certain amount of diligence.' Her sentences are as prim and poised as courtiers, occasionally granting you access to her mind palace and occasionally denying it. Interruption seems futile. She awes you gently.

Mantel prides herself on ambiguity. Rereading her diary has reinforced her doubts about memory: she has noticed that the most important things 'never made it near the page'. 'I think it's a real lesson to anyone concerned with history – how very hard it is to get the simplest things preserved.'

In her Reith lectures, Mantel objects to us treating the past as either horror film or fairy tale. The Tudors had teeth, ate vegetables, obeyed table manners; if they survived past five, they lived relatively long lives. They never knew industrial noise or pollution. 'I don't want to overfamiliarize the past,' she tells me. 'I want people to know it is alien – they were not like us. But at the same time I don't want my readers to condescend to the past. Sometimes people talk about our ancestors as if they were children and we're the grown-ups, and that's not the way it works.'

She celebrates history's messiness: she admires the brutality of the TV show *Game of Thrones* ('It might be fantasy, but it's a lot more like real history than some novels'). I ask if she is uncomfortable with Britain's doubt-free version of its past; probing the goat's cheese with her fork, she half agrees.

What does she make of comparisons between the Reformation and Brexit, five centuries later? 'Actually that's quite mistaken because the Reformation wasn't a break with Europe. It was a break with Rome.' England sought new alliances with German and Scandinavian rulers, who had also broken away. The strategy might even have worked had Cromwell, who knew Europe, remained in power, says Mantel.

It's a typically generous interpretation of Cromwell. In *Wolf Hall*, he is an accountant, a confidant, a fixer – 'as cunning as a bag of serpents'. He is wisdom personified: 'there is an art to being in a hurry but not showing it'; 'the heart is like any other organ, you can weigh it on a scale'. One of my friends treats the whole thing as a business self-help book; her colleagues should probably be warned.

Are there upwardly-mobile characters who fascinate Mantel today? Steve Bannon, Emmanuel Macron? She declines the bait. 'I don't particularly have a wish to use people who are living now in fiction, because I really value the idea of getting a bit of perspective.'

Indeed Mantel judges today's politicians differently. She once suggested David Cameron's welfare cuts were less enlightened than Cromwell's draft poor law from the 1530s. Why so cynical? 'I hate to be called cynical. I'm not. I'm in love with politics in a way.'

Cromwell's proposals – of employing the poor on road-building projects – marked 'the very beginnings of the welfare state', she argues. 'He was trying to get away from the concept of the poor as having a character defect.' Hold on, I say, if the Tudors deemed someone a lazy beggar, they chopped off the top of their ear. Is that really better than 2014 housing benefit changes? 'I just think it's pathetic that the 16th century could realize that poverty's not a character defect whereas the idea is being powerfully pushed today. I think it's immoral.'

She hasn't raised her voice – the fire comes naturally. What type of politician would she have been? Probably 'one of those outliers who, if anyone had ever elected me, simply grumbles from the backbenches, in permanent revolt against the leadership'. Ah, like Jeremy Corbyn? 'More of a Clare Short,' she laughs, referring to the international development minister who agonized over the Iraq war, resigned and disappeared from public life.

More plates arrive – the main courses – a deep bowl of mushroom risotto for Mantel, slow-cooked duck egg with asparagus for me. The ingredients echo those of the appetizer, like actors playing multiple roles in the same play.

Can Mantel see herself as the Booker judges saw her, as the greatest modern English prose writer? She shakes her head. 'You're only as good as your next sentence.' The line arrives too cleanly to have come from her inner sanctum, but she insists. 'There is no place you can rest. You are in a constant state of making yourself as an author.'

Wolf Hall and *Bring Up the Bodies* crescendoed to the deaths of Thomas More and Anne Boleyn respectively. *The Mirror and the Light* is relentless: Cromwell's fortunes turn; his memory misleads him. 'The third book is particularly taxing, it needs all my ingenuity . . . There are so many things happening on any one day that to do it truthfully in one way you'd have to divide the page into columns. I think it's the hardest thing for the historian or for the writer to convey to the reader – that things don't happen one by one . . . It all has to look as smooth as cream and as transparent as glass.' She laughs at her own task. 'Really, you're trying to give people a book that they can read twice.' (*Game of Thrones*, she notes later, cannot be watched twice, because 'you're just watching for plot'.)

The Mirror and the Light has been expected since 2014; 'the TV people want to get going'. Does it make Mantel anxious? 'If I think about the totality of it, it seems impossible. If I stick to the scene-by-scene, it does seem possible.'

The totality of the risotto is impossible, and Mantel places the remains to one side. The more of her you read, the more you see jabs at those in the know: priests, historians, criminal profilers. Where does that confidence come from? How does she not let criticism intimidate her? 'It's in a different world really from what I do when I sit down with a piece of paper. I'm not at that point thinking, what will the *Daily Mail* think of this? You can't let that kind of silliness get to you. They camped at the seafront, outside our house, and we just drew the curtains.' That is the solution – and the problem: if Mantel can shut herself in her world, her critics can stay in theirs.

Her husband is now her manager and her gatekeeper. 'I'll say to him, anything I need to know, just come and tell me, otherwise I'm getting on with my day . . . I remember during the [Kate Middleton] thing, his coming in to say, "Oh, David Cameron hates you," then coming in to say, "Oh, Ed Miliband hates you." '

How would such politicians have fared in a Tudor court? 'I think they would have learnt to guard their words a lot more carefully. The stakes were so high then – an incautious word could ruin you . . . It's one of the things that fascinates me about being a political animal in those days: part of you says, why would you risk it? Why would you not settle for life as a London merchant?'

An enthusiastic waiter approaches. 'Everything's fine, thank you,' says Mantel. She is 64, an age not attained by Cromwell or Henry, and certainly not by their wives. Only in her seventh decade have good health and financial success collided. 'If you're not ill every day, it's surprising how much time there is, how much energy you have,' she smiles.

Lympstone Manor
Exmouth, Devon EX8

....

Two-course lunch
  menu x 2   £90
Bottle of still water x 2 £8
Coffee and petits fours £8

....

Total
  (inc. service) –   £119.25

She once wrote that the loss of not having children 'keeps changing its shape'. Some people might see her books as the offspring she never had. 'I feel those people are a little emotional. They're downgrading the intellectual fascination.'

She looks at her watch and delicately excuses herself to speak to her husband, who she knows will now be waiting outside in the car. 'If I could just have a very quick word with him – he won't mind.'

When she returns, I ask if she thinks Prince Charles will be an adequate king. 'I think he'll be a very interesting king. I have actually a great deal of respect for him.' Mantel is a governor of the Royal Shakespeare Company; the prince is its president. 'He shows up. When you see his real interest and his real enthusiasm, you can't help but think how hard it must be to stay in that public role and . . . operate as a private human being.'

The hotel has emptied. The bill arrives, and somehow our alcohol-free lunch has come to £119. The Reformation would surely have come sooner if Rome had charged Henry £8 for an espresso. What did Mantel think of the food? 'I didn't notice it,' she says. 'I was interested in talking.'

We shuffle outside. As Gerald drives us to the station, I ask Mantel if she thinks artificial intelligence will soon conjure up credible fiction. 'I wouldn't mind a robot assistant,' she laughs. 'You've got one – me!' interjects Gerald, and for a moment they laugh in unison, forgetting I'm there.

On the train, I think how many such exchanges escape historians. There is a transcript we lose. There is a transcript we long to recover. There is a reason why Mantel works, even while she's sleeping.

Edna O'Brien

'I never wanted to be old but I couldn't stop it'

By Janan Ganesh

'All creativity comes from trauma and cuts.' Edna O'Brien gestures to her face, as though it were covered in wounds. In fact, the Irish novelist has lineless skin and hair the colour of a fox's pelt. The sole clue to her age ('86 and a half') is the range of experiences that infuse her conversation. 'You've got to have a cut of some kind, and I have a triple cut. From family, especially my mother, from country, from religion. And that's no small business to be going on with.'

Painful candour offset with lightness: the O'Brien sweetener. It marks her speech and her prose. When we meet, her first novel, *The Country Girls*, is just finishing a theatre run on the English south coast 57 years after its incendiary (and, in Ireland, prohibited) publication. Cooped up in their rural convent school, Cait and Baba, the girls in question, flee for a life of swish new clothes and romantic escapades in Dublin, which has another kind of disillusion in store. The book and its sequels upset conservatives with their scandalous insinuation that women quite like sex. By modern standards, the writing is chaste. It is the underlying theme of freedom that retains its sting.

Today, O'Brien is screened from London's mad heat by the marble and dark wood of the Delaunay, which serves Mitteleuropean fare from its corner spot on Aldwych. Over heftier portions than either of us bargained for, she becomes a production line of epigrams that balance light and dark: 'I'm not fickle but I can fall for a monster'; 'I never wanted to be old, but I couldn't stop it.' The effect, on me at least, is to elicit admiration for her endurance in life but to ward off anything as presumptuous as pity. It feels like an Irish flavour of the stiff upper lip.

I wonder if she fears being defined by her early work just as Philip

Illustration by Seb Jarnot

Roth, who has her down as the 'most gifted woman now writing in English', remains tied to *Portnoy's Complaint* half a century and several superior novels later. 'If you are defined at all, that's something,' she says. 'I'm proud of the book. It wrote itself in three weeks. It was a gift from God. L. P. Hartley said it was just two nymphomaniacs.' Apparently, he meant that in a bad way.

Free-love hippies in a few enclaves of London and California emerged with the credit for sexual liberation at the end of the 1960s. But the breakthroughs were hard-won at the start of the decade by brave (often female) artists from less celebrated places. Shelagh Delaney, who wrote *A Taste of Honey*, a drama about a mixed-race coupling in industrial Salford, was one. O'Brien was another, though she would go on to build a larger career.

From the general manager of the restaurant, a young Irishman with whom she has some acquaintance, O'Brien orders a goat's cheese flambé and a crab salad. I go for the salmon tartare and the wild boar wurst. When she refuses a glass of wine (she has to give a talk in Chichester, where the play is showing) I tell her I feel too guilty to have one myself. 'Don't,' she fires back. 'I have guilt to donate.' It is too good a line not to act on. I summon a red. She sticks to her cool ginger beer.

O'Brien was born and raised in County Clare, in the west of Ireland. Her strict parents sent her to a Sisters of Mercy school and later forbade her to study literature, prodding her into life as a pharmacist instead. At 24, she thought she had found freedom by marrying, against their wishes, the Irish novelist Ernest Gébler and moving to London. But he turned out to be a 'rather imperious man' (I sense she would like to use a harsher adjective) and their new home was the suburb of Morden, where 'you have to get a bus to get a bus'.

Through prodigious independent learning, she found a job as a reader of manuscripts for the publisher Hutchinson. On the basis of her reports alone, the firm commissioned her to write a novel. That was *The Country Girls*, which led to *Girl with Green Eyes*, *Girls in Their Married Bliss*, *A Pagan Place* – and to divorce, infamy, freedom and the London she had imagined. 'I had a bit of money,' she says, 'which I rapidly spent on parties.' Her social pace slowed – all those books to write – but she still prefers urban life to the countryside she describes so well in prose. 'I am less susceptible to loneliness in the city. Because I can if I want to go out, go to the pictures. The great Russian poet Marina Tsvetaeva said the same thing about cities. Poor Marina, she hanged herself.'

The goat's cheese flambé turns out to be more flambé than goat's cheese, and bigger than a pizza. 'You have to have some,' she begs, and I agree to share the carbohydrate burden.

From what I can work out, her relationship with Ireland has improved without achieving absolute harmony. I ask what she makes of the new prime minister, Leo Varadkar, an openly gay man with an Indian father. Impressive for a republic that banned her work two generations ago, no? 'Some more cultural change is needed,' she says, after agreeing. 'What about the abortion laws? If we're going to be liberal, let's get the whole policy on the table.' For Irish critics, distaste at her sexual themes has gone but another criticism has replaced it: that she does not quite understand the place that Ireland has become, alternately missing its material progress (in 2015's *The Little Red Chairs*, her latest novel, there are crafty priests and 'farms auctioned off for half of nothing') and worrying that it has gone too far. Ireland has lost its 'poetic soul', she tells me. 'But then so has England.'

O'Brien saw off the 1970s and 1980s, when flash prose ('absolute wizardry', she grants, of the likes of Tom Wolfe) edged out the communication of feeling as the most prized skill in literature. 'It's very brilliant but it's not for me. Give me the Russians, give me the Russians,' she says, with the hunger of someone who had to learn her own way around the canon. Her favourite writers of recent decades are W. G. Sebald and Roberto Bolaño: both foreign (German and Chilean, respectively), both dead when at the peak of their popularity, both excavators of the past. 'Memory and language are the two best things a writer has,' says O'Brien, who has also enjoyed Teju Cole's *Open City*. How quickly can she sense a book that lacks depth? 'I can tell within one minute.'

The Dorset crab arrives in a silver receptacle you can see yourself in, and is much more to her taste than the hubcap-sized starter. There is no buyer's remorse from my side either as the wild boar sausage is as good as you would expect from a restaurant that defines itself with these Ruritanian dishes. You imagine stern Junkers with names like Otto gorging on this stuff before horseback duels in the forest. Though just five years old, the Delaunay is a holdout against the small plate and the sharing concept. It is the bridge between the ossified London that O'Brien came to in the 1950s and the creative destruction of today.

Does she get enough credit for the body of work she has accumulated in between those eras? 'A male artist in the room is – for women and men – cultural Viagra,' she says. 'As for a woman, there may be one or two who are glad you are there but you don't make the same impact.' None of this is said with bitterness. If anything, she values being left alone to concentrate on her writing. 'For all my affability, I am also cold.'

You have to look after number one?

'Well no, you have to look after what is right. In the case of work, you have to look after the work. If someone comes into your life that you don't want and keeps nagging you with emails and things, the gate comes down.' She mimes a portcullis shutting in front of her face. This is Graham Greene's 'splinter of ice': the chill at the heart of the serious novelist. Writers cannot be with you all that much. And even when they are with you, they are not really with you.

In the 1990s, O'Brien's work widened to take in politics – though, she says in a post-lunch email, it was never about 'preaching or protest'. *House of Splendid Isolation* revolved around a member of the Irish Republican Army. *Down by the River* explored the abortion laws through a courtroom showdown. And in *The Little Red Chairs*, a charismatic healer who shows up in an Irish village turns out to be a Radovan Karadžić-style fugitive from a dirty war at the other end of the continent. It is her best book (take Roth's word, not mine), a highly evolved writer describing the species at its most basic: a man of violence, a woman driven to folly by want of a child. But there is always humour competing with pain for space on the page. Reading the book, it takes a while to realize it will not be a rural comedy.

'There's a great line in Beckett,' she says, searching for a quote to capture this equipoise of light and dark. 'I can't remember who says it. "You're on Earth. There's no cure for that." There's as much common sense in that as in all of Sophocles or Socrates or anyone else.'

She speaks in coherent paragraphs with the rich, sonorous husk of a continuity announcer on a high-end public-service radio station. She is also the most inquisitive person I have interviewed. She wants to know what will happen with this Brexit business (search me), whether I have tried LSD (she has, with the psychiatrist R. D. Laing) and what pick-up techniques go on in bars these days. Through one of her two sons, an architect who worked on the private members' club Shoreditch House and the Everyman cinema in Hampstead, she still knows her London. She knows her football, too, tuning into big European games of an evening. 'When Madrid are playing Barcelona, oh boy, that's a game and a half.' She has friends in the adjacent arts, including the film director Michael Haneke and his frequent star Isabelle Huppert (who, it occurs to me, has the poise and the features to play O'Brien in an eventual biopic).

This proliferation of interests makes me wonder why, after all the novels, plays and short stories, she has never been one for essays. O'Brien on Lionel Messi (she rates him over Cristiano Ronaldo), on Emmanuel Macron ('Jupiter himself'), on modern Ireland, would demand attention. I feel like crossing the restaurant to lobby her publisher, who by coincidence has booked a table of his own. 'The thing with essays,' she says, 'is the marriage of theme and writer. If that is vitiated in any way, then the essay is nothing.' She contrasts Saul Bellow's powerful early essays with his 'cranky' late stuff, when the writer exceeded the theme. If I did not know better, I would detect self-doubt here.

Or it may be that everything she wanted to say in non-fiction form came out with her 2012 memoir, *Country Girl*. In the book, pride in her defiance of those who sought to contain her – parents, church, spouse – vies with regret at her slowness to act. I press her on which she feels stronger.

The Delaunay	
55 Aldwych, London WC2	
....	
Goat's cheese	
flambé	£9.50
Salmon tartare	£12
Crab salad	£19.50
Wild boar	£16.50
Spinach oil	£4.95
Macchiato	£4.25
Sparkling water	£2.50
Ginger beer	£3.50
Valpolicella	£12
Diet Coca-Cola	£3.50
....	
Total	
(inc. service) –	£103.73

'I wish in my early life I had stood up a bit more,' she admits, 'but all things considered I was pretty brave. You know, if you start off with a pretty terrifying start, you have many handicaps. You have many handicaps.' The repetition is poignant. 'I would say, as regards my inner self, I am happier than I ever was, while naturally aware of death and decay and decrepitude. I am full of darkness, but I am also full of light. Do you know what I mean?'

Yes. All her readers do.

Memory and language – those precious writerly resources – are flowing as I ask for a coffee. 'Because of my religious saturation,' she recalls of her younger self, 'I believed that mortal man and Jesus Christ overlap. I wanted sensual love and spiritual sensibility. Well, you know what, you can't always have both.' Splinter of ice or what.

'You're young, you see,' she says, as I settle the bill. 'You're happy and you have original life.'

Original Life could have served as her memoir title. Her novels are bold, but not as bold as her own story. In literature, characters who escape an unpromising start to make their own way in the world tend to be male: David Copperfield, Julien Sorel, Augie March. O'Brien did not just invert this tradition with *The Country Girls* and subsequent books, she lived the inversion. The result appears to be a woman in love with the freedom she has won and conscious of what it has cost – but then life, as she says of literature in her email, 'requires layers of complexity'.

She leaves me with a copy of *The Love Object*, a collection of her short stories with an introduction by John Banville, her stiffest competition as Ireland's greatest living writer. And now she must head to Chichester. A car waits for her on Aldwych, London's hinge, where postcodes stop starting with W and start starting with E, where tourists, students, diplomats, barristers and chefs on a cigarette break compete for space on the paved bend. Into the scorched traffic she disappears, a city girl.

Fahad Albutairi

'I didn't want to be shocking from the beginning'

By Erika Solomon

A s I set out for lunch with the Saudi comedian Fahad Albutairi, my phone suggests the restaurant is out at sea. Then again, we are meeting in Dubai, home of artificial islands and an indoor ski slope.

The interior of the Al Qasr hotel, connected to the restaurant where he has opted to meet, looks like something from a harem painting: camel statues, marble archways and ceiling-high doors carved from wood and gold. Outside, a long pier leads out into the Persian Gulf and the Pierchic restaurant, a circular wooden building with glass walls and stunning views of aquamarine waters, and the alienesque but iconic Burj Al Arab rising from the shore.

Given the ostentatious setting and his laconic emails, I fret our lunch may be a stilted affair. But my anxieties melt the second Albutairi arrives, greeting me with a big smile and profuse apologies for being late. He is dressed in a grey shirt and frayed jeans, with black-and-grey-striped socks poking up from his boots.

Saudi Arabia is not exactly known for its humour. The austere kingdom attracts more attention for accusations of funding radical Islamists, the activities of its recently muzzled 'morality police', the use of beheadings in executions and a rule banning women from travelling without a male guardian's consent. Albutairi, however, is known for challenging both his country's ultra-conservative social mores and also westerners' interpretation of them – quite a double act.

'I can guarantee you this, the only bomb I can make is a Jägerbomb,' he says, reprising a line from his first successful stand-up routine, when

Illustration by
James Ferguson

he was studying abroad in the US, a few years after 9/11. 'People were laughing, but just a little laughter, because it was a little awkward. And I was, like, "Yeah, you guys didn't find that funny? The immigration officer didn't think it was funny, either. He told me, with three fingers up my ass: That's not funny."'

Albutairi, 31, was raised in the seaside town of Khobar, known for the laid-back attitude of many Arab coastal towns and an openness to westerners working at the nearby headquarters of oil company Saudi Aramco. His seaside upbringing fostered a life-long love of seafood, he says, which is why he chose Pierchic for our meeting.

He also grew up on a diet of Egyptian slapstick comedy films, Jim Carrey movies and an older Saudi TV sketch show, *Tash ma Tash*, known for breaking new ground with political parodies. In the early 2000s, he went to study at the University of Texas, Austin, where he picked up not only a geophysics degree but also a Texan twang.

His friends goaded him into his first stand-up attempt at the Cap City Comedy club in Austin. An audience of about 50 people stared in awkward silence. 'Horrible. Horrible performance. Completely weird. It was like reading off of a paper. I had a blonde joke in there – oh my God,' he groans, head in hands. 'I thought, hey, [blonde jokes] work for everyone else. And then I realized I was brown.'

The waiter delivers a basket of bread and butter. 'I'm not going for that,' he says, before describing his latest workout regime.

Albutairi's epiphany came through watching some of America's stand-up greats, such as Eddie Murphy, who drew on the experience of being African-American, and Richard Pryor, who channelled his struggle with drug addiction. 'I kept, like, having this little voice in my head: Try it again, just don't tell anybody. Because if you bomb on stage, nobody will know – oh, wait a minute, "bomb on stage" – that's funny, because I'm Arab. OK, let's try that, you know?'

From those humble Texas beginnings, Albutairi won an audition in 2008 to open for 'Axis of Evil', a Middle Eastern–American comedy tour, in Bahrain, after returning home to neighbouring Saudi Arabia for work. That same year, he did what any young Saudi aspiring to make it big would do: he joined Twitter (he now has well over 2 million followers), and started a YouTube show called *La Yekthar*, which means 'put a lid on it' in Saudi dialect.

With a trademark set of goofy thumbs-up and winks (which he also uses in face-to-face conversation) and well-honed comedic timing, he delivers Arabic monologues, often subtitled in English, in a way that takes delight in his society's absurdities as much as it mocks them.

To the rest of the Middle East – where many locals cling to the notion that the wealthier, showier Gulf is bereft of culture – it is Egypt, with its dominance of the film industry, that was long the king of comedy. But that is changing in an era of pan-Arab television channels where American programmes dominate entertainment and an obsession with social media has made Saudi Arabia one of the biggest users of YouTube and Twitter per capita. *La Yekthar* started in 2011 as a pioneer of Saudi social media entertainment. In its final season last year, it had more than 1 million subscribers and regularly received between half a million and 1 million hits per episode.

Dubai was not where I expected to meet Albutairi – he used to be based in Riyadh. I ask if his relocation has something to do with the local furores he has raised among hardline clerics and social commentators, one of which concerned a movie scene in which he appeared in his boxers, which they dubbed 'pornographic'. More recently he helped write and produce the music video 'No Woman, No Drive', mocking the ban on female motorists. It got 13 million hits on YouTube. In the video – to the tune of Bob Marley's 'No Woman, No Cry' – Hisham Fageeh, another comedian, performs a cappella, in mock deference to austere Islamic practices forbidding musical instruments. Albutairi rewrote the lyrics with lines such as: 'Ova-ovaries. All safe and well!' – a reference to those who say it's better for women's reproductive health if they don't drive.

He laughs, insisting he moved here for professional reasons. And anyway, he adds, many older conservatives liked the video, not detecting the irony. 'A lot of people were actually using the video to show international audiences we don't want women drivers. I loved the fact they were so confused. I'll tell you why: because if we kept it mysterious, everybody is going to retweet, everybody is going to share it . . . They might only realize later on when it's too late.'

His use of Twitter and YouTube in a country hungry for social media catapulted him to fame, and he has leveraged it to produce and star in his own television series. He starts to discuss this when the waitress comes by for a second time, practically begging to take our order. We dutifully peruse the menu. Albutairi asks for a description of the prawns. He decides to start with the yellowtail carpaccio and then – 'The prawns?' asks the waitress.

'No. No.' He shakes his head slowly and dramatically, and the waitress bursts into laughter. 'If I was paying, then yeah. But since it's on the *FT*, I'll go for the grilled Canadian lobster.'

As she convinces him to add a side of mashed potatoes, I gape at the price – 490 dirhams ($133.41) – and order some scallops to start and a sea bass from somewhere in South America, a comparative bargain.

Our orders taken, Albutairi says he only recently returned from Glendale, California, where he finished filming what he describes as Saudi Arabia's first ever sitcom, to be aired this year on a regional channel he cannot identify yet. The show is in English and Arabic, with a mixed American and Saudi cast, detailing the misadventures of four Saudi men studying at an LA film school to make movies for a country that notoriously still bans public cinemas.

'I want to link this region to the global scene. People have already started doing that in France. French comedians, Gad Elmaleh and other comedians, are actually bridging the gap between French comedy and the US,' he says. The actor Christoph Waltz, who was in *Inglourious Basterds*, is another example. 'Hollywood is now, more than ever, opening up to the rest of the world to become more politically correct . . . It's an opportunity for us.'

He comes off far savvier than the scrawny nerd with the shock of curly hair that first endeared him to fans, a look he says got him branded by an Emirati newspaper as the 'Seinfeld of Saudi Arabia'. 'It's because of the Jewfro and the eyes and the glasses, and just the whole thing – the schnozz. And it's because I work safe and I work clean on stage,' he says, noting that he quickly abandoned his early foray into the vulgar jokes. 'I want my mom to watch.'

His mother is supportive but it is his grandfather, a local writer, who is his biggest fan. His father and siblings are a tougher sell. 'They're like: we're already dealing with a big ego, we don't want to inflate it too much,' he laughs.

At this point we realize we have barely touched our appetizers. Albutairi's carpaccio is sprinkled with petals, candied orange peels and an electric-blue goo. My scallops are buttery and tender, but I skirt around a dollop of foie gras.

When he first started doing stand-up in Saudi in 2009, it was so new that organizers were unsure what the reception among more conservative parts of society – or the morality police – would be to this western-inspired entertainment. They hosted the first shows in residential compounds and then moved into bigger tents in the desert to accommodate larger crowds.

Arabic stand-up itself was a new concept, and Albutairi and other comics who were starting out rehearsed and produced sketches together, finding ways to transfer American stand-up delivery into Arabic. 'It was like walking around in a dark room and having people following behind and turning on the light at some point. And some doors you open and then you close immediately – like, OK, I don't want to go in there. And for me that was: one, overly vulgar material, and two, overly political material. I really wanted a certain degree of popularity. I didn't want to be shocking from the beginning.'

Pushing back on the country's most extreme conservative practices is, he insists, actually more daring in a country where Salafi clerics have long dominated society. 'A lot of people have been able to practise activism to a certain degree. Some of them did get jailed' – including, briefly, his own wife, a women's rights activist – 'but if it's just political, there's more room to get out with it . . . If it's religious, that's when it gets really, really tricky. There's still a little bit of a struggle on a governmental level to a certain degree, but not as much as society.'

He learnt that through reactions to his show. The first episode to cause an uproar poked fun at the Saudi religious police for hunting down men who had gone out to sea to drink. Albutairi was deriding fake news long before it became an American media obsession, for example in a sketch mocking a Saudi video gone viral of a man insisting western countries are trying to contaminate food with chemicals that destroy male chromosomes.

Our waitress brings out the main meal. My sea bass is soft and flaky, perfectly grilled with green beans doused in pesto. Albutairi is wrestling with his lobster, which he approves of but notes is not quite as tender as the lobsters in neighbouring Oman. We both gorge on a side of creamy mashed potatoes.

Albutairi says his stand-up has lately been influenced by the darker style of American comic Louis CK, after his wife, Loujain Alhathloul, was arrested and jailed for 73 days for trying to drive into the kingdom. He recites the first bit he did after her release: 'I say: "I haven't done stand-up comedy for a while. I got married, kept busy with the marriage. My wife was pretty busy, too . . . being in jail." Because they all know. It's the elephant in the room.'

But, contrary to the complaints of his Saudi critics, Albutairi is no cheerleader for American-style democracy and 'self-righteous Americans'. 'I get pissed off at people back home who push a no-change agenda, that we don't know what we're doing and should be a certain way to be good Saudis. But it's also very frustrating to see Americans do the same thing,' he says. 'A lot of people think Saudi Arabia is a totalitarian monarchy and it's horrible. What is that? Why do you think monarchies are horrible? Because you're not a monarchy? We could become a constitutional monarchy.'

He sees the election of Donald Trump as a 'wake-up call'. 'Like, hey, maybe not everything is flowers and breezes and getting a cold brewski on July Fourth. No, there's an ugly side to America. An ugly side that got this guy up there.'

As he is prying out the last piece of his lobster, I tell Albutairi that I was intrigued by his only sketch on the Arab Spring protests of 2011, when people thought democracy was coming to the region. One of *La Yekthar*'s recurring characters, a crocodile puppet, waves a lighter as if at a concert and tries to lead the audience in a protest against Albutairi. A protest sign in the background says, 'No to armpit hair'.

He was never sure what to make of the Arab Spring protests. 'Sure, we don't trust our governments, but we don't trust the population, either. I had just read something by Gustave Le Bon about the

---

Pierchic
Al Sufouh Rd, Al Qasr,
Madinat Jumeirah, Dubai

....

San Pellegrino x 2	Dhs70
La Scolca Gavi	Dhs80
Dorado carpaccio	Dhs160
Scallops	Dhs210
Lobster	Dhs490
Sea bass	Dhs220
Mash potato	Dhs45
Pearl for two	Dhs120

....

Total –	Dhs1,395
	(£295)

psychology of the masses and I was like, I don't know if this is going to be a classic social-science thing, where it's a pure example of tyranny of the majority, or is it going to be actually positive?'

This question seems apt in the days of rising populism in Europe and America, too, I say. He nods vigorously. 'It keeps supporting the whole notion, though we hate to admit it – like, that kind of a democracy, if it were to happen in Saudi, someone like Trump would definitely win. But he would be even worse!'

Our dessert arrives: 'The Pearl' is a ball of chocolate and vanilla mousse placed inside a chocolate cage. I am not a fan but soldier on, and point out he has surely broken his calorie count. 'I know,' he grins. 'It was worth it.'

On our way out, we walk down the pier, through palm-shaded canals, to the hotel, and I feel we have opened up enough to share the reactions I received from friends I told about our interview. Some joked they didn't believe Saudis had a culture. A Lebanese colleague quipped: 'I didn't think Saudis had a sense of humour.' (The stereotypes aren't just for westerners.)

'That's BS,' he laughs. 'If anything, in the Gulf, we're the troublemakers.'

Jonathan Franzen

'I'm a poor person who has money'

By Lucy Kellaway

I sit alone at a reproduction antique table under a fake chandelier in the dining room at the Gore Hotel in Kensington. There is no sign of Jonathan Franzen; nor of anyone else. The place is entirely empty.

While I wait, I look at what people are saying about Franzen on Twitter. There is a *Times* columnist moaning that *Purity* is a load of tripe. Someone else points out that Franzen has no black people in his novels. Others are incensed by his recent performance on *Newsnight*, in which he did what he often does – disparage the internet.

All this loathing is baffling. I have read and loved *The Corrections* (2001), *Freedom* (2010) and now *Purity*, the latter billed as a cross between Charles Dickens and *Breaking Bad*. It has kept me up every night for a week, and now that I'm done, I'll miss its wit, its messed-up characters and its emotional complexity. It is a mystery how the man who wrote it could have become, in the words of the *Los Angeles Review of Books*, 'with the possible exception of Kanye West – the most bitched about artist in America'.

It is nearly 2pm when the door opens and the great American novelist makes a modest entrance. He's in an old navy fleece. His dark hair is tousled and even though it is going grey he looks closer to 40 than 56. He is wearing the same heavy black glasses that, last time he was in London promoting a novel, were snatched from his nose by a prankster who proceeded to jump into the Serpentine lake, just minutes round the corner from where he stands now.

Franzen has barely sat down when the waiter, evidently excited to be given something to do at last, is bearing down on us, pad in hand. 'I

Illustration by James Ferguson

would love some still water if I may, please,' says Franzen, all politeness and diffidence. 'And maybe something along the lines of a Diet Coke?'

Does he know about Lunch with the *FT*, I ask? 'I think my eye has literally fallen on it.' Franzen speaks slowly and sounds so uncomfortable, I conclude he's trying to be nice but is a rotten liar.

I make some disparaging remarks about the restaurant's frumpy decor but he declines to join in. For him its unpopularity is an advantage. 'There's a certain sameness to high-end restaurant experiences, at least in New York, I'm kind of nauseated by the clientele. They're total 1 per centers and they're doing it every day and there's something kind of just disgusting and like the pigs in *Animal Farm* about the whole thing.'

But since the rip-roaring success of *The Corrections* 14 years ago, isn't he a 1 per center himself? 'I am literally, in terms of my income, a 1 per center, yes,' he says, his eyes not on me but on the empty table next to us. 'I spend my time connected to the poverty that's fundamental to mankind, because I'm a fiction writer.'

He doesn't write about poverty, I protest. He writes about the angst of people like him and the people he knows. Franzen gives the neighbouring tabletop a weary look. 'That's a quotation from Flannery O'Connor, by the way.'

While I smart, he goes on: 'I'm a poor person who has money.'

Franzen doesn't spend anything. The fleece he is wearing is 10 years old. He doesn't like shopping and hates waste. Upstairs in the fridge in his hotel room are the leftovers from meals, all of which he will eat in due course. His only luxury is expensive kit for birdwatching.

'I don't like to hire people to do work that I can do,' he says. So that means he does his own dusting in the New York apartment he shares with his girlfriend? Franzen looks slightly shifty. 'We do have a cleaner, although even that I feel some justification because we pay her way more than is standard and she's a nice Filipino woman who we treat very well and we're giving her work.'

In a way this middle-class guilt is sweet. But it's also absurd. By the same argument he should be employing as many people as possible.

'Something doesn't sit well. It seems to me that I don't want to lose touch with . . . Like I repainted our guest room this summer in our rather small house in Santa Cruz.'

Bingo, I want to shout. I love decorating too and start trying to interest him in my thoughts on masking tape, but he continues deadpan: 'If I had hired someone, it would've been done better, and I was very sick of doing it by the end, and yet it seemed important. The first two coats I enjoyed and the third coat I was getting tired of it and the fourth coat was just sheer torture.'

While he has been talking we have each been given a large white bowl with a pair of tiny, shrivelled pastries in them and a jug of tepid, cloudy liquid on the side. Franzen eats his without comment, and I ask: does he understand why he makes people quite so cross? 'Well, I have to acknowledge the possibility that I'm simply a horrible person.'

He recites the line with a practised irony. Evidently he acknowledges no such possibility at all.

'My other answers would all be sort of self-flattering, right? Because I tell the truth; people don't like the truth.'

He tells me about a piece he wrote in the *New Yorker* in March about climate change and bird conservation in which he managed to alienate everyone, including bird watchers. 'I pointed out that 25 years after humanity collectively tried to reduce its carbon emissions, they reached an all-time high last year; further pointed out that the people who say we still have 10 years to keep the average temperature from rising more than two degrees Celsius are, charitably, deluded or, uncharitably, simply lying. And, therefore, maybe we should rethink whether we want to be putting such a large percentage of our energies into what is essentially a hopeless battle.'

His idea of himself as a truth-teller is only partly why people find him so aggravating. There is something about the man himself, and his variety of superior maleness, that also annoys. *Purity* – which has a clever, lovably sarcastic woman as its heroine – has, nevertheless, enraged some feminists because there is a mad manipulative wife in it who makes her husband wee sitting down. The journalist Jenni Russell, for example, writes about how all Franzen's books have dutiful men trapped in relationships with manipulative women. 'It's, like, where do you even begin with stuff like that? People who don't know how to read fiction, they just shout words like "loathsome" and "misogynist" because they can't deal with it. I fail to conform to the brutish, white, male stereotype and that is actually more enraging than the brutish, white, male stereotype. It's the middle ground which is precisely what's upsetting to people on the extremes.'

Our starters have been replaced by an almost entirely grey dish. The grey mullet lies on a grey bed of puréed artichokes with some whitish almonds.

This tastes weird, I say. 'I'm not fussy about my food,' he says, taking a forkful. 'It's not bad.'

I ask if he saw the review of *Purity* in the *Financial Times*, which called it 'middlebrow'. He says he never reads what people write about him. 'I don't know what "middlebrow" even means. I think it's threatening to commercial writers that someone who's selling well is also getting literary respect, and it's threatening to literary writers who don't sell that somebody who's literary also is getting commercial success.'

The thing that bothers me about his prose is not the popular bits but the clever-dick ones. In *Purity*, I took exception to a bilingual acrostic that allows Franzen (a Fulbright scholar in Berlin in the 1980s and translator of the work of obscure Austrian satirist Karl Kraus) to prove he's smarter than his reader. 'My agent didn't get it, either,' he says. 'Many, many people didn't get it, and yet if the whole book were like that, you could say the writer's being insufferable. But I think you have to have a few things that you have to kind of chew on to get.'

As if on cue, a loud cracking noise comes from his mouth. 'Teeth hitting each other sort of sideways, glancing, catching,' he explains.

I ask if his teeth are bad, but he says they are very good. 'I'm an American.'

He laughs and at once the ponderous gloom lifts. I get a glimpse of what are very good teeth indeed.

The levity doesn't last: have I read *Sapiens* by Yuval Noah Harari, he asks? When I say I haven't, he explains how the agrarian revolution was a mistake and argues we were happier as hunter-gatherers. With the internet, he implies, the same may apply. Is he really saying people were happier before the internet? He ducks the question and says instead: 'I wasn't. But I didn't start feeling happy, really, until my forties.'

Happiness for Franzen is slightly problematical. He has often said the best writing comes from discomfort. He has had his share of pain – he has referred to the unhappiness of his 14-year marriage to writer Valerie Cornell – so I wonder, if he had always been as happy as now, would he ... He cuts me off. 'I was,' he says. 'I was a smiling, smart, healthy, straight, Midwestern American male who went to decent public schools, what we call public schools, and an excellent college. I had everything it took.'

I have the feeling he's playing with me, but still I plough on. Doesn't he believe that if you haven't felt pain you can't write good fiction? 'Apparently Paulo Coelho can.' He gives another dazzling smile that manages to be both beatific and slightly nasty. 'I'm giving you a hard time. We're talking about real novelists, who are going to be very sensitive, experience things intensely. That's basically a recipe for pain. Things that a less sensitive person may experience as nothing create lasting scars.'

There is a lot of scar tissue in *Purity*. At one point the narrative switches into the first person, and a man and his wife have an exchange on the phone that is so mad, miserable, undignified and perverse, no one could have written it without having experienced something similar. When I read the passage I was slack-jawed with admiration, but couldn't help wondering what his ex-wife would make of it. 'I'm not the only one who's been in a kind of nutty relationship. And so simply the fact of writing about a nutty relationship is not compromising anyone.'

So it's fine, then? 'No, there's blood on the floor. It's never fine. In a way, the thing I feel worst about is writing about my parents, even though I did all my writing after they were dead. It has more to do with their not having had an education that would have enabled them to appreciate what I was doing and why I was doing it.'

Then why betray people he loves? 'Well, there's a utilitarian argument to be made. People feel grateful and feel less alone with what had been a private torment, a private sorrow, a private shame.'

The waiter brings him a bowl of fruit salad so large he looks at it in dismay, as if fearing the inevitable waste.

'Would you like a little bit of this? Even just one bite would help,' he pleads, shovelling fruit on to my plate.

In *The Corrections*, Albert, who was based on Franzen's father, was a benign if stern parental figure. In *Purity*, parents get a tougher time of it. One mother shows a seven-year-old son her vagina. Another inflicts psychological violence by manipulating and stifling. I wonder if he would have written anything quite as dark if he had children himself?

Franzen sighs. 'I'm sure everything would've been different. Maybe I would've been retired and working on a historical novel about the civil war and teaching fiction at Portland State University if I had had kids.'

I get the reproach, but it's only later that I get the snobbery. There was a time, though, when Franzen wanted to have kids. According to the *Guardian*, for a while he considered adopting an Iraqi orphan so he could get to know young people. Was that true? 'The story was the work of a nasty personage,' he says, then tells me what really happened. 'There came a point when I was struggling with my fourth novel and I suspected the reason was that I had lost touch with the world, that I came from a strong family, and maybe I was meant to be a family man. But it's a long way from that to adopting a war orphan to study young people. It fed into what everyone wanted to believe, which is I am an absolutely horrible person.'

He seems so weary of all this that I ask if he finds fame a burden. Has success made him less nice? No; he says it has made him less angry, and much less envious. 'Writer's envy is insane and knows nearly no bounds, but at some point it becomes obviously inappropriate.' These days if anyone else writes a good novel, he doesn't feel upset; he is glad. The only trouble is that it hardly ever happens.

'I am very grateful to Haruki Murakami for writing *The Wind-Up Bird Chronicle*; I feel the same way right now about Elena Ferrante. I have trouble finding books that really do it for me.'

Envy is something his girlfriend, the writer Kathryn Chetkovich, is more straightforward about. In 2003, after the triumph of *The Corrections*, she wrote a devastating essay for *Granta*, on just how hard it was for her to bear her boyfriend's success. If the boot had been on the other foot, Franzen says he would have felt differently, partly because he roots so seriously for 'whoever I'm living with' but also because he is usually only competitive with men. In any case, he says, if he hadn't been successful as a writer, he would have given up.

The waiter asks if he'd like coffee. 'I'm good, thank you, right now.' It's

Bistro One Ninety, Gore Hotel	
190 Queen's Gate, Kensington, London SW7	
Pre-theatre menu (tortellini, grey mullet) x 2	£49.90
Fruit	£8
Diet Coke x 2	£7
Mint tea	£4
Total (inc. service and VAT) –	£77.50

only when I see the transcript of our lunch and notice the phrase 'I'm good' to mean 'No, thank you', I wish I'd challenged him on it. Franzen has strong feelings about certain words. He has written a whole essay on the evils of 'then' as a conjunction, which strikes me as entirely baffling.

I try out a sentence: 'Jonathan Franzen leant forward, then he leant back again.' What's wrong with that? 'That's just a run-on sentence,' he says. 'What you will find in bad English prose is, "He leant forward then spoke again."'

Sounds OK to me, I say. 'Read my essay,' he says.

Lunch is nearly over, and there is one more thing I want to ask him. He has said that all decent novelists are changed by every book they write. So how did *Purity* change him? He stares at the table for so long with his eyes closed that I wonder if he has gone to sleep. 'How I changed was I realized that I really am a fiction writer, I don't have all that many years and that I've got to find a way to write another couple of novels.'

As he gets up to leave, I tell him that we have covered so much ground in 90 minutes it will be a nightmare trying to write the lunch up. 'Ask for more space,' he says. 'Maybe they'd let you do a two-parter, the appetizer and the main course. Just saying.'

Woody Harrelson

'I had to go out and fire up a hooter'

By Matthew Garrahan

Woody Harrelson is explaining why he recently began smoking pot again after more than a year off. 'I gave up giving up,' he says in a slow drawl. Redolent of so many of his movies, it is pitched somewhere between his childhood homes of Texas and Ohio. In interviews last year the Hollywood hellraiser said it was time to quit after three decades of hard partying but Willie Nelson, his close friend and neighbour in Hawaii, where he now lives, seems to have turned his head: the country music star is perhaps America's most famous stoner (he even has his own cannabis brand, Willie's Reserve). 'He was a corrupting influence,' Harrelson says with a slow, low laugh: even his chuckles seem to be at half-speed. Some people self-medicate with pot to get through the day when life is too hectic, but not Harrelson. 'My life is not too hectic now,' the 56-year-old says. 'In fairness, it's pretty great. But everything can be slightly augmented.'

We are in Farmacy, a Notting Hill vegan restaurant filled with plants that is a regular hang-out when he is in London: the owner, Camilla Fayed, daughter of Harrods' former owner Mohamed Al-Fayed, even comes over to give him a hug when she spots him. A vegan since 1990, he says he likes the place because the food he eats these days is mostly raw. 'I got hip to raw food probably more than 20 years ago and was like . . . damn! What a cool thing.' He starts riffing about a book he read on healthy eating and the importance of enzymes. 'If you cook or process food then you kill those enzymes.' They are, he says, the 'life-force' of food. A raw meal for him it is, then. He laughs again: although he may not be fully baked today he gives the confident impression of being lightly toasted.

Illustration by James Ferguson

Then again, maybe not. Before our lunch I watched clips of interviews he gave during his weed hiatus last year and his manner was just the same: stoned or not, a friend of his later tells me he is like this all the time. We are supposed to meet at 12.30pm and he is there early, wearing a blue T-shirt and a blue baseball cap embossed with *Lost in London*, the title of the film he produced and starred in last year. The movie was shot in one take and streamed live in cinemas on both sides of the Atlantic. It is a fictionalized account of the worst night of his life, bringing together two episodes that happened to him in 2002 when he fell foul of a *News of the World* sting and was arrested after an altercation with a London cabbie. *Lost in London* is being released on iTunes this weekend and on the Hulu streaming service in the US but is likely to be overshadowed by his other new movie, *Solo*, the latest *Star Wars* spin-off; in a summer of blockbusters this will be one of the biggest. He had made his fair share of big studio films, such as *The Hunger Games* series and last year's *War for the Planet of the Apes* – not to mention his Oscar-nominated performance this year as a small-town police chief in Martin McDonagh's sparkling *Three Billboards Outside Ebbing, Missouri*. But nothing tops the scale of *Star Wars*. It's 'the biggest you could dream of' for its sets and 'all the other stuff', he says. In *Solo* he plays Beckett, a criminal and mentor of sorts to Alden Ehrenreich's young Han Solo, with Donald Glover starring as the debonair smuggler Lando Calrissian. Harrelson breaks off from riffing about the movie to salute Glover, whose recent rap video 'This is America', delivered by his persona Childish Gambino, has been widely acclaimed for its searing look at race in America. 'It's got something like 180 million views on YouTube. He's phenomenal. One of those artists who has the ability like Michael Jackson to recognize the pulse of America.'

A waitress has arrived to take orders. Harrelson immediately orders an adaptogenic latte (the menu reveals that its ingredients include reishi and chaga, two types of Chinese mushroom, and the ho shu wu herb). 'Don't worry about all that Chinese herbal stuff, it's really good,' he says. A round of adaptogenic lattes it is.

He knows the menu well but asks the waitress to recommend something for me, given that I am more of an enzyme-destroying carnivore. She rattles off a list of items and I choose a vegetable quesadilla; he goes for the Asian salad with a side order of avocado. Slightly concerned that the quesadilla may not be enough, I persuade him to share a mac 'n' cheese with me (made with rice pasta, naturally, and a non-cheese sauce described in the menu as 'cheese'). 'Some people who actually eat mac 'n' cheese on a regular basis might say, "Well this ain't mac 'n' cheese,"' he says. 'But it's beyond delicious.'

The waitress asks if we want the dishes to come all at once or the mac 'n' cheese on its own to start, and Harrelson is momentarily confused. 'I never understand when they ask that,' he says when she's gone. 'Do you want this first or that? I'm sitting here and those decisions are way beyond what I understand. Psychologically, I just don't get it.'

The adaptogenic lattes arrive promptly and I am relieved to discover it tastes more of coconut milk than Chinese fungi. He tells me how much he likes London, having spent a lot of time filming here in recent years. 'I even got that registered traveller thing because I'm coming in so much. I dig it.' He also likes the variety of English accents, listing some of his favourite local words, such as 'knackered' and 'chuffed'.

I want to know about the journey that took him to Hollywood – a journey that would itself be worthy of big-screen treatment. He lives in Maui with his wife, Laura, and their three daughters but was born in Texas and lived there until he was 12, raised by his mother in a Presbyterian household. Presbyterianism 'is like Catholic-lite', he says. 'Half the ritual but all the guilt.'

He didn't have much time with his father, who spent most of Harrelson's childhood in prison: he was a contract killer associated with organized crime. I tentatively ask him about his dad, who died in 2007. He confirms he was in prison for much of his life but he clearly doesn't want to elaborate. 'We were poor,' he says of his childhood. 'But my mom always took care of us [and] we always had food. It was a lot to raise three kids on her own as a secretary but she did it and she sure did look after us.'

After school he went to Hanover College in Indiana, where one of his fellow students was one Mike Pence, now Donald Trump's vice-president. 'He was two years ahead of me,' he says. 'I liked him. He was a pretty nice guy.' Both men were religious and Harrelson, who was studying theology, reveals that Pence once assisted him in arranging a sermon. 'We had Wednesday night services and I did a sermon and he helped me with it, just trying to make sure everything was on point and all of it worked.'

I'm going to need something stronger than a mushroom latte to picture the right-wing evangelical vice-president collaborating on anything with one of Hollywood's most renowned potheads, let alone a religious sermon. Understanding what led to their lives diverging then is also intriguing, given what I know about Harrelson's long-standing belief in environmentalism (in 1996 he was arrested for scaling the Golden Gate Bridge to protest against the destruction of a redwood grove) and his politics, having spoken in the past about his belief in anarchism. 'Politics is businessmen working for bigger businessmen and it's never going to be any different,' he says. What about his former fellow student, Pence? 'It's 35 years down the road. One of us still has his soul intact.'

The mac 'n' cheese arrives and he does not appear to hear the waitress's warning about the bowl being very hot. 'Ow, ow, ow, that's hot as shit!' he exclaims as he burns himself on it. It looks pretty cheesy for a non-cheesy dish, I say. 'Nah, try it, man,' he says, taking a forkful. 'You're going to love it.'

As we tuck in, I ask about his other connection with the current US administration. In 2002 he had dinner with Trump, who had invited Jesse Ventura, the former wrestler and then governor of Minnesota, to Trump Tower in Manhattan. Ventura, an old friend, asked Harrelson along. Trump, he says, 'is not afraid of talking. Now, being overly talkative is not an uncommon trait. But he's one of those people who start talking and literally three hours have gone by and they haven't noticed that no one else said a word.'

Sounds like tough going, I say. 'Yeah, it was heavy sledding. I had to go outside and fire up a hooter to summon the courage just to get back in for the second half.'

We have made short work of the mac 'n' cheese, which tasted just like the real thing. As the main courses arrive, I ask how he went from Hanover to Hollywood. The more he learnt about religion, the more he realized it was 'a man-made construct', and the theatre was beckoning. He had done some acting at college and a friend asked if he wanted to move to New York. 'It was perfect timing. Right as I was moving to New York, I shifted from being a Christian to a hedonist. I wasn't an atheist . . . I was an agnostic and a hedonist.'

Almost immediately, he landed some theatrical roles and, in 1985, while visiting Los Angeles, won a part on *Cheers* playing Woody, an affable naïf from Indiana. He would appear in almost 200 episodes on the hit show, which made stars of its cast and teed up Harrelson's subsequent career in movies. The cast seems to have been a close-knit group. I tell him I saw Ted Danson, one of his co-stars, on a late-night chat show recently recounting the time he and Harrelson took hallucinogenic mushrooms on a boat trip to Catalina off the coast of Los Angeles. 'He said that?' he says, apparently unaware. 'There are a lot of stories from back then that I thought would never come out and now one of them's out, so that's good.' The boat trip must have 'needed some augmentation'.

He spent eight years on *Cheers* but avoided being typecast, going on to star in a flurry of movies, among them *White Men Can't Jump*, *Natural Born Killers* and *The People vs Larry Flynt*, for which he received his first Oscar nomination. In the past decade he has hit a real purple patch, from his hired gun in the Coen brothers' *No Country for Old Men* in 2007 to his turn as a Louisiana detective hunting a serial killer in HBO's magnificent *True Detective* series, to his Oscar-nominated role in *Three Billboards*. I haven't seen *Solo* yet but ask about the change in directors midway through the production, when Phil Lord and Christopher Miller, who had been filming for more than two months, were abruptly replaced by Ron Howard. 'We'd already been shooting 70-something days and Ron came in. Not an easy thing for him.'

Why did Lord and Miller leave? 'It really was creative differences. You hear that a lot but I think they were making a different movie and the powers that be did not necessarily want the kind of movie they were making and they didn't want to keep butting heads.' He says he loves the film. 'I thought there were a couple of things I did, little chuckles that could have been in there that I would have liked but I understand that it needs to be edited.' Still, Howard 'made something fantastic'.

I wonder when an actor knows that the film they are making is going to be any good. On *Three Billboards*, 'I don't think any of us knew. I don't even think Martin [McDonagh] knew. I thought it was really good writing but I wasn't madly in love with the part. I would have been psyched to play Sam Rockwell's part but I wasn't that psyched about playing Chief Willoughby.'

This is surprising, because his understated performance as the stoic, small-town police chief suffering from cancer – and trying to rein in

Frances McDormand's tyro of a bereaved mother – is one of the film's highlights. 'It turns out the part wasn't so bad,' he says. 'And then as it turns out the whole movie wasn't just good on the page. You watch it and suddenly – when did Martin McDonagh become one of the Coen Brothers?' He remembers seeing it for the first time with McDonagh on a tiny monitor in a London editing suite. 'I sat there next to him and watched the whole thing and afterwards I just looked at him and said: "Martin, I don't even think you realize how great this is. You're too close but you have something great." I was blown away by it.'

Ninety minutes into chewing our vegetables, I ask if he wants dessert, but he demurs. 'I can be very gluttonous with food. I shouldn't even have had the mac 'n' cheese.' I wonder how he squares drinking alcohol with his strict rules about food. 'It's one of those little things that doesn't really sit with my philosophical straight-edge healthiness idea,' he says. 'There's just no squaring it. I drink beer but I try to drink the lightest drink possible.' He pauses, considering what he has just said. 'On the other hand, sometimes you've just got to say, "F*** it."' He is about to embark on a European break. 'I'm going to go hang out in Italy, Greece, Norway, Sweden.' That's a good itinerary, I say. 'I like to call it a friendship tour. A sweet name for a bender.' Even Hollywood's most laid-back star needs some downtime.

Farmacy
74–76 Westbourne
Grove, London W2

....

Mac 'n' cheese	£10
Asian salad	£13
Quesadilla	£12.75
Avocado	£3.75
Adaptogenic lattes x 2	£12

....

Total (inc. tax and service) –	£57.09

Gwyneth Paltrow

'I'm a real person'

By Jo Ellison

G wyneth Paltrow arrives at Marcus, the Michelin-starred restaurant at the Berkeley Hotel, London, just as the lunch service is getting started. Perfectly blonde, tanned and freckled, the Oscar-winning actress and founder of the online wellness empire Goop radiates the sort of golden aura possessed only by the really, truly famous. But even she can't take the edge off the froideur in the private dining room, which, with its tasteful greys and air of whispered deference, feels a little frigid.

We politely study the menu, a delectation of seasonal recipes whose highlights include a lamb's neck, cooked for 36 hours, served with miso and girolles, and roast bream with Dorset snails. It all sounds deliciously inedible.

'Oh my God,' says Paltrow in that familiar flat-vowelled American drawl. 'What the hell are we going to eat?' She looks at the menu once more before announcing: 'I can't eat this shit. Let's just go up to my suite and order room service . . .' Turns out the author of five cookbooks, including the about-to-be-released *The Clean Plate*, a collection of meal plans, detoxes and cleanses, quite fancies a club sandwich instead.

Minutes later, we step into an apartment-style penthouse overlooking Mayfair. It encapsulates the greige luxury one might find in a romantic comedy by Nancy Meyers. Better still, it's toasty warm. 'I mean, it seems kind of a shame not to make the most of it while I'm here, right?' she says. She kicks off her sneakers and starts sorting prototypes of clothes being developed for Goop's range, G Plan. I wander into the living area to have a closer look at planet Goop.

The dining table is spread with hair and make-up products, all waiting to get Paltrow photo-ready for the opening of a pop-up Goop store. Beside that sits a bouquet of white flowers. Its card reads: 'Missing you. Your husband. x'.

Illustration by James Ferguson

The husband is Brad Falchuk, the scriptwriter and television producer Paltrow married 10 days earlier in Amagansett, New York. Paltrow has been enjoying something 'vaguely' resembling a honeymoon ever since. Tomorrow she will travel back to the US and her children, Moses and Apple, from her previous marriage to the British pop star Chris Martin. The details of the ceremony are only made available a few days later via a post called 'The Wedding Party', on Goop.

From its launch in 2008, Goop was designed to be Paltrow's own breaking news service. It is where, in 2014, she announced she and Martin were 'consciously uncoupling' following 12 and a half years of marriage. And where she decided to go public with her engagement to Falchuk. But from being a 'place to solve my own problems', as she describes its early years, the business has since become a sprawling multi-category business with a staff of 220. It was given a valuation of $250 million during its last round of funding last February.

Goopers still go to the site for advice on everything from 'how to teach kids financial literacy' to the 'merits of having a smart shoe wardrobe'. Some of the advice is fairly benign; other titbits, such as its advocation of coffee enemas or consulting a 'shamanic energy medicine practitioner', have invited widespread criticism and anger. But true Goopers aren't deterred. They buy Goop-endorsed books, accessories, vitamin tablets, clothes, skincare products and sex aids. And increasingly, they meet other Goopers at Goop summits (the next will be in London this spring), where they pay up to $2,000 to take part in wellness workshops, yoga sessions and meditation classes. Not bad for an actress with little or no experience in internet publishing who conceived her business plan at her kitchen table in Belsize Park.

OK, so she wasn't exactly an unknown when she decided to launch. Her brand was already global, she had more than a decade of magazine covers behind her, and when she talks about 'seeing a marketing guy in New York who gave me the name [Goop], and hooked me up with a guy to get it going', one must appreciate that hers is a circle that includes people like Steven Spielberg (who is her godfather) and Brian Chesky, the internet billionaire and co-founder of Airbnb, whom Paltrow still 'calls up for advice'.

'It's bizarre to think back on. I had such a different life then,' says Paltrow of the 'life crisis' that precipitated Goop. 'I was completely burned out. I had done 40 films in a decade, and even though there were aspects of it that were incredible, it was also pretty lonely. I was on the road alone a lot. And I had had my daughter and I thought, I don't want to do that any more. And then I started to realize I was very interested in the digital space. I certainly had no idea what I was getting myself into,' she adds. 'I was trying to figure out WordPress alone in my kitchen. It was ridiculous.'

We are waiting for the room service. Paltrow has ordered a club sandwich, fresh tomato soup and French fries; I have chosen a Niçoise salad and tomato soup, with tea. Is she on any diet right now? 'It sort of goes in phases,' she says. 'Right now I don't know what I'm going for. I eat whatever I want and then I clean up my act for 10 days.' She sighs. 'French fries are my favourite food. And I love alcohol. So it's a balance. I'm a real person who wants to eat delicious stuff.' Annoyingly, she has few of the physical flaws one might expect of a real 46-year-old. Yes, she has the faintest of crinkles around the eyes, and years of intense exercise have sculpted her physique from waifish fragility to svelte athleticism, but she looks pretty much the same as the woman who leapt to global fame in the 1995 thriller *Seven*.

Not everyone was convinced by her early homilies to the benefits of skin cupping and juice fasts. But Paltrow, who first became interested in clean living while investigating alternative treatments following her father's diagnosis with oral cancer in 1999, forged ahead. As a spokesperson for wellness, she was a pioneer, and considering that the market is now estimated by the Global Wellness Institute to be worth some $4.2 trillion, one imagines she feels quite smug.

'I started writing about this kind of stuff when it was ahead of the curve, and we are still ahead of the curve. Even when I started to do yoga, pre-internet, I remember there being very cynical articles about how yoga was culty and weird and for freaks. It's been great watching the sea change. I had this funny experience the other day where I went to a yoga studio in LA and the beautiful 22-year-old girl behind the counter was like, "Have you ever done yoga before?" And I was like: "Bitch, you have this job because I've done yoga before."' It's an anecdote I've read before. But I like it because it sums up precisely the kind of sororal candour that has won her both fans – and a good few detractors. No matter how real, hands-on and 'Hey, let's just order French fries' she may be, people take issue with her life of vitamin blasts and blithe entitlement.

'But this is bullshit,' she says of accusations that Goop represents privilege. 'This idea that wellness is aspirational, and for rich people, it's absolutely not true at all. At the crux of it, the true tenets of wellness – meditation, eating whole foods, drinking a lot of water, sleeping well, thinking good thoughts, trying to be optimistic – are all free.'

Paltrow doesn't pretend that her lithe figure and glowy complexion are genetic gifts. But in sharing the extent of her exercises and skin-brushing techniques, she can seem quite extreme. 'I think the reason why people get pissed off with me is because I'm like, "No, I actually work my ass off in all areas of my life,"' she says. 'Some people are really inspired by that and some people are annoyed by it.'

Lunch is served, arranged prettily by two waiters who are quite giddy to be around her. The tomato soup is fresh and flavoursome. The club sandwich is a towering classic of the five-star-hotel school. Paltrow gets stuck in.

Was she always so driven? 'I think I'm very competitive with myself,' she says, flicking a bit of bacon from the sandwich. 'Part of that is really healthy and I think part of it is really unhealthy. Part of me has a real perfectionist streak and it's punishing and it's not great, but the upside is I always want to be squeezing the marrow out of life.'

Goop is a tidy little business. It was incorporated in 2013. Paltrow raised $10 million in 2015 and a further $15 million in a second round. Her investors include the venture capitalist firms Felix Capital and New Enterprise Associates (NEA); she was made chief executive of Goop in 2017. What is it like, I wonder, to 'be Gwyneth Paltrow' while pitching for investment? 'Oh, it's hilarious. And so brutal,' she replies. 'Firstly, every investor will take the meeting. And then, for about the first 90 seconds, I am Gwyneth Paltrow and maybe they want a selfie for their wife and maybe they tell me about how much they loved *The Royal Tenenbaums*. And then you sit down to do the presentation it's like: "Oh shit, this is what it's like to be an entrepreneur." It's such a great lesson, because when you're a famous person . . . people are always treating you with kid gloves and removing obstacles for you. Investor meetings were a huge wake-up call, in the best way. It was when I realized I'd been treated like a fake person for 20 years.'

Paltrow has now been running the show for three years, but she is unequivocal about the chief executive job. 'No question,' she says. 'It's the hardest thing I've ever done.'

One lesson she has had to learn is greater rigour. In a much-publicized lawsuit last September, Goop was forced to pay $145,000 in fines for unsubstantiated marketing claims regarding the sale of her stone 'eggs' – one jade and another quartz. Goop literature said that, when inserted into the vagina, the eggs could fix hormone levels and aid bladder control. The consumer protection lawsuit filed by Santa Clara County district attorney Jeff Rosen and nine other state prosecutors found those claims to be bunkum.

'As you grow, you realize you have a lot of responsibility and accountability,' says Paltrow. 'We're getting very buttoned-up about all that stuff now,' she adds. 'I think the scariest thing for me is not knowing what I don't know. I have made huge mistakes because I didn't know those particular mistakes were even conceivably possible to make.'

She segues briefly to another misstep, migrating to a new email server – not the sexiest of subjects, considering I'm talking to a woman who actually knows what it's like to date Brad Pitt. But Paltrow seems to care far more about her MailChimp woes than she regrets acting opportunities she might have lost. Does she feel more fulfilled by her work today? 'No. It's apples and oranges,' she replies. 'Acting is so myopic and emotional. When you're acting, you're in your little silo, and you're learning your lines and you're doing your part, and you're an important part but you are still only an important cog in the wheel. Creating and executing a business strategy is far more stimulating.'

That said, Paltrow did recently revisit her role as Pepper Potts for the upcoming Avengers outing of the current Marvel franchise. Was being on set a holiday – or did she sit in her trailer with a tonne of Excel spreadsheets? Obviously, the latter. 'And thank God I have my spreadsheets because I would go crazy now in a trailer,' she says. 'I was on set with my lovely chief of staff and she was like, "I can't believe how much we're sitting around." And I was like, "I can't believe I used to do this with no internet and no business to run on the side."' Film sets have changed in other ways as well. As the princess of Miramax productions, Paltrow was once the prized asset of Harvey Weinstein. When allegations of sexual misconduct first arose about the producer, Paltrow went public with her own story about how Weinstein had tried to make a pass at her in 1995 when they were alone in a hotel room. At the time, Brad Pitt threatened to kill Weinstein if he did anything like it again. And he didn't. But, until last year, Paltrow was silent. Has the culture of Hollywood changed? 'For sure,' she says. 'You can see it, smell it, taste it; it's different. We used to roll our eyes or grit our teeth and be like, "Oh, that's gross," and shake it off. But now, if you were to do those things to a 24-year-old in the workplace, there would absolutely be repercussions. I think it's very healthy and long overdue. And I'm proud I played a little part in it.'

As for Goop, can it grow beyond its founder's image? 'Ultimately, I want to get out of people's faces,' she says. But there are clearly huge gains to be had from a Paltrow endorsement. 'You have to be very judicious about when you pull that lever,' she says.

She is confident, however, that the brand will outgrow her. 'I think you could say that for any founder business, even if they're not a consumer-facing CEO,' argues Paltrow. 'But you can always point to somebody like Coco Chanel or Walt Disney, brands that have always been associated with people. I mean, I didn't name Goop "GwynethPaltrowLifestyleBlog.com". I always knew that I wanted it to be much bigger than I am and to be more of a legacy.' She talks of Stella McCartney, an old friend, whose label is 'so much bigger' than McCartney herself because it stands for some 'amazing values'.

I ask what Goop's amazing values might be. 'I think people see we're trying to solve problems for the modern woman,' she says. That might be getting better sleep, feeling more energetic or eating more healthily. Often, it means improving their sexual health as well.

'Absolutely,' she says. 'When we write about female sexual health, people always get completely up in arms. I always think to myself, why

---

The Berkeley

Wilton Place,
Knightsbridge,
London SW1

....

Room service:

Club sandwich	£24
Tomato soup x 2	£28
French fries	£9
Niçoise salad	£26
Tea	£7
Water	£4.50

....

Total (inc. tax and service) –	£130.94

is this so threatening? I think women really appreciate our content because we're trying to create a space where there's no shame and you can ask questions. I think it's also refreshing, as a woman who considers herself a respectable professional woman, that I have an article about anal sex on the website. It gives people permission to ask a question, or to be curious about it. That's a great thing.' She smiles. 'It's a very small aspect of what we write about, but it gets a lot of coverage, as you can imagine.'

Lunch is over. A team of stylists has arrived to prepare Paltrow for her next appointment. Things are on the move. 'Oh, God. Why did I eat so much?' Paltrow moans as she poses for a mandatory selfie. 'My stomach feels enormous.' It looks tiny. Of course.

Her eyes fall on the flowers. 'Do you want them? I'm leaving tomorrow and they'll only go in the trash.'

I take the flowers. Flowers from Goop. I'm cock-a-hoop.

The Revolutionaries

'A lot of people who care about me tell me to shut up'

Edward Snowden

'I sleep in Russia but I live all around the world'

By Alan Rusbridger

E dward Snowden is not the easiest lunch date. The former National Security Agency operative doesn't fancy talking in a Moscow restaurant so – via an intermediary – we settle on meeting in my hotel and risk the room service. He will present himself at the agreed time. That's all I need to know.

In the end he's 20 minutes late, dressed casually in black jeans and black V-neck, buttoned-up T-shirt, carrying a pair of unbranded dark glasses. He eyes up the small, dimly lit room 203 of the Golden Apple 'boutique' hotel – half an hour's gentle stroll from the Kremlin – with the look of a man who has spent too much time in such places.

How does it compare with room 1014 of the Mira Hotel in Hong Kong, where in June 2013 – having shared many of the NSA's most closely guarded secrets with a few handpicked journalists – Snowden spent a week as the most wanted man in the world?

'A bit smaller, but not dissimilar,' he says. 'The Hong Kong room had a glass bathroom wall here,' he adds, pointing to a bland wall featuring an obligatory hotel watercolour.

The interior of the Mira hotel room is about to become much better known with the US release next week of Oliver Stone's biopic about Snowden, which stars Joseph Gordon-Levitt in the whistle-blower's role. Much of the tensest, most claustrophobic action is filmed in a reconstruction of room 1014 built inside a hangar-like studio in Munich.

During that intense week three years ago, Snowden and two *Guardian* reporters worked on those first stories disclosing the full capabilities that intelligence agencies can now deploy against populations. When he revealed himself as the source he was acclaimed as a hero by some – others recommended the electric chair. I had never met him and was

Illustration by James Ferguson

entirely reliant on the judgment of our veteran reporter Ewen MacAskill, who rang to report (in pre-arranged code owing something to Hollywood) that 'the Guinness is good'.

I first saw his face about an hour before the rest of the world, when MacAskill filed his video interview to New York. Like everyone else there I was struck by his stubbled youth and impressed by his thoughtful articulacy. Today, at 33, there's a touch less stubble, and the hair is a smidgen longer. He says he moves freely around Moscow, seldom recognized, which is surprising since he has changed little since that first picture of him etched itself on our consciousness.

Reading the laminated room service menu card, complete with English translations, he is tempted by the spicy chicken curry with rice and chilli sauce. I go for the risotto with white mushrooms and a 'vinaigrette' salad with herring. Snowden – skinny thin – decides he can't resist the crab cakes, too. We telephone the order for the food, with mineral water.

He has been unwillingly marooned in Moscow since 2013 when – the subject of a giant manhunt – he was forced to leave Hong Kong. How's his Russian coming on? He confirms it's up to ordering in a restaurant, but is reluctant to elaborate. 'All my work's in English. Everybody I talk to I speak to in English,' he says. 'I sleep in Russia but I live all around the world. I don't have a lot of ties to Russia. That's by design because, as crazy as it sounds, I still plan to leave.'

He lives 'mainly' on Eastern Standard Time and spends most of his waking hours online – 'but it always has been so'. He admits he misses the 'sense of home' represented by America, 'but technology overcomes most of that divide. For me, I'm a little bit of an outlier to begin with because, remember, I signed up to go work overseas for the CIA and overseas for the NSA. So it's really not that much different from the postings that I had for the US.

'The only difference is that I'm still posted overseas and I work for the US but they don't realize it.' As anyone who follows him on Twitter knows (he follows just one account: the NSA) he is capable of a very dry wit.

He has seen a version of the Stone movie on one of the director's trips to Moscow, during which Snowden says he would talk to Stone's co-writer, Kieran Fitzgerald, about 'trying to keep the film a little bit closer to being reality'.

'But,' he shrugs, 'I know it's a drama, not a documentary.'

How would he score it out of 10? He avoids a rating. 'On the policy questions, which I think are the most important thing for the public understanding, it's as close to real as you can get in a film.'

He met Gordon-Levitt in Moscow and thought him 'an amazing guy . . . we had lunch together, talked for several hours just about every-thing, our personal lives – what we think about, what we care about. At the time I thought it was just a social visit but, after the fact, he told me that he was actually scoping me out, trying to get my mannerisms.'

Having interviewed Gordon-Levitt's 'Snowden' as part of my own cameo in the film, I can vouch for how well he captures the real thing. Snowden was impressed, too: 'His characterization of me makes me uncomfortable, with the super-deep gravelly voice, but that's because you never hear your own voice the way other people do, right?'

Was he moved by the film, which in flashback revisits the episodes in his life that led to what he calls his 'tortured' decision to engineer the biggest leak of classified documents in history? 'There's always going to be something emotional about seeing something that you did retold as a story by other people. It shows a reflection of how your choices matter to them. Three years later, seeing what we thought was going to be a five-day story still being reported on [makes me think] that I wasn't crazy.'

There's a knock on the door – which would have caused a spasm of paranoid anxiety in the Mira in 2013. Now it's just room service. The floor is so small the waiter balances the tray on the bed and Snowden has to perch his chicken curry on his knee. The water is missing. My vinaigrette salad turns out to be cubed beetroot. I avoid the herrings.

Once he nods at the iPhone recording our interview and expands on a point 'in case someone is listening'. The first time I met him – to see how he was surviving in his new circumstances in spring 2014 – my iPhone had displayed a giant red thermometer, a sign of alarming over-heating. Snowden had observed mildly it was because so many different people were trying to listen in.

He confirms he received no money from the movie, adding of his tan-gential experience of Hollywood: 'When I was told that there was going to be a film made about me, it was a scary thing, one of the most terrify-ing things I can imagine. But, looking back, I hope it helps. I'm cautiously optimistic that it will.'

He looks back over the period since the revelations and reflects that all three branches of government in the US – Congress, courts, president – have changed their position on mass surveillance. 'We can actually start to impose more oversight on spies, rather than giving them a free pass to do whatever simply because we're scared, which is understandable but clearly not ethical.'

What of subsequent developments in the UK, where the government's response has been to propose laws that not only sanction, post hoc, the intelligence activities that were revealed to be happening, but extend them? He says it was not his intention to tell the world how to structure their laws, but to give people a voice in the process. 'The laws have gotten worse in some countries. France has gone very far, so too, of course, countries like Russia, China. In Britain there's an authoritarian trend.

'We don't allow police to enter and search any home. We don't typically reorder the operation of a free society for the convenience of the police – because that is the definition of a police state,' he says, mopping up the last of the rice. 'And yet some spies and officials are trying to persuade us that we should. Now, I would argue there's no real question that police in a police state would be more effective than those in a free and liberal society where the police operate under tighter constraints. But which one would you rather live in?'

He has finished his curry and pronounces it 'quite good'. The crab cakes are abandoned after a bite. 'Less good,' he says. We order ice cream – vanilla, strawberry and chocolate for him, sorbet for me. The voice on the phone launches into a complicated explanation of why, with five scoops in all, we can have a discount.

Does he never lose sleep at night wondering whether Isis terrorists might not have gained some useful advantage from the information he disclosed?

Well, firstly, he says, in all the recent European attacks the suspects were known to the authorities, who thus had the ability to target them without having to scoop up everyone else's data as well. Secondly, he points out, Osama bin Laden stopped using a mobile phone in 1998 – not because of leaks to newspapers but because 'there is an aggressive form of Darwinism in terrorist circles. Long before we, the public, know about any of these surveillance measures, they have already known for years because, if they had not, they are already dead.'

'But,' he goes on, 'let's say that the newspapers had decided this should not be public. Let's say the intelligence services had been able to continue using these programmes in secret. Would it have stopped any of the terrorist attacks that have occurred in the last three years? There's no public evidence that that's the case. In fact, there's no classified evidence that that's the case, or else we'd be reading it in the newspapers.'

We move on to talking about stories alleging Russian hacking of the NSA itself and of the Democratic party's governing body, the Democratic National Committee. The former involved a group calling itself the Shadow Brokers, who threatened to auction very sophisticated alleged NSA surveillance tools. The latter was a collection of DNC emails published – to general embarrassment – by WikiLeaks in July.

The Shadow Broker leak, says Snowden, 'doesn't strike me as a whistle-blower: that strikes me as a warning. It's political messaging being carried out through information disclosure.' And the DNC hack, where, as he observes, the conventional wisdom is that it was the Russians? 'This is part of the problem of this surveillance free-for-all that we're allowing to occur by refusing to moderate our own behaviour. We've set a kind of global precedent that anything is possible and nothing is prohibited.

'Now, the fact the DNC got hacked is not surprising and interesting. We're hacking political parties around the world, so is every country. What makes it interesting is that some of the things taken from this server were published afterwards. That's quite novel. I think.'

Which makes him think what? 'That it's for political effect.'

He says – as someone who used to try and do this sort of thing to the Chinese – that it would be easy to attribute the hack to whoever had done it. 'But this creates a problem because, let's say, the NSA has the smoking gun that says the Russians hacked the DNC, and they tell us the Russians hacked the DNC, how can we be sure? It presumes a level of trust that no longer exists.'

The ice creams arrive along with an espresso, replacing the first set of dishes on the bed. Snowden spills a bit of chicken curry on the duvet and apologetically mops it up with a towel.

Aren't we beginning to discover that no digital databases are secure? 'We are living through a crisis in computer security the likes of which we've never seen,' he says. 'But until we solve the fundamental problem, which is that our policy incentivizes offence to a greater degree than defence, hacks will continue unpredictably and they will have increasingly larger effects and impacts.'

The answer, he thinks, is that there ought to be some form of liability for negligence in software architecture, such as would apply in the food industry. He adds, drily: 'People from my tribe will be extraordinarily mad at me for suggesting regulation in the terms of negligence for software security.'

He has finished his ice cream and declines coffee. Life in Moscow is getting better, he says: 'I'm more open now than I've been since 2013.' He sees few people – such meetings as this are rare – and divides his time between public speaking (which pays the bills) and devising tools to protect the digital security of journalists. He would rather not go into 'the family stuff' or how often he sees Lindsay Mills, his partner, who was left behind in Hawaii when he quit his job for the NSA there and disappeared to Hong Kong.

His American lawyer, Ben Wizner at the American Civil Liberties Union, is reported to be preparing to launch a petition to President Obama to grant Snowden a pardon before he steps down. Snowden will only say: 'Of course I hope they're successful but this has never really been about what happens to me. No matter how the outcome shakes out, it's something I can live with.'

Golden Apple Hotel
11 Malaya Dmitrovka str.,
Moscow, Russia

Room service:

Spicy chicken curry	£5.60
Crab cakes	£6.35
Risotto with white mushrooms	£5.20
Vinaigrette salad with herring	£5.60
Ice cream	£3.35
Sorbet	£3.35
Espresso	£3.35
Total –	£32.80

His chances of a happy ending under President Donald Trump would be zero, I observe. What about under President Hillary Clinton? 'You're trying to drag me into a political quagmire,' he protests. He collects himself, looking intensely at the ground, before sidestepping the question: 'I think we should have better choices. We're a country of 330 million people and we seem to be being asked to make a choice between individuals whose lives are defined by scandal. I simply think we should be capable of more.'

If he's tough on the options in US politics, his willingness to tweet criticism of Russian politics to his 2.3 million followers has not gone unnoticed. 'A lot of people who care about me tell me to shut up, but if I was married to my own self-interest, I never would have left Hawaii.

'I can't fix the human rights situation in Russia, and realistically my priority is to fix my own country first, because that's the one to which I owe the greatest loyalty. But though the chances are it will make no difference, maybe it'll help.'

He gathers up his dark glasses: it's time for him to melt into the Moscow crowds. A final question: the Stone film shows him spiriting his trove of secrets out of the NSA on a micro-SD card hidden in a Rubik's Cube. True or false?

'Oliver confirmed in an interview recently that that's a touch of the dramatic licence, but that's only because I wouldn't confirm or deny how it really happened. I will say that I gave Rubik's Cubes to everyone in my office, it's true. I really did that.' And with that he is gone.

Bana al-Abed

'Just a small girl in a war zone'

By Mehul Srivastava

During the four-year battle for Aleppo, the world was flooded with images of the toll it took on the civilians trapped between the Syrian regime and opposition militias. As the siege tightened, the ancient city was dubbed Syria's Stalingrad, enduring relentless street fighting, indiscriminate barrel bombings and deadly 'triple-taps' – that killed civilians, killed those who came to rescue the wounded and finally destroyed the hospitals that the few survivors could reach.

It was a siege smothered in myth and propaganda. With few independent journalists left to document the collapse, it had to be archived on social media – immediate, unfiltered and often inescapable. In the deluge of those images, one voice cut through the noise, like a clarion call broadcasting our failure to protect the weakest. It belonged to Bana al-Abed, a precocious young girl whose Twitter feed – managed by her mother – captured in painful granularity the confusion and fear of being a child caught in a war. Each tweet felt like a frame in a horror film – one in which her followers worried constantly she might be killed. She became for many the face of Aleppo.

And here she is in front of me, wide-eyed in a shopping mall in Ankara with her mother, Fatemah, as my lunch guest.

'My name is Bana, I'm seven years old . . . This is my last moment to live or die.' So wrote Bana on 13 December, amid one of the heaviest bombing campaigns. Three days later, as the bombing drew closer, she wrote: 'Please save us now.' A few weeks earlier she had posted: 'I am sick now, I have no medicine, no home, no clean water. This will make me die even before a bomb kill me.'

In those terrible weeks, the Twitter feed @AlabedBana went viral. It

Illustration by James Ferguson

brought fame: J. K. Rowling, author of the Harry Potter books, shared Bana's tweets with her millions of followers. It brought danger: for the Syrian regime, it was a daily reminder of the suffering they wrought upon civilians, marking her first for character assassination and finally, her mother felt, for death. Eventually, it brought her to Turkey.

Now, she is one of 3 million Syrians here, after the largest human exodus since the partition of India. An object of fascination – child, social media legend and witness to war – she is also a pint-sized prop in a geopolitical propaganda game. Both, I explain to Fatemah, are good reasons for me to have lunch with them. But, as any parent will tell you, choosing a place to take a seven-year-old for lunch is fraught with peril: too formal, and the child loses interest; too adventurous, and the child is put off.

For advice, I ask a six-year-old, Mira, the daughter of a colleague. We have settled on the Kent Mall in Ankara – what it lacks in fine dining, it makes up for with a huge playground – and ice cream.

Bana approves of the choice. Her hands are swiftly entwined with Mira's, who I have brought along to help break the ice. We walk through the shiny mall, the sort of place young Turks so love, struggle with an elevator and eventually reach a cul-de-sac that leads to Gelato Ice & Caffé, which has pop music on the stereo and a decor that tries – and fails – to evoke a 'Ruby Tuesday' in the American Midwest. Our table is a latter-day Tower of Babel. Bana speaks Arabic and a little English; her new friend, Mira, speaks Turkish and English; Bana's mother speaks near-fluent English and Arabic; I speak neither Turkish nor Arabic; and my Arabic translator, Jihad (who jokes later that he better change his name if he wants to move to America), is so excited to meet Bana that he often forgets to translate.

We order quickly: a burger with onion rings and a Coke for her; a mushroom pizza and chicken wings for mum; fajitas for me; manti (cheesy ravioli, covered in yoghurt) for her new friend, Mira. Simple and unexciting – but a feast compared to the fare in her months under siege.

For many months, Bana has been an Anne Frank-like figure, a visceral, online diary of the rawest of human emotions. But she has also been accused of being a tool of propaganda. In the version of the Aleppo siege propagated by pro-Assad groups, including the machinery of RT (formerly Russia Today) and cyber trolls, Assad was a brave leader fighting terrorists and defending the world from Isis. Bana's story helped puncture that lie and for months her mother has been hounded by people claiming they were faking their tweets, that Bana spoke no English, and was being manipulated to generate fake sympathy for terrorists. There were death threats and the fear of being singled out for execution.

Behind this global profile is a girl we know so little about, other than the fact that she loves Harry Potter and didn't want to die. She may have captured the inhumanity of war for millions, but she remained veiled, a totemic image of every child in war. In possibly a first for Lunch with the *FT*, we strike a deal – we'll eat something first and talk, and then, we'll all share ice cream.

Bana is proud of her English, which she speaks like any child talking in a foreign language would – sometimes haltingly, sometimes in a rush of words unconnected by grammar. But she is thoughtful right now. She says it was her and her mother's idea to go on Twitter and that she wanted to share a picture of herself with the world. That first tweet, on 24 September 2016, was three words long. 'I need peace,' it read.

After dozens of television interviews in the early days, many of her sentences sound like stock phrases ('I want to help the children of Aleppo'; 'I want to be the voice of children of Syria'). We switch to the translator, hoping she will open up more. I ask her if she understands how different her life has been to those of other children her age.

She thinks for a while, and then delivers a rush of words, tangled up in emotion. 'In Aleppo, I couldn't feel like a child,' she says. 'I couldn't sleep, I couldn't find a safe place. There were bombs dropping overhead, in the morning, afternoon, night. I couldn't find any food – biscuits, or normal food, like normal children. We were always worried – when will a bomb come on our heads? I wanted to go to school, but my school was bombed.'

She and her family had a particularly close call. Their kitchen was destroyed one evening in a bombing raid when they happened to be taking shelter in the living room. Her mother shows me photos on her phone of a shattered room, and her children covered in dust and dirt. The timestamp said 27 November 7.55pm. She describes what happened. 'My husband and his brother and my mother-in-law were sitting with Bana, there is a family conversation. Suddenly, the rockets came down, like birds in the sky. I was in the kitchen, I was cooking. Thank God I just moved for two seconds from the kitchen.'

Bana starts to tell me about her friends. 'I had a friend, her name was Yasmin, and I had another friend, her name was Fatma, and we were the same age and we played with each other all the time . . . My friend Yasmin is dead. Fatma's still alive, but we cannot contact her,' she says. Yasmin's death inspired one of her most powerful tweets, with a picture of a young girl's bloodied and lifeless face. 'Oh dear world, I am crying tonight, this is my friend killed by a bomb tonight. I can't stop crying.'

It seems like a cruel moment for our food to arrive. Our waitress bustles around, bringing Bana her burger, Fatemah her pizza and wings. The wings are spicy, and Fatemah is pleased. Bana's burger is too big to fit into her mouth. She loves it, she loves the onion rings, she loves her Coke. I notice she's missing a few teeth. She counts them out in English – seven – and then flashes a big grin.

I remember a tweet of hers from October, when she smiled into the camera, holding a tooth that had come loose. The next morning, she tweeted again. 'The tooth fairy is afraid of the bombing here, it run away to its hole. When the war finishes, it will come.'

Fatemah explains how the tweeting worked. She would ask Bana how she felt, or what she was thinking, and would type out her words for her. Even towards the end, they had solar panels to charge their phones and they could sometimes pick up a mobile phone signal from government-held Aleppo or from the satellite internet provided by Turkish and other NGOs.

Bana has her mouth full, so I speak with Fatemah. She's 27, and had been training to become a lawyer when the war came to Aleppo. I have to ask her how she feels about her child being used 'as a tool for propaganda' – first for the anti-government forces and now by the Turkish government. When the Turkish government brokered the chaotic retreat of fighters and civilians from east Aleppo, they found Bana and her family in a makeshift camp in the north-western Syrian province of Idlib, and flew them by helicopter to Ankara. She and her two younger brothers ended up in front of the cameras, sitting on President Recep Tayyip Erdogan's lap. Now, even as Turkey sends in its own military, arms opposition fighters and demands the overthrow of Syrian

President Bashar al-Assad, they are presented as symbols of his magnanimity.

Fatemah has been thinking about this, she says. She worries what it will do to her child. Her sons, aged three and five, have known nothing but war and even today are scared to be alone, crying in their sleep. 'Bana wants to help, but also I want the world to understand that Bana is a child,' she says. 'We want her to be a normal child, and live like a child of the world, without war, without anything.'

But Bana has a strong personality, she adds. 'For my Bana, it's different because when her father and I raised her, we gave her her own personality. We don't want to make her what we want – we don't want a robot, do like this or do like that,' she says.

'The war itself, it's a big teacher,' she adds. 'Even for the children. They know and they recognize that when they hear the bombs, they know the sound, which bomb it is. They know if it was a cluster bomb, if it was a barrel bomb, if it was phosphorus bombs. They know everything.' They pick it up, from listening to adults, from reacting to their fear, from what they hear on the television. 'If you ask a little one, three years old, where's your house, he'll say it's destroyed. Why? Because of the bomb. Who sent this bomb? The war plane. He knows.

'But they don't know real life. If you say, "Draw something," maybe they will draw a rocket, maybe they draw a bomb. [Normal] children draw flowers, butterflies, because they imagine life.'

Bana is full and she wants ice cream. We reach another compromise – she can go and play in the amusement centre with Mira. The two girls run off with Mira's mother and, as Fatemah and I keep talking, my phone pings with pictures of Bana on the swings, on a rock wall, playing an arcade game. She is laughing – Mira is her first new friend in Turkey and, although they can barely understand one another, they have bonded.

I return to my question, about the balance between being a little girl, a siege survivor and a global symbol. As a mother, does she feel torn? Fatemah answers cautiously. She is used to the fact that her daughter is an object of fascination but daunted by the idea that she is now seen as a little girl who speaks about big issues, maybe without fully understanding them. Now in Turkey, all Bana talks about is going back to Aleppo, she says, about saving the children of Syria. Fatemah herself is more circumspect – she is considering a life in Turkey, learning the language, looking for schools for her children.

'She is a child of war, and a child of war knows more than adults and cares for others more than adults do, because they feel there is something lost,' she says. 'During the war, she was the daughter, but also the big sister to two younger brothers, and she wanted to be the angel, the saviour for them. She was always afraid to lose one of us, so she had a lot of energy to do something. But now she is free, but she almost has to continue what she started during the war – she talks about returning to Syria, that Syria is free, and she is going back to her street, her school, her house.'

Fatemah wonders aloud how the war and her celebrity status have made her daughter want things she herself does not. Fatemah wants a normal life, to shop in a mall, to finish her degree. Bana, she says, wants greater things. She giggles as she thinks of an example. 'If you ask her, "Why did God put you on earth?" she says, "My God created me to help people." I don't know how she thought of it. We asked her, and she answered like that. We were surprised that she talks like this.'

She says Bana's answer made her laugh at first, and her husband, too. 'If we try to ask her this question again, she feels angry. "Why are you all laughing?" she asks.'

Perhaps the most magnetic thing about Bana's tweets was that they were, for the most part, a mirror of shattered innocence. Most days, they were simply a reflection of how she had survived, what she had done, what she had seen. They were the windows of childhood, opened up to a gruesome world. I ask Fatemah if she was surprised that her tweets got so much attention, that even J. K. Rowling paid attention to them.

Gelato Ice and Caffé
Kent Mall, Ankara

....

Cheeseburger x 2	TL46
Funghi pizza	TL22
Steak fajita	TL44
Butter manti	TL19
Penne pesto	TL21
Hot wings	TL18
Combo platter	TL22
Coke x 3	TL19.50
Fanta	TL6.50
Tea	TL6.50
Ayran	TL6
Bottled water x 5	TL15
Turkish coffee x 2	TL15
Coffee	TL9
Ice cream x 5	TL51

....

Total (inc. service) – TL360.50 (£79)

'When Bana was talking on Twitter, she was talking about her life, not politics. There is no agenda in there, there is nothing, just a small girl in a war zone. She wants to live, she wants to go to school. At night, she heard bombs; in the morning, she heard bombs; in the afternoon, she heard bombs. She saw her friend dead. She wanted to leave. She showed people the garden in which she was playing, but she can't now because it's bombed. Showed the world that, "Look, this is my window, and look what I see: I see bombs."'

Bana and her new friend have returned. She picks out a waffle cone, with sprinkles on it, and two scoops – one strawberry, one vanilla. Fatemah asks for a Turkish coffee. She puts a small hairband on her daughter's long hair, and braids Mira's so it matches Bana's.

And suddenly, ice cream in hand, hairband in place, fresh from a play-ground, giggling with her new friend, Bana is just a seven-year-old child. Nothing more.

Maria Alyokhina

'Don't quit what you've started'

By Max Seddon

Maria Alyokhina is the closest thing modern-day Russia has to a rock star. And the diminutive 29-year-old, clad in black with mousy blonde hair spilling out from under a beret, isn't even a musician. For the past four years, she and Nadezhda Tolokonnikova, fellow founder of the feminist punk art collective Pussy Riot, have travelled the world with the story of their time in remote prison camps – where they were sentenced to two years for their extraordinary protest against Vladimir Putin on the altar of Moscow's main cathedral. They have made music videos with Chloë Sevigny and posed for photographs with celebrities from Yoko Ono to Hillary Clinton. They even had a scene-stealing cameo in a Putin-themed episode of *House of Cards*. Yet in her native city she cuts a low-key figure.

'Who could ever have thought all this'd really happen,' she sighs, as I turn on my tape recorder.

I arrived at Dom 12, an unassuming café tucked into Moscow's expensive Golden Mile district, to find her waiting for me with her 10-year-old son, Filya, who has just got out of school, and Sasha, a friend-cum-assistant. It's a rainy Thursday, and the place is nearly empty. If the few customers have recognized Alyokhina, they're not paying any attention. We address each other with the informal *ty* in Russian, even though we have met only once before, when I kicked her and Tolokonnikova out of the *FT* bureau in the late hours of our office building's summer party. (I'm still not entirely sure how they wound up there.)

The café, which vaguely attempts to emulate a smoky French brasserie, is a favourite late-night haunt of Moscow's liberal intelligentsia. It's also just a short walk from Christ the Saviour, the site of the

Illustration by James Ferguson

infamous protest that made Pussy Riot's name. Poignancy aside, the real reason we are here is because Filya needs to pick up his kit for football practice from his father's place down the street.

In February 2012, Alyokhina and three other young women in bright tights and balaclavas crashed the cathedral altar to stage a 40-second performance, 'Virgin Mary, Drive out Putin!' 'None of us thought there would be charges or a sentence when we did it,' she says – but a week later they were on the run. After a bizarre trial that evoked Soviet-era proceedings against dissident artists, they were sentenced to two years in prison for 'hooliganism motivated by religious hatred'. 'We joked that, if they caught us, we would be the new dissidents,' says Alyokhina, 'which was just what happened.'

Pussy Riot owe their stardom foremost to the Kremlin. After tens of thousands of middle-class liberal Muscovites had taken to the streets in the dead of winter to protest against Putin, the Kremlin stoked a culture war aimed at convincing Russia's 'silent majority' that the opposition were a bunch of louche, wealthy perverts. Pussy Riot were the perfect poster girls. State TV ran endless denunciations from vituperative hard-liners. The case inspired new laws that banned 'offending religious believers', as well as 'gay propaganda', attending unauthorized protests and reposting allegedly 'extremist' content, measures that have been used to jail hundreds.

Pussy Riot were always received much more warmly in the west, where Putin has become a bête noire of the feminist and LGBTQ movements – largely thanks to them. In Russia they continue to divide opinion even among fellow opposition activists, some of whom see them as a garish distraction.

But Alyokhina is now a rebel with a different cause. She divides her time between work on behalf of Russian prisoners at home and travelling the west to tell their stories. In August, she was arrested by police in the far-flung city of Yakutsk for protesting on behalf of a political prisoner; three months later, she was performing in London's Saatchi Gallery. She faces the classic punk rocker's dilemma, I think: how to stay true to your roots while being embraced by the mainstream. 'Maybe some people live according to a pre-prepared plan in the form of school, university and a career somewhere,' she says. 'That's just not me.'

Alyokhina and Tolokonnikova spent their first year of freedom trying to bring their message about Russian political prisoners to the world. Although the group made as much as $700,000 in 2014 from donations and appearances at places such as Glastonbury, the money that Alyokhina saw went to two organizations she had helped to set up: Zona Prava, a human rights NGO, and Mediazona, an excellent news site that focuses on the myriad injustices of Russia's court and penal system. 'We didn't make any money,' she says. 'I had some savings. I'm not the sort of person who needs a lot. I rented a room. That was it.'

The waitress arrives and, in keeping with the café's faux-euro theme, I order the French onion soup and chicken schnitzel. But Alyokhina demurs: 'I don't really want to eat, I don't know if that's all right,' she says, asking simply for water and a large Americano.

'I should tell you that I've actually got huge problems choosing things. Choosing something is a whole adventure for me,' she adds.

'Especially clothes,' Filya chimes in.

'That's why I limit myself to one colour in my life,' she says.

Sasha, meanwhile, orders the onion soup and a falafel plate, and Filya chooses a risotto, apple juice and a chocolate cake. Alyokhina balks at the risotto before I explain that the *FT* will be picking up the tab. 'Seriously, that costs Rbs700 [£9]?' Alyokhina says. 'I've brought you to a bourgeois place. Now I'm starting to feel ashamed.'

Her opposition to Putin may have defined her life as an activist, but she has no interest at all in talking about him. 'We have this habit to talk just about the changes that the state provokes – the repressions, all the horrors we are living through,' she says.

But doesn't it worry her that Pussy Riot's main audience is outside Russia? A long pause follows. 'I've got five huge cardboard boxes in my attic with all the letters that people sent me for the two years I was in prison,' she says. 'They told their own stories. And for many people our story became the reason for changes in their life.'

The furore around her trial has clearly affected her less than her time in prison in Berezniki, a town in the northern Ural Mountains. Her memoir, *Riot Days*, is largely devoted to that period. It was in prison, she says, that she discovered what has become the Pussy Riot project's main purpose. 'People came up to me and Nadya and said, "Girls, if you don't change this, if you don't tell people about it, then no one will."'

Alyokhina's childhood was all too typical of Russia's turbulent 1990s.

She grew up without her father – she only met him after seeking him out at 21 – and was raised by her mother. Her teens were spent hanging out in a dormitory in the Hotel Ukraine, a Stalinist skyscraper whose lobby was full of mafia types and prostitutes, and going to poetry readings in a heroin addict's burnt-out flat. She changed school four times, then went hitchhiking as her classmates sat university exams.

'They discourage people from thinking and asking questions, they only teach you to follow the rules and submit without explanation or, most importantly, reason,' she says. 'Obviously I didn't like that. Who would?'

While she was at one of those schools, Alyokhina was introduced to a lesbian couple who asked her to look after their cats in a grim Moscow suburb when they left Russia. Gradually, the apartment became a hangout for members of the underground art collective Voina, or War. They shocked Russia with politically charged performances, crowned with a brilliant escapade where they snuck out in the dead of night to draw a penis on a bridge over St Petersburg's canal so it would raise, erect, to face the local FSB headquarters.

The political point was often muddled – they were more anti-authoritarian than doctrinally anti-Kremlin – but Voina always delivered in shock value. In one notorious performance, a woman shoplifted a frozen chicken from a hypermarket by partly tucking it into her vagina. Voina's radical action made them the *enfants terribles* of the Russian art world, but Alyokhina was more interested in political protest. While a student, she took Filya to environmental demonstrations in a sling, then a stroller. As Voina fragmented between its Moscow and St Petersburg cliques, some of the women hit on the idea of Pussy Riot as a showier spin-off inspired by feminist theory and riot grrrl bands. Or as she puts it: 'Filming a frozen chicken being pushed up a c*** was good, but it wasn't for a mass audience.'

Food arrives for everyone except Alyokhina. The onion soup is surprisingly authentic, given that Putin has passed 'counter-sanctions' against the Gruyère with which it is ostensibly dressed, along with all other western cheeses. The slightly soggy schnitzel is decorated with a cabbage-and-dill 'salad' and sits on top of a goopy yellow mass that I think is mustard sauce.

I realize Alyokhina – who went on hunger strike in prison to protest about the lack of vegetarian meals – has forgotten to order anything. At a loss, she asks Filya to pick. 'I chose onion soup for you!' he says. 'I don't want soup,' she replies. 'I chose risotto for you!' says Filya, having just devoured one himself.

'I don't want that either. So then I don't need anything,' Alyokhina sniffs, before turning to me. 'Do you smoke?' I don't, but agree to accompany her outside. She asks for a second Americano, before we convince her to order a beetroot salad.

By the time of her release from prison, Pussy Riot had become a global sensation. The two women spent the next year taking their message to the international jet set. Alyokhina and Tolokonnikova had never been particularly close friends, had only done one performance together before the cathedral, and served their sentences in different prisons. The remaining members of Pussy Riot, whose identities are mostly unknown, spoiled an Amnesty International bash in Pussy Riot's honour in New York by disowning Alyokhina and Tolokonnikova in an open letter.

Many lofty plans never came to fruition. Madonna wanted to make a movie about them, but the idea fell apart over creative differences. 'It would have been a very particular film,' Alyokhina says, without elaborating. They scored a hefty advance for a book from Penguin, but spent it without delivering a manuscript (Alyokhina ultimately repaid the debt by producing a book by herself). Alyokhina then went to Cambodia with Tolokonnikova's husband, Pyotr Verzilov, who had masterminded their support campaign while they were behind bars, to write it. Instead of producing a manuscript, they had a brief affair.

Though friends describe their marriage as more of a business arrangement, Tolokonnikova was furious. She and Alyokhina have performed separately since 2015, though they insist they are still friends. Now, Tolokonnikova spends much of her time in the US making music revolving around Putin, Trump and the word 'vagina'.

Alyokhina's latest project is a play, *Burning Doors*, developed with the Belarus Free Theatre, who put on underground shows in a garage in their repressive homeland. The play is often uncomfortable viewing thanks to its unflinching depictions of the physical violence and psychological pressure Alyokhina endured while in prison.

She filed dozens of appeals against the prison wardens and went on hunger strike several times. She was eventually transferred to a better prison, while several of the wardens were fired. Since public attention died away, however, things have taken a turn for the worse. In November, Mediazona reported that three women had killed themselves at the prison this summer under duress from sweatshop-like conditions in its sewing factory. Does she not wish she'd had more of an effect on the system?

'It's not about the state. It's about the people who were touched by this story and the changes that have happened,' she says, before asking for another coffee, her third. 'I try not to drink more than eight,' she says.

It's getting dark. Sasha runs off with Filya to football practice. 'I asked him once, at school, do they ask you where I am? . . . He says, I tell them my mother's in prison because she sang a loud song against Putin in church. And I realized you need to keep things simple sometimes,' Alyokhina beams. After we go for another cigarette, I take the opportunity to ask her about her personal life. Last year she started an improbable romance with one of her biggest detractors when she began dating Dmitry Tsorionov, leader of the hardline activists who lobbied for harsher sentences against her.

She met Tsorionov at a party last autumn, curious to find out what had motivated him. After a two-hour theological discussion, they went to buy a bottle of wine; one thing led to another and they became an item. He was recently kicked out of his own Christian group, God's Will, for failing to disown her. Her circle was also shocked; Tolokonnikova made a thinly veiled reference to a 'friend f***ing

Dom 12	
Mansurovsky Pereulok, Moscow	
Onion soup with Gruyère x 2	Rbs700
Risotto with white mushrooms	Rbs700
Chicken schnitzel with cabbage	Rbs590
Falafel with grilled vegetables	Rbs450
Chocolate cake	Rbs370
Chocolate fondant	Rbs430
Beetroot salad with cheese mousse	Rbs400
Mint tea	Rbs200
Cappuccino with cinnamon	Rbs230
Double americano x 3	Rbs600
Milk x 3	Rbs90
Still water	Rbs300
Black tea	Rbs250
Thyme	Rbs50
Fresh apple juice	Rbs350
Total (with discount) –	Rbs4,568 (£60)

a fascist'. I think the story, which recently hit the Moscow hipster press, is a suitably touching conclusion to Alyokhina's mission – winning over her biggest detractor so much that they fell in love. But it turns out they have already broken up. 'We had a fight,' she says bashfully. 'Because of different stuff. It's hard to say. It's complicated.'

She needs to go and pick up Filya, then pack her bags for a trip to Berlin and the UK. The constant touring must make it hard to keep her grounded, I say. But she sees Pussy Riot as a community she takes wherever she goes.

'When you do something, you realize that people immediately show up and stand up with you,' she says. 'The point is that it's better to be brave and honest than just to be a function of this system, which is going to wear itself down in the end. It's important to be consistent. Don't quit what you've started, don't give up, don't walk away. It's important that those aren't just words.'

We walk over to Filya's father's house, where Alyokhina gives me a samizdat copy of her memoir, which has a quote from feminist icon Chris Kraus on the back: 'This book is freedom.' I think of Alyokhina's final sentiments as I leave: 'At every stage, you have to do everything you can. Everything you feel.'

Hyeonseo Lee

'In my life there are so many what-ifs'

By Victor Mallet

Hyeonseo Lee bursts into the quiet warmth of the traditional Korean restaurant, bringing with her a blast of sub-zero air from the wintertime streets of Seoul. A miniature hurricane and a woman of strong will – 'obstinate' is how she puts it herself – she is not at all the doll-faced persona suggested in photographs. Now 36, she escaped on foot across the frozen Yalu river into China from her home in North Korea at the age of 17. For the next decade, she survived abusive Chinese pimps, gangsters, importunate marriage suitors, informers and police interrogators, and then escaped again to seek asylum and a new home in South Korea.

Her traumas and adventures did not stop there. She returned to China in 2009 to smuggle her mother and brother out of North Korea and eventually had to extract them from a prison in Laos. She is now one of the most prominent global voices of the subjugated North Korean people, a bestselling author and public speaker and a campaigner against the thriving Chinese trade in Korean sex slaves. With North Korea developing nuclear weapons and long-range missiles, and Donald Trump questioning America's existing security commitments to its Asian allies, there has rarely been a more important time to hear the truth about the secretive, paranoid state of North Korea and its symbiotic relationship with the neighbouring Chinese superpower.

Lee has arrived 15 minutes late to Sosonjae restaurant. Since our dinner appointment was set for 5pm, early even by Korean standards, I am hardly complaining as she flings her coat aside and we order a Korean set meal, starting with vegetable pancake and *japchae*, a salad of glass noodles made from sweet potato and flavoured with sesame oil. The restaurant's name means 'house of simple food'.

Illustration by James Ferguson

I start by asking about identity and truthfulness, an issue that has haunted North Korean exiles – and played into the hands of Pyongyang's propagandists – ever since the most prominent among them were found to have lied or exaggerated their already gruesome experiences in their memoirs.

Lee, according to those who first heard her story and helped her tell it to the world, is different, not least because she openly loves her home-land and is able to evoke the cosy normality of family life in the north as well as the horror of public executions, the mindless worship of the Kim dynasty and the famine of the 1990s. Lee's North Korea is not just a country where peasants starve to death and denounce their neighbours – though it is that place, too – but one where people fall in love, friends gather to (illegally) watch foreign videos and a young girl delights in a new pair of shoes.

Some memories, she admits, are 'very painful', especially those of her narrow escape from servitude in a brothel in the north-eastern Chinese city of Shenyang and her harrowing journey to smuggle her family out of North Korea and across China to freedom. But she is conscious of being peculiarly lucky, perhaps even the recipient of the kind of miracle attributed to the Christian God.

'In my life there are so many "what ifs?" What if I was repatriated by the Chinese police when I was caught by them? What if I was raped by the Chinese gangsters? What if when I brought my family out of the country . . .'

Her voice tails off. 'My mum and my brother and me, even today we are not talking about that experience.' A few months ago, a fellow defect-or arranged the extraction of her own parents from North Korea via China; the Chinese police caught them and repatriated them, and the mother committed suicide by swallowing poison on the bus before recrossing the border. The father's fate is unknown.

Lee is *The Girl with Seven Names* (her autobiographical book describes how she escaped detection in China, learning the language and living under a series of assumed identities), and unless the two Koreas are reunified, I will probably never know her real name ('A girly name,' is all she will say), which must remain secret to protect relatives and friends left behind under the dictatorship of Kim Jong Un. She chose the name Hyeonseo – whose two parts mean 'sunshine' and 'good luck' – to celebrate her emergence from the 'long tunnels' of darkness into her new life of freedom in South Korea, and insists that even her mother must use it all the time.

'Because if they use the old name at home, then they are going to get used to calling me by my original name and make a mistake on the outside when we are around with people. She says I'm trying my best to erase my name. Of course we can't forget about the name but you just get used to it.'

The dangers are real. South Korea's National Intelligence Service has warned Lee that Pyongyang's agents may try to kidnap her – it has happened to other critics of Pyongyang and Beijing – and make an example of her in North Korea.

With chopsticks, we are delicately wrapping slices of boiled pork – one of Lee's favourites – with tiny raw shrimp and radish kimchi into a pickled leaf and popping the rolls into our mouths.

'That's why the NIS tells me, every event, when you receive an invitation, better check if that's a real event. And the one thing they told me is, don't go to Southeast Asia, including China.' After her book was published in 2015 and while she was in New York, she says, the NIS told her that Pyongyang had sent a message to its embassies abroad accusing her of slandering North Korea and ordering them to 'do something'.

After just two generations of separation since the end of the Korean war in 1953, the ill-nourished people above the 38th parallel north are on average a couple of inches shorter than those in the prosperous south. Lee herself witnessed devastating famines. Yet at 5ft 2in – 'very small,' she says – she seems always to have been determined and resourceful, driven to survive first by curiosity about the bright lights of China over the river from her home, then by the urge to find her family again, and now by her mission to speak out for the voiceless 25 million inhabitants of North Korea.

'I think I have some strong something that maybe other people don't have,' she says, recalling the TED talk she gave in 2013 that propelled her to stardom. It has so far been watched 7 million times; and her book is being translated into at least 18 different languages. 'The TED talk I gave, that gave me another character I didn't know about. I'm not saying the mind of a hero, but a kind of responsibility. Every word I'm speaking, it's not from myself. I'm speaking for and representing the people of communist North Korea.'

With constant public appearances, by the end of last year she had driven herself into a state of exhaustion, 'torturing myself', she says, in 'mental agony' and with a sense of inadequacy for the task she had undertaken. 'People in the past, they used to tell me you need a vacation, vacation, vacation – I didn't know what they meant.'

To cheer ourselves up, we turn again to the food, including a large and delicious uncooked crab, its gooey flesh marinated in the restaurant's secret sauce.

Food is a difficult subject for North Koreans who survived the famine of the 1990s. Hundreds of thousands, possibly millions, died, and Lee left the country just as the disaster reached its peak. I ask her whether it still feels strange to be able to eat whatever and whenever she wants. 'The food makes me the most sad,' she replies, pointing out how often we leave it behind on the table. 'For us, it's nothing. For people in North Korea, only for one bowl of rice – not this kind of fancy food – they don't have it and so many people have died . . . We are unlucky. We're born in the wrong country, with the wrong leader.'

As she settled into the high-tech economy of South Korea eight years ago, Lee was astonished to discover from television and from Google that there were things called 'human rights', even 'animal rights'. She suddenly reaches across the table and shows me a picture of a cat on her smartphone.

'In New York, last week – it's my friend's pet. And on her birthday, often, actually, she eats nice sushi. She loves sushi.'

The cat? I ask, incredulous. 'Yes. She loves sushi. Then whenever I see those pictures, I feel so sad. People who live in North Korea, they die for food, but living in the free world, the cat even eats expensive sushi.'

Yes, but that's not really sensible, is it? 'I'm not criticizing the cat or the owner,' she says. 'I'm not. It's just reminding me how North Koreans live.'

The memories come tumbling out, some good but mostly bad: her disbelieving mother – lost and now found again – running towards her in a prison yard in Laos; the corpses of famine victims floating down the Yalu; the handcarts to take away the dead so that Chinese visitors would not see evidence of North Korea's shameful failure; a weakling flung on to the heaps of dead because he was probably going to die anyway and a passing Chinese driver laughing at the sight. Lee's hands are fiercely twisting her long necklace of black beads as though she is trying to strangle the recollections.

'Sometimes the dead bodies wouldn't be moved, so the smell of the decomposing flesh was everywhere, especially under the bridge and near the train station, because under the bridge is where not many people can see.'

I suggest we celebrate the good memories and the reunification of her family (her brother is studying at Columbia University in New York) and order soju, the local rice liquor. She rejects it as too ordinary and so we opt for a plump bottle of Korean black raspberry wine, a sweet drink that tastes to an Englishman like neat Ribena.

We need the painful testimony of escapers such as Lee – who barely touches the wine – to understand the reality of life in North Korea and China's essential role in propping up the Kim regime. She does not want to dwell on other defectors such as the torture victim Shin Dong-hyuk or Yeonmi Park, a prominent young woman escaper, whose stories have been subject to scrutiny having been shown to contain inconsistencies. All she will say over dinner is that it 'makes me so angry' because the exposing of 'fakers' helps the regime and undermines the credibility of those who do tell the truth.

The importance of Lee's story rests on her intimate understanding of China. The country's communist rulers supported Kim Il Sung during the Korean war, but they worry today about the nuclear ambitions of his grandson Kim Jong Un. They also oppose reunification for fear of seeing US troops along the Yalu river.

The communist government in Beijing treats North Korean refugees with varying degrees of cruelty and indifference, depending on the winds of geopolitics. Even in South Korea, North Koreans find it notoriously hard to succeed in such a hyper-modern society, brainwashed as they are since birth and almost wholly ignorant about the outside world. (The north is seen by southerners as their 'mad uncle in the attic. A subject best avoided,' Lee wrote in her book.)

'We refugees, we become always a punchbag,' she says now, as we turn to dessert, a large slice each of crisp and juicy pear. 'A political punchbag between China and South Korea and North Korea. China has all the keys right now. On unification, China also has the answer. So if China wants North Korea to completely end, if China stops supporting North Korea, within one week or 10 days they can make North Korea chaos. I wish they could do more, but they are not doing it at all . . . Certainly North Korea is not easy to handle. And the west, including South Korea, they see North Korea in a wrong perspective. They see them as weak while western media make jokes about the Dear Leader's ridiculous hairstyle. What they've done over time, they've developed more the nuclear missile system, while we make fun of them. And right now it becomes a real threat. I don't know if the Trump administration can really have something change.'

Lee wants reunification, she wants to be able to go back to her hometown on the Yalu, and she worries that young South Koreans do not care as much as their parents whether or not it ever happens. ('Many people in the past, they never predicted German reunification,' she says hopefully, 'but it did happen very abruptly.')

Her immediate goal is to build an NGO to stop the trafficking of desperate North Koreans in China as brides and sex-workers. She estimates that about 30,000–40,000 of the 200,000 North Korean defectors hiding in China are sex slaves. 'As a woman who actually survived from there, I should be their voice. I want to end sex slavery in China, although I know it's really difficult to make it happen. One day maybe it's possible.'

Sosonjae
113–1, Samcheong-ro, Jongno-gu, Seoul

....

Set meal x 2   Won76,000
Korean black
  raspberry
  wine   Won17,000

....

Total (inc. service) –
          Won93,000 (£65)

I ask Lee what she has learnt about North Korea since she escaped, but I quickly realize it is the wrong question. North Koreans flee because they realize there is something wrong with their homeland. It is the lies they have been taught about the rest of the world that are deeply ingrained. 'We learnt that Americans are our primary enemies and all human scums live in America,' says Lee, who stunned her mother and brother by entering a relationship with an American man called Brian, before marrying him four years ago.

'South Korea was described as the poorest country in the world, where beggars were filling the streets. And then the most shocking thing for us was the Korean war – it was created by the American and South Korean enemies together. We never learnt it was actually started by the North Korean regime. My mum, who was brainwashed for more than 60 years, she still asks me: "Show me the proof".'

In South Korea, Lee also learnt about freedom. 'Breathing in South Korea, even though the life here is not easy, makes me so happy. I feel that sitting in a coffee shop, having a cup of tea and looking out of the window at the blue sky – this is happiness. Truly happiness. I could never have this moment when I was living in North Korea for 17 years and when I was hiding in China for 10 years. I don't think many people, when they are having a cup of tea, go: "That's freedom. It's the joy of life." But me, I have that.' For the first time in two hours, she laughs.

Jaron Lanier

'The enemy of the future is the complacent person'

By John Thornhill

Jaron Lanier arrives a little late for our lunch at a Peruvian restaurant in London's Fitzrovia, having been distracted by a Ukrainian shepherd's flute. As excuses go, that one is certainly novel.

His polite minder had warned me of the delay, explaining that Lanier had been 'sucked into the vortex' of Hobgoblin Music, a shop for rare musical instruments next door. When Lanier finally emerges, he says the Ukrainian flute would be 'disturbing if I were a sheep', but is still kind of interesting. 'There are a few temptations there but I'm undecided at the moment.'

Lanier is not the type to remain undecided for long. An imposing bear of a man with long, tangled brown dreadlocks, Lanier rarely passes unnoticed, even in an anonymous black T-shirt and black trousers. He sends the cutlery flying on the adjacent table as he settles into his seat but does not seem to notice.

As well as being an obsessive collector – and player – of several hundred musical instruments (favourite: the Laotian khaen), Lanier is a Berkeley-based composer, computer scientist, virtual reality enthusiast, author, Microsoft-affiliated researcher and scourge of social media. To revert to epithetic journalese, he is a one-man polemical polymath.

In a Silicon Valley culture that mythologizes youth and creative destruction, the 58-year-old Lanier can sometimes seem like the eccentric uncle in the room, worrying about the impact of technology on humanity and determined to keep society in the loop. He was one of the early pioneers of virtual reality, founding VPL Research in the mid-1980s and developing VR goggles and gloves. But he never fully bought into the tech sector's 'magical thinking' and later sold out to Sun

Illustration by James Ferguson

Microsystems. If you do not believe in the Silicon Valley myth of the great man, he later wrote, it is hard to aspire to be one.

In a series of subsequent books and essays, Lanier has been both evangelist and heretic, enthusing about technology's creative possibilities while warning of its destructive effects. He was among the first to raise the alarm about the harmful fallout of social media on our lives, a theme developed with passionate force in his latest book, *Ten Arguments for Deleting Your Social Media Accounts Right Now*. We would all have a clearer understanding of our world, he claims, if we relabelled the likes of Facebook and Google as 'behaviour manipulation empires'. His argument is that 'pervasive surveillance and constant, subtle manipulation is unethical, cruel, dangerous and inhumane'. In short, this weaponized form of advertising is polarizing society, destroying democratic debate and turning us into 'assholes'.

I had read that Lanier considered music his first love. He tells me how his mother, Lilly, taught him Beethoven piano sonatas as a young child, even if he insisted on playing in his own 'comically overwrought style'. That emotional connection has fuelled a lifelong fascination with performing music, which he describes as a kind of 'instantaneous creation of the future'. 'For the most part, the world of music is joyous and generous,' he says, noting that even the Laotians indulge his idiosyncratic khaen-playing style.

Such passing joy contrasts with Lanier's childhood, which reads like one of J. G. Ballard's bleaker novels. His beloved mother, a piano-playing prodigy from Vienna and a Holocaust survivor, was killed in a car crash in the US when he was nine. He and his father then moved to the New Mexico desert, where they lived in a tent for two years while they designed and built a home in the form of a geodesic dome. Later, while studying at university, Lanier paid for his tuition by breeding goats and selling their milk and cheese.

According to a *New Yorker* profile, Lanier's girlfriend was so disconcerted by his dishevelled appearance that she took him to a laundromat on their first date. You can perhaps see why the *New York Times* columnist Maureen Dowd has described Lanier as the 'most unusual person I've ever met'. Lanier's traumatic early life, nomadic intellect and fascination with technology have given him an unorthodox perspective. As an *FT* columnist who writes about the impact of technology, I had long been intrigued to meet the writer who has done so much to delineate the contours of our shape-shifting digital world. First, though, I decide we had better order some food.

The light, airy Pisqu seems strangely quiet on a Friday lunchtime in the heart of London. It is located just off Oxford Street on Rathbone Place, where the great 19th-century essayist William Hazlitt once lived. Pisqu is, however, well suited to cater to Lanier's emailed list of dietary restrictions: 'No meat. No cephalopods. No sugar. No alcohol.' Lanier has developed an obsession with the octopus, which he values both for its intelligence and amazing ability to morph. We both order the ceviche of sea bass, sweet potato, coriander, Inca corn and lime tiger's milk, a pleasing contrast of tastes and textures. Given that alcohol is off-limits, we stick with tap water. I am intrigued by how Lanier can be so productive across so many different fields. He describes his work style as 'compressed procrastination', switching from one activity to another, like cross-training. 'You can get away with feeling like you're being lazy all the time and yet at the end of the day all the things have gotten done,' he says.

Fortified by the ceviche, Lanier launches into an unsparing assault on the Big Tech companies – although he stresses that the problem is not so much the technology itself or even the corporate leadership as the economic incentive system in which we operate. Sadly, the early libertarian idealism of the internet has resulted in the creation of 'gargantuan, global data monopsonies'. Like many internet pioneers, Lanier wants to revive the technology's original promise. 'I miss the future,' he says.

Lanier argues that these platform companies are using their colossal computing power to gain a vast informational advantage, keeping the economic rewards for themselves while radiating risk out to everyone else. 'It's reminiscent of a gambling economy where the only sure position is in the casino.'

He is particularly damning of social media companies, even if he accepts that their services have real benefits: connecting patients suffering rare diseases or helping users find lost pets. The trouble is, as he puts it, that Facebook, Google, Twitter, YouTube and Instagram all have a 'manipulation engine' running in the background, working to the advantage of unscrupulous advertisers, scammers or Russian spies.

'The current incentive structure is that any time two people have any contact, it's financed by a third person who believes they can manipulate the first two,' he says, sweeping his dreadlocks off his shoulders like some demure debutante. 'There's never before been a society in which everybody is under constant observation, constant surveillance, and in which they're constantly receiving this stream of experience that is being dynamically adjusted to find ways of manipulating them.'

He says his wife, Lena, who has been successfully battling cancer, has found it hard to track down useful information about her condition online because the internet is so crowded with garbage from hucksters and fakers. 'It's like a labyrinth of deception.'

He accepts that his campaign will not persuade many people to delete their apps. Social media has been designed to be addictive and its dominant companies enjoy 'preposterously grand network effects' that make it hard to quit. But he hopes enough people will disentangle themselves for long enough to ensure there is a small, sheltered island of alternative public debate.

How can he write so sweepingly about the effects of social media if he long ago stopped using it? That, he concedes, is a 'valid, inevitable criticism', but counters that 'those people who are in prison will know more about prison life than the reporter writing about prison life. Yet we need the reporter to be outside or else there will be no report at all.'

One of his biggest critiques of social media is that it decontextualizes and mashes up meaning. Every statement is chopped up into algorithmic-friendly shreds and recontextualized, often triggering a 'cranky backlash' that renders it meaningless; the election of Donald Trump was the natural outcome of this cognitive confusion. Lanier says he has met Trump several times over the past three decades and has always regarded him as a typical New York conman. But, he argues, Trump has been reprogrammed by his interactions with social media. 'What has happened with Trump is that he's taking on a personality disorder that's associated with social media addiction, the snowflake personality, where the person is super-insecure, super-ready to jump into a bizarre social pissing match.'

According to Lanier, Trump's election has shaken the social media companies out of their complacency. The subsequent scandal surrounding Cambridge Analytica's abuse of Facebook data has further rattled Silicon Valley and left the sector open to outside thinking. 'I'm still considered a bit of an outlier, and my ideas might be somewhat radical but they're definitely treated as a normal part of the conversation now.'

Despite growing talk about the need for state intervention, Lanier does not have much hope for regulation, fearing that it might only strengthen the incumbents. Somewhat surprisingly, he says Facebook and Google are more likely to reform themselves, partly in their own self-interest and partly under pressure from their own ethically minded employees. 'The one thing that will kill them totally is if the good engineers start leaving. Then the companies will die.'

Lanier has been working with a group of radical economists to design an alternative information economy. He is an eloquent champion of the Data-as-Labour movement, arguing that if people do use social media then they should at least be paid for their posts and photographs. He hints that he is involved in backroom dialogues with the tech companies to bring about such a restructuring. 'I don't see how any society can hope to survive unless there's at least some degree of alignment between society's interests and economic incentives.'

In his darker moments, he wonders whether we might have lost control to our digital creations. 'I've started to think of social media a little bit, you know, how Richard Dawkins suggested that we think of the gene as if it had a will of its own.' Is it a coincidence, he asks, that social media is trying to undermine the politicians who are trying to tame it? Just when European governments are moving to regulate social media and data privacy, they are assailed by populist movements. The test case may come in Germany, which Lanier describes as 'the centre of resistance to a lot of the madness' today. He sees evidence of the same destabilizing process at work in Italy, Poland, Southeast Asia, India and Africa. 'If somebody wants to disrupt a particular area, they just make everybody cranky and paranoid and cynical in the way that you can using these tools because that's what the tools are precisely optimized to do. And so we've entered a world of insanity. The Trump election is only one example. There will be many more until we fix it.'

Lanier speaks in enthusiastic waves of well-modulated paragraphs but still polishes off his avocado risotto with gusto. My grilled fish are delicate, if somewhat dry, spiced up by the criolla sauce. He shoots a glance of disapproval when my fork wanders near a piece of octopus.

Since completing his book, he has come up with a new metaphor for the interaction between social media and politics: toxoplasmosis, a parasitic disease that rewires rodent brains to make them less fearful of cats. Once the reckless mice are devoured, the parasite reproduces itself in the cats' guts. He suggests that Trump – or the Russians – eat the metaphorical mice only because the social media parasite is making people crazy. As I raise a sceptical eyebrow, he laughs: 'I'm expecting the metaphor commandos to fire into this restaurant at any minute and put me under arrest.'

Lanier retains credibility among many West Coast technologists because of his pioneering work on VR. He became fascinated by VR as a 'lonely, traumatized kid' seeking a way to connect with people through shared imagination. In his quixotic book on VR, *Dawn of the New Everything*, he described wanting to replicate the trifecta of his childhood sensory delight: the art of Hieronymus Bosch, the music of Johann Sebastian Bach and Mexican chocolates tinged with cinnamon.

Lanier debates with himself whether Mexican, Brazilian or Peruvian cuisine is the finest in Latin America but declares himself happy with Pisqu. We've been talking so intensely that we don't find time for dessert. That's a shame because the Amazonian chocolate mousse with passion fruit sounds pretty tempting.

As a VR pioneer, Lanier has argued for 'post-symbolic communication' in which symbols such as words fade away to be replaced with a form of communication through improvising a shared reality. But he also came to realize that such a powerful technology could alter people's behaviour. 'This was a very terrifying realization. Inherently, VR is the most purified form of both the best and the worst of technology's potential.'

Hard as it is to credit at times, Lanier calls himself an optimist. But I

Pisqu
23 Rathbone Place,
London W1

....

Two-course set
    lunch x 2   £24
Ceviche with sea
    bass, sweet potato,
    Inca corn and lime
    tiger's milk
    £2 supplement x 2   £4
Avocado risotto
Grilled seafood
Side dish of yucas
    (deep-fried cassava) £3.50

....

Total (inc. tax and
    service charge) –   £35.44

admire the personal credo he described during a prize acceptance speech in 2014 in which he argued that death and loss were inevitable and so boring. 'It is the miracles we build, the friendships, the families, the meaning, that are astonishing, interesting, blazingly amazing. Love creation,' he declared.

He supports the idea that the world is broadly healthier, better educated and happier. But he argues this has only come about because of the activism of the discontented. His stark criticisms serve a higher purpose. 'At every increment of improvement in human history somebody got pissed off and said, "This can be better, this must be better." To be an optimist has to mean being a critic. The enemy of the future is not the pessimist but the complacent person.' And with that final rhetorical flourish, the happy but discontented critic heads back to the music store – to check out that Ukrainian shepherd's flute.

Sport's Greats

'You can buy everything except passion'

Eric Cantona

'You can buy everything except passion'

By Leo Lewis

Sometime between the potato gratin going cold and my guest refusing coffee, the main section of the Commune Social tapas bar in Shanghai falls silent. It is tempting to imagine that the whole city has done the same.

Eric Cantona – the actor and philosophical sketch artist perhaps better known as one of the finest and most combustible footballers in history – closes his eyes and starts whistling Edith Piaf's 'Hymne à l'amour'.

It is somehow unsurprising. This is exactly why Britain fell in love with Cantona in the 1990s and why his years at Manchester United were the centrepiece of one of the most thrilling epochs in the beautiful game. It takes only moments of meeting the 51-year-old Frenchman to discover that he remains, first and foremost, a performer. On the field, in his pomp, he could electrify tens of thousands of fans every time he made contact with the ball. Off the pitch the performance was even more audacious – a scene-stealing role as the French pseud surrounded by barbaric Brits.

His reign defined not just the stunning success of a dream team that featured David Beckham, Roy Keane and Ryan Giggs, but the tectonic shifts – led by huge TV deals – that reshaped English football. There was a swagger that infused the era, and Cantona's was the biggest and most brazen. The game was then in the throes of becoming a global, televised circus. His superstardom, he says, arose in part because 'I understood before the others what the circus was'.

When the whistling comes to an end, 32 seconds later, the Frenchman's expression is unmistakable: that defiant, imperious flare of entitlement that accompanied every sublime goal, every telepathic pass,

Illustration by James Ferguson

every thoroughly deserved red card and every enigmatic pronouncement flicked towards the media. Two decades since his retirement from the professional game, and even with his once trademark upturned collar neatly turned down, he could still ignite a stadium.

'The whistling? My kids used to like it. Nowadays they tell me to stop,' he shrugs, convinced of its brilliance but acknowledging, as one dad to another, that we can sometimes be embarrassing to our children. He asks whether I would also like to hear a more piercing whistle he uses to summon dogs. I don't, but he does it anyway. It is quite fabulously piercing. Heads around the restaurant jerk to attention. No dogs appear.

Cantona, the Marseille-born son of a nurse and a dressmaker, did not need to whistle to be the centre of attention. An hour and a half earlier, he had arrived, rather late, at the Commune Social to find me halfway into a Bloody Mary. He does not accept the offer of something similar, opting instead for a mug of hot water, a gesture towards his larynx and a display of his professionalism as an actor. There is no point arguing: after appearing in more than 25 films since 1997, Cantona now takes his acting as seriously as he once took his football.

Asked whether he would ever consider a return to the game, he replies immediately. 'No. Only to manage Manchester United . . . They won't ask me. Maybe that's why they didn't win the Premier League. Only I could have made them succeed [after Sir Alex Ferguson's retirement]. Nobody else. Only me.'

We are meeting at a friendly, higher-end Shanghai brunching spot beloved of expats – cramped and informal enough that one of the three bankers at the next table is cheerfully earwigging our conversation. Various people, including one of the bankers and several Chinese kitchen staff, interrupt our lunch for selfies. The restaurant, built into the brick-work confines of a former police prison cell, has been recommended to me by a British diplomat as Cantona enters the final days of a two-month film shoot in China. It is a Franco-Chinese production called *Magic*, about which Cantona is tight on details – he says he will play 'a nice man, but when you see him you won't think that'.

For the most recent stretch of the project he has been in Turpan, a beautiful but remote city in the country's north-western deserts. The various noises of appreciation – '*magnifique!*' and '*parfait!*' – that later punctuate our lunch suggest that the restaurant's meaty, comforting,

Mediterranean spread is stuff that he has missed. After retiring from United in 1997, Cantona left football altogether rather than seeing out his thirties in one of several countries with 'a lot of money but no history of football'. He took up acting and has appeared in what is now a decent list of films (*Elizabeth*, as well as an assortment of French dramas and comedies). To British audiences, his most famous post-football work is Ken Loach's *Looking For Eric*, a 2009 film in which Cantona plays a hallucination of his Man Utd-era self experienced by a football-obsessed postman. The film brims with lines of soulful machismo ('I am not a man, I am Cantona') that would not be unexpected coming straight-faced from him now, and he reveals, proudly, that he made important contributions to the script.

Loach, and Ferguson, he says, were geniuses who had a similar impact on his life. 'Director. Manager. Football. Film. It's just a different game, but still play, play, play,' he says, embarking on a more general thesis about work hierarchies. 'I think the boss has a bad image,' he says, after an uncharacteristically long pause.

'In the media we need to make a good image for businessmen. Some of them are nice. Some are very creative . . . but if you ask the person on the street about the boss, he says "he's shit". Why? Because we all say that.' I note that Cantona did, in fact, say that of Henri Michel, the for-mer manager of the French national team who, in 1988, Cantona publicly described as a 'bag of shit' in a TV interview. The window is small, but I see an open goal. What about his own relationship with managers? 'I respect the boss. I loved some of my bosses,' says Cantona, weaving out of danger. 'That was the secret of Alex Ferguson. We loved him and we respected him. That is the job of the boss – to be loved and respected.'

And how about Guy Roux? I ask, speaking of the manager of Auxerre who gave Cantona his first job in professional football, but had to deal with his protégé punching a teammate in the face.

'Yes, I was like a son. We had a very strong father–son relationship. That doesn't mean everything was nice. No. I was like a teenager. He was like a father and we had a lot of fighting together but in the end we loved each other.'

But, I begin to say . . .

The waiter, who is French and crimson with excitement, materializes at the table and I realize we haven't ordered. There is a brief to and fro, during which Cantona rapidly agrees to all the waiter's recommendations, before steering conversation to the evils of mobile phones and why he bans his children (aged four and eight, by his second marriage) from going near them. 'I don't want to live in the world of phones,' he says, suddenly sniffing at the air like a deer and tasting some imaginary food plucked from the forest floor, 'I want my senses to be always activated. I want to feel nature. I want to focus on smells, nature, the sound of words, the sound of birds –' he runs out of inspiration and glares at the table – 'a fork . . .' The food – all sharing plates – conveniently starts arriving and, suddenly, the flinty professionalism behind this digital debunking dawns. Cantona has just released a book called *My Notebook* that shows off some of the thousands of sketches he makes, as a constant hobby, in a Moleskine. He archly suggests this habit is the antithesis of the mobile phone – a pen-and-ink engagement with the world, rather than the seditious virtuality of the screen.

Cantona historians will surely identify in this artistic oeuvre echoes of the press conference he delivered in 1995 at the end of an eight-month ban from the game, the result of the inglorious night at Crystal Palace when he aimed a flying kick at a racist fan. As he now recounts it, he didn't want to say anything. The rules (in this case Manchester United's lawyers) required something, however. 'They said I should just say anything, so I said anything,' he says.

His 21-word response ('When the seagulls follow the trawler, it's because they think sardines will be thrown into the sea. Thank you very much') remains among the most memorable lines ever uttered by a footballer, and sealed Cantona's image as a Gallic pseud in shorts. He remains sniffily unsure how many of the journalists in the room understood that they were the seagulls in question.

I induce him to explain, with 20 years of hindsight, what drove his career. 'I was just someone who always, totally wanted to give everything to the game all the time. That's it. And to be on the field with everyone who wants the same – that is unity. That is beauty. The outperformance of the individual in service of the team. It is the most exceptional education,' he says, forking scrambled egg and salmon towards his plate after checking that I have had my fill.

'But at Manchester, even that was different. That is why I have always said it was like going home. A different energy. More energy. You have more passion for football in England than in France. I felt that immediately. Of course the game is loved everywhere, but in England it is real passion,' he says, pausing to check whether this is profound enough. 'You can buy everything except passion,' he ends, just to be sure.

This leads neatly to his thoughts on the transfer of Brazilian star Neymar from Barcelona to Paris Saint-Germain for €222 million – the biggest in history. It is an insult, as Cantona sees it, against the argument he has just outlined, and an excuse to trash the passionless French league. How, he asks with a look of straight-backed horror, can a player like Neymar go to the French championship? 'He will be playing games against [lowly] Lorient and [even more lowly] Guingamp. How is it possible? To be a great player and go . . . somewhere . . . just . . .' He groans, temporarily speechless. 'How old is he? Twenty-five? From Brazil to Barcelona to the French championship. It disappoints me so much.'

He builds from this fury into a more full-bodied assault on the way that the monetization and consumption of football evolved so dramatically during his time in Manchester. The system in which Neymar has made this disastrous choice, he argues, forces players into a permanent, painful contest between their undiluted passion for the game (which he wholeheartedly believes most players have) and the mindset of commoditization into which they are forced by the money sloshing around the industry. He sees the root of this malefaction in the very innovation that propelled Cantona's superstardom – televised availability of all matches.

'We kill the desire. I think so,' he starts, sphinx-like on whether this is a wind-up. 'We killed the desire to watch a game. When I was young, when the only game was the cup final or the national team games, that was it. On Sunday night we had to wait all the way through the programme to see five goals from other countries like England and Italy. Now, they have everything. Kids need frustration . . . if you give everything to everyone, they don't learn frustration. I'm talking about football, but it is the same with everything.'

A discourse on the football manager as father figure – 'do you respect him because you love him, or do you love him because you respect him?' – switches abruptly into a stream of consciousness, partly fuelled by an excellent beef cheek empanada, on the mysterious phenomenon whereby children who share the same father can turn out completely differently. 'The viewpoints are different,' he says, pointing to the windowsill and a small candle in his line of sight, 'I will remember a candle in a window. You will remember me.'

Worried that he has at last clocked me as a trawler-following seagull, I ask him what has troubled me all along – whether he has any regrets about a career that, despite the astonishing things it has delivered, could have delivered so much more without a long list of lunacy, topped by that flying kick.

'I would change nothing. You know why? Because I am very optimistic. All the roads you take, even when they have barriers and difficulties, they lead somewhere better. Everything that I lived through, good and bad, pleasures and traumas – if I were unhappy now then I would regret parts of this, but I don't. I drew this [he shows one of the pictures from *My Notebook* depicting two arrows facing in opposite directions]. I called it "evolution". Yes, I had a bad time, but I decided to use it . . . like a painter or director or writer. You use trauma to make a work . . . so no, I don't regret anything.'

In *Looking For Eric*, Cantona reveals that in fact he used his eight months of suspension to learn to play the trumpet. I ask if he has kept it up, and he replies that he hasn't – but that he now has another musical passion in his life. That is when the whistling starts.

Commune Social
511 Jiangning Rd, Jing'an District, Shanghai

. . . .

Bloody Mary	Rmb88
San Pellegrino	Rmb60
Brunch of three dishes: Potato gratin, Scrambled eggs, Zucchini	Rmb188
Beef empanada	Rmb98
Pork and foie gras burger	Rmb98
Espresso	Rmb25

. . . .

Total –	Rmb557 (£62)

another musical passion in his life. That is when the whistling starts.

Just as he is rising to leave, he has another stab at my question about regret. 'You know, the circus. Either you endure it, you suffer from it or you use it. I used it. I had fun.'

Vanessa Selbst

'Poker is like an annoying brother that just keeps nagging at you like, "Come play with me"'

By Stephen Foley

The world's most successful female poker player has picked a neighbourhood Greek restaurant for lunch. Yet when I arrive at Faros, in Brooklyn's Park Slope, it is deserted, not just of diners but apparently of staff. Is this another of Vanessa Selbst's elaborate bluffs, I wonder?

The 31-year-old has taken home more than $11 million from live tournaments and wowed TV viewers of the game with her aggressive play and apparently reckless betting on weak hands. I have been looking forward to our meeting for weeks, so I am not willing to fold immediately. I go hunting for a waiter and find one twiddling thumbs at a table tucked in the back. Contrary to impressions, the kitchen is open, so I pick a spot near the window and await my guest.

When Selbst arrives – without a coat, since she lives only a few blocks away – she glances round in horror and suggests we find another venue. She explains that she has been looking for a replacement Greek restaurant since her go-to, Okeanos, a few blocks down, shut; she had remembered an enjoyable summer evening at Faros when the outdoor garden was rammed with patrons.

We decide to stick it out, in the service of culinary investigation. 'I like Greek because it is usually really fresh vegetables,' she says. 'I just like to eat light food.'

A modest local restaurant is a world away from the brattishness and bling of the professional poker circuit, and from the hedonistic antics of

Illustration by Luke Waller

stars such as Dan Bilzerian, filmed last year throwing a naked porn star from a roof into a swimming pool. But Selbst, a gay woman who prefers campaigning on social justice issues to collecting guns and motorbikes, is not your typical poker star.

'I never really considered myself a poker pro,' she says. 'I think poker is more like a theme in my life. It's like an annoying brother that just keeps nagging at you like, "Come play with me." I'm always trying to get away and do my own thing and the sibling is just like, "No, come back." It is addictive, in a way. I know some people struggle with gambling addiction. For me I find it really addictive in the same way that I find Candy Crush really addictive. It's not about winning and losing money.'

Indeed, Selbst sometimes drops out of competition altogether. Having previously taken a break from poker to complete a law degree at Yale Law School in 2009, this year she passed the New York bar exam and has been considering extending her work with non-profits such as the Innocence Project, which works to overturn miscarriages of justice, and Make the Road New York, a group of community organizers.

Lately, though, she has felt the little brother tugging her sleeve once again. She will be on the professional circuit more often in 2016, she says, although she prefers domesticity in Brooklyn.

Even after a decade and three World Series of Poker bracelets, the game's most coveted non-monetary prize, Selbst says she feels like an outsider on the tours, where players spend days on end playing for prizes that can reach into millions of dollars.

'I don't actually hate them,' she says of her fellow players. 'It's just kind of seedy. Men around other men, they're just at their worst. It's gross, the way they talk to and about women. Whereas when other women are at the table, they might restrain themselves because there's a – I'm using air quotes – "lady present", with me, because of the way I look, it's like I'm some weird grey area.'

Has she, I ask, experienced discrimination? 'I have been discriminated against but not for being a woman. For the way I look as a gay woman, I've had opportunities not be presented to me for sure.' She says she knows of at least one TV presenter role where this happened. 'They say we wouldn't get as many viewers, or whatever,' she says. 'That might or might not be true. I don't care enough. It's not my battle. It could be, but I don't want it to be.'

The underemployed waiter has quickly taken our order: salads to start, then octopus for Selbst and a *souvlaki* dish off the specials menu for me. Lunch specials come with a beer – a bargain $15 all in – and Selbst orders a coffee.

Perhaps our presence has emboldened passers-by – by the time the first course arrives, the restaurant has attracted three other covers. Selbst's classic *horiatiki* is a huge pile of tomato hunks and slabs of feta; my Faros *salata* includes avocado and dried cranberries as well as mixed leaves and crumbled feta. Both are dauntingly large.

Selbst has worked hard to separate poker the game (good) from poker the lifestyle (unhealthy) – yet it was not always so. She had a comfortable upbringing, first in Brooklyn and then in Montclair, New Jersey. Her parents were talented card players – they met at a bridge game – and kindled an interest in logic puzzles in her and brother Andrew. Her mother, an options trader by profession, taught her Mastermind and cribbage.

At high school, inspired by the Matt Damon movie *Rounders*, Selbst and friends started playing poker and when she took up the game again as a political science undergraduate, it coincided with the online poker boom.

'We were the first generation of online players, the first really good poker players,' she says, in the tone in which one delivers statistical fact. 'Most of the poker pros in the past were these rough-and-tumble guys that didn't have a great opportunity in their lives who were like, "I don't see myself having a traditional career, so I'm going to go out and try my luck in Vegas." They're not these nerdy math guys and girls who were sitting at home or at college with plenty of options but who then started making a lot of money by doing statistical analyses. That's a different generation and that's what we were.'

It has been clear from the minute we sat down that Selbst is terrifyingly smart, but what seems to have pushed her to a level above the rest of the 'nerdy math guys and girls' is something else: a tragedy.

When her mother died suddenly from an intestinal condition in 2005, Selbst was on a Fulbright scholarship to study gay marriage in Spain. In turmoil, she effectively abandoned her studies for all-night poker sessions and what she has described as a near-depression which, in a dark sense, made her a great player. It prompts me to ask if she ever fears her present happiness and balanced approach to poker could be upended. 'It's an interesting question. My gut reaction is "No", but if something happened to my wife or something, I guess it's not unheard of that I would be so miserable that I would just retreat.'

She continues, 'Not that you should only play if you're miserable, but it was such an escape. If I hadn't had such a difficult year, I'd maybe never be at this level. That was my most intense year of playing poker, which is a kind of weird, morbid take on the whole thing.'

Questions of addiction and life choices are once again current in the US. Online poker really took off in 2003, when an unknown called Chris Moneymaker became the first world champion – and a millionaire – to have qualified for the World Series of Poker from an online site. The so-called 'Moneymaker effect' led to a huge rise in the numbers of poker players worldwide yet, for the past decade, this has not included players from the US.

In 2006, Congress shut down access to online poker sites for US citizens, citing concerns about money laundering and a rise in addiction, and the US authorities prosecuted several companies and executives. Now the industry is going state by state to try to persuade local authorities to legalize and license poker sites within state borders. Selbst hopes this is just a precursor to another poker boom.

'Anything's dangerous but we don't live in a paternalist society. Some gambling's legal and some is not. A lot of policies are just based around which lobby gave them more money,' she says. 'Online poker is so great because you have access to a billion people. Now your pool is cut down to a few million. The network effects are really big. We're hoping that, if enough states regulate it, then they get their act together and realize they're not getting the traffic that they could be getting [so] they'll pass a resolution to allow interstate poker.'

Reconnecting the US to the rest of the world could also help the professional game – including Selbst and her sponsor PokerStars, an online card room – by bringing back viewers who have deserted televised events and drained money from TV licensing deals.

Our main courses, which arrive while we are still scaling our salad mountains, are more sensibly sized. My cubes of pork come in a delicious, tangy marinade. Selbst expresses enthusiasm for her octopus, which is charcoal-grilled and presented with a red wine vinegar. She is a keen cook and says that preparing the perfect octopus remains an elusive goal, despite many attempts – one of which was when she was dating her now-wife, Miranda, a teacher who she met on the website OKCupid.

The meal was designed to impress, early on in their relationship. 'She was the least adventurous eater ever so I was testing her and she ate it. It was terrible, too. I was, like, "OK, you must really want to get to know me because you ate that and it was really bad."'

While Selbst is looking for Greek cooking tips, I am rather hoping to come away from lunch with a cute poker trick or two, anything to improve my timid occasional games of ultra-low stakes Texas hold 'em with friends. The truth, I'm not surprised to hear, is that there is no substitute for study. In fact, my question on how to tell if a rival is bluffing is greeted with the verbal equivalent of an eye-roll.

'People always want to know, "What are the main tells?" Let's just say it doesn't work like that. One thing that you look for: is someone's heart racing? It often means that they're nervous, but sometimes they're nervous because they just have a really great hand. You have to look, to see what hand they turn over, and then you can associate.'

What I do learn is that Selbst's own aggressive style is partly a made-for-TV fabrication. In her major TV debut in 2006, a disastrous bluff lost her all her chips and knocked her tournament prize money down from $800,000 to $100,000, but gained her a reputation that she has been cashing in ever since.

In fact, she says she plays relatively tightly when the cameras are not rolling. 'There was a number of years where, whenever I was on TV, if there was an option between a crazy play and a not crazy play, I just always made the crazy play because I was like, "I can just keep bolstering this image,"' she says.

'I don't mind saying it now because, first of all, I'm sure the people that I'm going to be exploiting aren't probably going to be reading this. No offence. Also, it should be clear to everyone that I'm not playing every hand crazy, but it doesn't matter. You can tell them that I'm exploiting this and doing this and people are still like, "No, I won't get bluffed, and I especially won't get bluffed by a girl."'

Selbst turns down dessert but, since she is under no particular time pressure and I still want to hear about her life beyond poker, she gets her coffee refilled and I nurse my beer. When, eventually, I return to the office it is to learn that Mark Zuckerberg, who is the same age as Selbst, has promised to give all but a sliver of his Facebook fortune to philanthropy. Selbst shares this millennial desire to impact the world for good.

In the past, that meant student activism – during Selbst's law studies she led the Queer–Straight Alliance at Yale and railed against what appeared to be discrimination in the way police responded to complaints against gay and straight student parties – and volunteering for community organizations.

'I was working on behalf of people who hadn't paid their electric bill of $60. I'm spending seven or eight hours on the phone trying to get this bill paid or trying to get them to waive it, and meanwhile I'm gambling thousands of dollars and I'm like, "This is so stupid."'

Since then, Selbst has gone on to establish Venture Justice, a foundation that funnels her poker winnings to dynamic young entrepreneurs starting up nonprofits aimed at tackling inequality. As some commentators took care to point out to Zuckerberg last week, setting up the foundation can be the easy part; finding the change-the-world ventures, which she expects to begin in earnest next year, will be the real, time-consuming work.

So that'll be a 'no' to going into hedge funds, then? 'A lot of bored poker players go into hedge funds or vice versa,' she says. 'I imagine it would be fun, but I just feel like I've already spent enough time playing a zero-sum game. I'm also anti-capitalist at heart, so it doesn't really fit in with my values, I guess.'

A first step is to bring philanthropic work to the professional poker community. Recently, she organized a 'Blinds & Justice' charity tournament for the Urban Justice Center, which provides legal services to the poor. The event, which she co-hosted with fellow poker star Daniel Negreanu, attracted several big names and raised $160,000.

Faros

84 7th Ave, Brooklyn,
New York

....

Horiatiki salad	$9
Faros salad	$10
Octopus	$15
Pork souvlaki special	$15
Coffee	$3

....

Total (inc. tax) –	$56.62

According to Selbst, poker stars often do not realize how privileged they are, and have been tricked into thinking that they are winning through innate ability alone. 'I had the safety net of my family. If I lost my money playing poker, there wasn't an actual risk because I know I would have something to fall back on,' she says. 'But [the reason] you're not afraid to take risks comes from the fact your parents brought you up in a world where you didn't have to be afraid. You probably were from a white upper-middle-class background where you weren't getting harassed by the police. There weren't gangs or whatever, where one wrong step was going to land you somewhere you shouldn't have been.

'In poker, the cards are the same for everyone, and anyone can sit down in a game, so people extend that to think it's all meritocracy.'

I pay the bill and we prepare to head out into Park Slope, the neighbourhood in which she was born and to which she has returned. With rows of beautiful brownstones and pricey apartments, it could not be a better illustration of New York's 'tale of two cities' and the inequality she wants to help tackle.

'I feel I live such a comfortable life that I feel like a fraud every day,' she says. 'I don't feel selfless at all. If I were really selfless, I wouldn't come to a restaurant like this; like, what have we spent? $60 on a lunch we could have had for $6 and that money could have been a lot better spent on something else.'

Sepp Blatter

'I am a very generous man'

By Malcolm Moore

S epp Blatter likes to start the day just before 6am. He skips breakfast but drinks a cup of coffee and does a little dance to stay in shape. 'Rhythm, rhythm of life is very important. Also in football, but everywhere,' he says.

But on 27 May, 15 minutes after he woke up, his morning routine was broken by a phone call. Swiss police, acting on extradition requests from the US Department of Justice, launched a raid on Zürich's Baur au Lac hotel and arrested seven senior Fifa officials on suspicion of taking more than $100 million in bribes between them.

The arrests, which were followed by another raid on Fifa's headquarters on a hill above Zürich, came as hundreds of football officials were gathering in Switzerland for an election to choose a new Fifa president. 'I felt like a boxer who was just going into round 12 and said, "I'm going to win." But then: BONG!' says Blatter, 79, mimicking a knockout blow.

The effect was seismic: although the vote went ahead two days later, and Blatter was re-elected for a fifth term, he stepped down the week after, claiming he needed to 'protect Fifa'. It was not enough. Swiss prosecutors put Blatter under investigation and, on 8 October, he was suspended from all football activities and evicted from his office at Fifa. While you can physically remove Blatter from Fifa's headquarters, separating the man from the organization he has built in his image for the past 40 years – first masterminding football programmes in Africa, then becoming general secretary and finally president – is a tricky proposition.

We meet at Sonnenberg restaurant, which in its literature describes itself as the 'Fifa Club', run 'under the patronage of Joseph S. Blatter' and as a place 'where football fans from the worlds of Swiss business, politics and sports meet with their guests for business lunches, exquisite

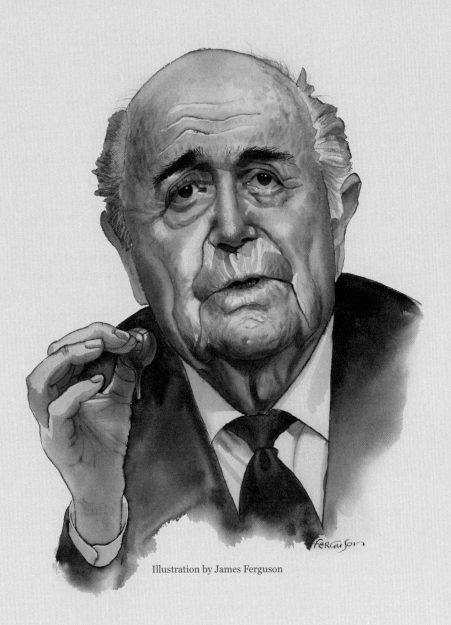

Illustration by James Ferguson

dinners and networking'. I arrive early but Blatter is already waiting, chatting to the restaurant's head chef, whose white jacket is embroidered with Fifa's blue logo. We are ushered into a private room with magnificent views over vineyards, then over the city and all the way down to Lake Zürich.

The door shuts behind us and there is an awkward silence. The man who has served for years as a lightning rod for so many shocking accusations of corruption and backroom-dealing suddenly seems frail as he fidgets with his cutlery and rubs his hands together. It turns out that he has a great deal to get off his chest, and several grenades to toss into the fragile process to find his successor, but it is difficult to know where to begin.

We clink glasses of a Swiss sauvignon blanc and I ask him how he feels now that the end is in sight. In February, he will permanently leave Fifa after a fresh presidential election. Others have told me that it will be an existential crisis for Blatter and hinted darkly that he may not be able to bear it. He freely admits that he is a monomaniac who cannot, and will not, stop thinking about Fifa.

He lives alone in an apartment in Zürich and works from a 'very small' office with a desk, a computer, a football and a picture of the Matterhorn on the wall. 'I regret I cannot go back to my office [at Fifa HQ], because my office [there] was a little bit more than an office; it was the "salon" we were living in,' he says in accented and slightly topsy-turvy English (he is most comfortable in German or French but also speaks Italian and Spanish).

Blatter still wakes early, however, and scans the news for any developments about Fifa. 'I answer my personal mail; there is a lot of mail. I am following very carefully what is happening in the office of Fifa and around this office. For the time being, I have not had any possibility to say, "Now I go a few days on holiday", he says. 'I am following everything. I cannot just say I switch off because I am not any longer in the office. Because my office is my memory,' he says, tapping a finger to his forehead.

A waiter enters with a treat from the head chef: plates of salmon, cucumber and caviar. But Blatter is allergic to seafood, he says, shooing the dish away. 'They know this. I do not know why they serve it.' He orders cured beef instead, which he eats with his hands, together with some bread.

As we settle into our conversation, he quickly pinpoints the moment when Fifa's troubles – and his downward spiral – began. 'It is linked to this now famous date: 2 December 2010,' he says, referring to the day he pulled Qatar's name out of the envelope as host of the 2022 World Cup.

'If you see my face when I opened it, I was not the happiest man to say it is Qatar. Definitely not.' The decision caused outrage, even among those who do not follow football. 'We were in a situation where nobody understood why the World Cup goes to one of the smallest countries in the world,' he says.

Blatter then drops a bombshell: he did try to rig the vote but for the US, not for Qatar. There had been a 'gentleman's agreement', he tells me, among Fifa's leaders, that the 2018 and 2022 competitions would go to the 'two superpowers' Russia and the US; 'It was behind the scenes. It was diplomatically arranged to go there.'

Had his electoral engineering succeeded, he would still be in charge, he says. 'I would be [on holiday] on an island!' But at the last minute, the deal was off, because of 'the governmental interference of Mr Sarkozy', who Blatter claims encouraged Michel Platini to vote for Qatar. 'Just one week before the election I got a telephone call from Platini and he said, "I am no longer in your picture because I have been told by the head of state that we should consider . . . the situation of France." And he told me that this will affect more than one vote because he had a group of voters.'

Blatter will not be drawn on motives. He says he has only once spoken to Sarkozy since the vote and did not raise the issue. He does admit that the vote for the World Cup, carried out by a secret ballot of Fifa's executive committee, was always open to 'collusion'. 'In an election, you can never avoid that, that's impossible . . . when you are only a few in the electoral compound.'

One month after Fifa's 22-strong executive committee voted 14–8 in a secret ballot in Qatar's favour, the Arab state announced that it had begun testing French Dassault Rafale fighter jets against rival aircraft for a fleet upgrade. In April 2015, Qatar bought 24 of the jets for $7 billion, with an option to buy 12 more.

The waiter arrives with our 'Fifa salad', a mix of lamb's lettuce, croutons, lardons and diced egg. 'This is Mama Blatter's salad,' Blatter says cheerily. 'We always made it with whatever greens were in season, and you put some croutons and a little bit of bacon.'

Blatter is from the small Alpine town of Visp (population: 7,500), about two hours from Zürich by train. A Roman Catholic, he plans to return there this weekend for All Souls' Day. His father worked in a chemical plant and his only daughter, Corinne, still lives there, teaching English. He has a 14-year-old granddaughter called Selena. Blatter admits that his troubles have hit her hard. 'I think she was suffering more than me,' he says, indicating that he lets criticism wash over him while she takes it personally.

When I ask Blatter what he thinks of Platini, he sits back in his chair, pauses and then gives a diplomatic, if strained, response. 'Platini was an exceptionally good player. He is a good guy. He could be a good successor, yes. It was foreseen, once, that he shall follow [me].'

Platini is still in the race for the Fifa presidency, but his campaign was effectively derailed following his suspension, at the same time as Blatter, after a payment of 2 million Swiss francs from Fifa to his bank account in 2011 came to light. 'You do not need to have a contract written down [...] according to Swiss law,' Blatter says of the Platini payment, adding that even witnesses are not necessary. 'Handshake contracts are valid. The Anglo-Saxon system is not the same as the system here in central Europe.'

He is correct – Swiss law does provide for oral contracts – but I point out that this is not the way that large companies behave. 'But we are a club,' he responds. When I point out that the payment was not accounted for, he shuts down the conversation.

While Blatter pays lip service to the idea of reform at Fifa, saying there 'must be more than a few changes', he remains brass-necked about the culture of handshakes, favours and secret deals that he encouraged. 'The system is not wrong,' he says, adding that if he had been allowed to remain as president, 'then we would be in the right way'. His successor, he believes, should not try to change what he has created.

I ask him about the money, the allegations of bribery and corruption that have dogged him for years. Did he, or people working on his behalf, ever hand out cash to win the support of Fifa's members?

He invokes his parents as he denies it all. 'We have a principle in our family. The basic principle is to only take money if you earn it. Secondly, do not give money to anybody to obtain the advantage. And the third one is if you owe money, pay your debts. These are the principles I have followed since [I was] 12 years old,' he says. 'That is why I am claiming that my conscience, as far as money is concerned, I am totally clear and clean.'

Is he a rich man? No, he says, he only earns what Fifa pays him – a sum that he refuses to disclose because Fifa releases its leadership payments only in aggregate; last year it paid $39.7 million to its 'key management personnel'.

'What do I do with my money? My daughter has an apartment. I have an apartment, one here and one there. That is all. I am not spending money just to show I have money. If you look at the richest Swiss people, I cannot approach the richest 3,000, because they are up to $25 million.'

The waiter returns with our main courses. For me, a surprisingly large veal chop; for Blatter, a plate of boiled beef and julienned vegetables. He picks at it slowly. 'I have to tell you that I don't eat so much because you cannot eat more than you burn,' he says.

After a pause, he sketches out what he thinks were his two main achievements at Fifa: the Goal project, which sends millions of dollars to the world's poorest countries and claims to have built more than 700 football facilities since 1998, and the decision to rotate the World Cup around the continents and, especially, to bring it to Africa in 2010.

He bats away my suggestion that the development money was another way of distributing favours and was a source of money for corrupt officials: 'There is a percentage, perhaps 2 per cent or 3 per cent which have not worked.'

His success in maintaining an iron grip on Fifa hangs partly on the support of African countries, which he has courted assiduously. The shadow of colonialism still lingers, and African football officials often feel that Europeans treat them as second-class. Blatter, by contrast, is unwavering in his vocal support for African football and worked tirelessly to bring the World Cup to South Africa. He has also delivered commercial success: in the four years leading up to the 2014 World Cup in Brazil, Fifa had total revenues of $5.72 billion.

In his view, he has created a virtuous circle: Fifa helps kids in developing countries play football by building them pitches and then benefits when they get home and watch big matches on TV. This work, he insists, cannot be undone: 'My reputation is spoiled, because I was bitterly attacked, as responsible for everything. But it will not damage my legacy.' With the benefit of hindsight, he wonders whether it might have been better for him to stand down after the high of the 2014 World Cup in Brazil.

When I ask about the ISL case, in which it was revealed in 2008 that a sports agency founded by Horst Dassler of Adidas had paid 138 million Swiss francs in bribes to senior Fifa officials, Blatter refuses to discuss it. He was not found guilty of any wrongdoing and, he says, the case is now closed and he jokes about double jeopardy: 'In American law it is said you cannot be condemned twice!'

I bring up the case in the US in 2006 where Fifa paid a $90 million settlement to MasterCard for reneging on a contract in order to sign a more lucrative sponsorship deal with Visa. 'We were not very very clever,' admits Blatter. 'It was wrong. But sometimes, because you were working hard you make mistakes. You cannot just hang somebody.'

As we pass over the thorny questions about his wealth, about Fifa's corruption and secrecy, Blatter is calm. He believes he is a man more sinned against than sinning, and he repeats that he has little control over the behaviour of Fifa's executive committee, whose members were not appointed by him, but by the six continental football federations.

'Regrets? I do not regret,' he says. 'The only regret I have is that in my life in football I am a very generous man in my thoughts and I think people are good and then I have realized that most of the time I was, let's say, trapped by people. You trust someone 100 per cent and then you see that all this trust was just to get some

---

Sonnenberg
Hitzigweg 15, 8032 Zürich

....

Passuger sparkling water x 2	SFr22
Bottle of Clavien Sauvignon Blanc	SFr73
Fifa salad (Mama Blatter recipe) x 2	SFr30
Veal chop	SFr59
Potato rösti	SFr9
Boiled beef with julienned vegetables	SFr37
Espresso x 2	SFr13

....

Total (including tip SFr20) –	SFr263

advantage. I have done it not only once, I have done it more than once. I have to bear that and I bear it.'

Meanwhile, he lambasts Switzerland for not protecting him. 'I am a Swiss citizen. I was even a soldier! I was the commander of a regiment of 3,500 people. I served my country!' he protests, referring to his service in the 1960s as colonel in command in the army's supply unit during the cold war.

These days, he has few allies left. He says he counted on one hand the number of friends he could call on for help when deciding whether to step down after years at the top of football. He admits his reputation has been destroyed. But he cannot stop. He remains proud of his life's work. 'Could somebody else have done it? If he was fool enough to only live for football, then he could have. But it is difficult to find people that have been in the game with not only their body, not only their mind or with their heart, but with their soul. And I was therein. And if you ask me what I am doing later, I am still therein.'

We do not order any dessert, simply a cup of espresso and some petits fours in the shape of small footballs. Blatter is looking forward to the evening, when his girlfriend, Linda Barras, a 51-year-old with two children, is flying in to see him. She lives in Geneva, but Blatter is happy with the situation.

'The distances are not detrimental to a good understanding,' he says. 'Perhaps it is even better for the guy who has devoted all his life to football. When you are 100 per cent in your job and your job is really something you believe in, then obviously even by being a generous man, at a certain time the person living with you cannot be happy,' he says.

Then he stands up, suddenly small and frail again, signs a football for the restaurant's manager and disappears into a black Mercedes.

Letters to the Editor

All aboard the in-house Commission gravy train

1 April 2017

Sir, I always enjoy the Lunch with the *FT* articles, not least because it's interesting to read what the interviewees order and what the cost is. Some of the choices are almost stereotypical and I can't help thinking that some are made in the knowledge that they will be printed for the world to see. So, we had Michael O'Leary (chief executive of Ryanair) ordering a chicken salad and coffee from the canteen for € 14.60 (for two), and Nigel Farage, being honest (if a bit excessive) about his preferences, sinking a few pints, washed down by a bottle of red, costing around £135. And who could forget Richard Desmond, who ordered a bottle of Château Palmer 1983 at £580 – total bill, including service, £758.81.

Then in last week's *Financial Times* the stereotype to top them all. European Commission president Jean-Claude Juncker, eating at the Commission's in-house restaurant, sips a glass of Languedoc to accompany the carpaccio and tender veal fillets. And the price: complimentary. Someone in the tax-paying community must have paid, and 'complimentary' says a lot about the European Commission's – literal – gravy train.

Nice work if you can get it, Jean-Claude.

Peter Brookes

Penang, Malaysia

Living in the pub

16 April 2016

Sir, What a genius spark of serendipitous synchronicity that the editor of last weekend's Life & Arts (9 April) should feature both a deliciously indulgent bibulous Lunch with UK Independence Party leader Nigel Farage, and Jethro Tull's 'Living in the Past' in the Life of a Song column in the very same issue. Please renew my subscription immediately.

Dr Alan Bullion
Tunbridge Wells, Kent, UK

Homo economicus, stripped down to basics

4 November 2016

Sir, David Crow's luncheon interview with Martin Shkreli ('Nobody stopped to punch me', Life & Arts, 29 October) is the finest portrayal of Homo economicus, that model of neoliberal thought, that I have seen in print – to the point and totally stripped of academic and ideological claptrap. Mr Crow has done a great service to economic thought and as a reward he deserves to go out to lunch next time with someone who drinks.

Leonard S. Hyman
Sleepy Hollow, NY, US

Disappointed by bad language and a lack of good manners

19 June 2015

Sir, Although Henry Mance gave an excellent description of Richard Desmond (Lunch with the *FT*, Life & Arts, 12 June), I wonder if it was necessary to quote his derogatory language? I would not expect a quality newspaper like yours, with a high standard to maintain, to print the f-word in its articles.

Willem Mock

Amsterdam, The Netherlands

The power of parentheses

17 February 2018

Sir, Rana Foroohar, aged 47, describes Rebecca Solnit as 'beautiful (still) at the age of 56'.

The power of those brackets! Surely even by the age of 47 one knows that real beauty is life-long and comes from within?

Edward Knighton

Bromley, Kent, UK

Homer would have loved to be invited to Lunch

20 March 2015

Sir, I am sure that the poet Homer would have appreciated an invitation to Lunch with the *FT*. As he showed in the *Iliad* and the *Odyssey*, food, wine, laughter, conversation and friendship were essential for a meaningful life.

Somewhere in the Elysian Fields, this wondrous poet must be feeling somewhat envious of Murad Ahmed's lunch with Demis Hassabis (31 January) and Gillian Tett's with Ginni Rometty (7 February). Artificial intelligence was the central topic of conversation at both meals. This is not a new idea. As Homer wrote of Hephaestus/Vulcan: 'There were golden handmaids also who worked for him, and were like real young women, with sense and reason, voice also and strength, and all the learning of the immortals' (*Iliad*, Book 18, Butler translation).

I hope there are copies of Homer in the offices of DeepMind and IBM.

Miguel Monjardino
Mentor, Republic,
Angra do Heroísmo, Azores, Portugal

More pressing claims on the Dangote billions

20 July 2018

My compliments to David Pilling for the brilliant interview with businessman Aliko Dangote (Lunch with the *FT*, 14 July). Mr Dangote is contributing immensely to Nigeria by creating jobs. On an extended business visit in Nigeria recently, I travelled in the interior and the villages of the country. Mr Dangote's name evoked respect everywhere. He is networked with trade even in remote villages.

My request to Mr Dangote is not to waste his time and money in acquiring a football club. Everywhere I travelled in Nigeria, I noticed small children aged between five and 12 standing at street corners, outside places of worship, at gas stations, traffic signals and so on, even in his birthplace Kano, with plastic bowls and metal tumblers, seeking some coins or food. It was heart-rending. These children should be in school, I told myself repeatedly.

I urge Mr Dangote to spend his riches in starting as many schools and colleges as possible. The children of Nigeria will be grateful to him for a better future.

Rajendra Aneja
Aneja Management Consultants,
Mumbai, India

Ancelotti's wine choice was difficult to stomach

27 May 2016

Sir, I was surely not the only reader to wonder how such a 'gourmand' as Carlo Ancelotti (Lunch with the *FT*, Life & Arts, 20 May) could order a Tuscan blend of Cabernet Sauvignon and Merlot to drink with tagliolini and lobster?

Ben Hunting
Brooklyn, NY, US

Silly snobbishness about red wine

3 June 2016

Sir, Ben Hunting (Letters, 27 May) wonders how such a 'gourmand' as Carlo Ancelotti could order a Tuscan blend of Cabernet Sauvignon and Merlot to drink with tagliolini and lobster (Lunch with the *FT*, 20 May).

Perhaps Mr Ancelotti is merely suffering from a bad case of red wine *snobisme*, a gustatory disease whose main symptom is the boring insistence that a decent red wine can be successfully paired with any food.

Once confined to the Paris metropolitan area of France, it has now spread its silliness throughout the EU – and even as far as California.

Stan Trybulski
Branford, CT, US

Contributors

MURAD AHMED

Murad joined the *FT* in 2014 as European technology correspondent. As a reporter, he covered the rise of Silicon Valley and the internet for the best part of a decade. In 2018, he became the paper's sports correspondent.

JOHN AUTHERS

John joined the *FT* as a graduate trainee in 1989 and stayed for 29 years. His *FT* roles included US markets editor, global head of the Lex Column and chief markets commentator. He is now a senior editor at Bloomberg.

LIONEL BARBER

Lionel is editor of the *FT*, assuming the post in 2005 after serving in Washington, Brussels and New York as a foreign correspondent and senior editor. He has lectured widely on US foreign policy and Europe and interviewed many world leaders. He is chairman of the Tate and a member of the board of Trustees of Carnegie Corporation.

ANNE-SYLVAINE CHASSANY

Anne-Sylvaine is the *FT*'s world news editor and former Paris bureau chief. Before joining the *FT*, she worked for Bloomberg, Dow Jones and *La Tribune*. She is the co-author of *Enron, la faillite qui ébranla l'Amérique*, published in 2003.

GUY CHAZAN

Guy is the *FT*'s Berlin bureau chief. He has previously worked as the paper's energy editor. Prior to joining the *FT* in 2012 he spent 10 years working in Russia, latterly as the *Wall Street Journal*'s Moscow correspondent.

CHLOE CORNISH

Chloe spent part of her two-year *FT* graduate traineeship in San Francisco. She is currently the *FT*'s Middle East correspondent based in Beirut.

DAVID CROW

David is the *FT*'s banking editor, formerly a senior US business correspondent covering the pharma industry for the paper in New York. He previously worked on the *FT*'s main news desk in London.

MARTIN DICKSON

Martin was deputy editor of the *FT* from 2005 to 2012 and US managing editor from 2012 to 2014.

ANDREW EDGECLIFFE-JOHNSON

Andrew is the *FT*'s US business editor. In more than 20 years with the *FT* he has worked as its US news editor during the 2016 election, its global media editor for eight years and other reporting and editing roles on both sides of the Atlantic.

JO ELLISON

Jo is the *FT*'s fashion editor. Prior to joining the *FT* in 2014, she was the features director of British *Vogue*. She writes a weekly column called Trending.

ALICE FISHBURN

Alice is editor of *FT Weekend Magazine* and deputy editor of *FT Weekend*. Prior to this she worked at *The Times*.

STEPHEN FOLEY

Stephen is deputy US news editor at the *FT*, based in New York, and also author of *FT Wealth* magazine's Ambitious Wealth column. He has previously covered the investment industry and markets for the *FT*.

JONATHAN FORD

Jonathan is City editor of the *FT*, having previously been chief leader writer and written for the Lex column. Before that he worked at the financial commentary service Breakingviews of which he was a co-founder.

RANA FOROOHAR

Rana is an associate editor and global business columnist at the *FT*, as well as the author of *Makers and Takers: The Rise of Finance and the Fall of American Business*.

JANAN GANESH

Janan is the US political columnist for the *FT*, based in Washington. He also writes a column in the *FT Weekend*. He previously wrote the UK politics column in London and served as the political correspondent for *The Economist*.

MATTHEW GARRAHAN

Matthew is the *FT*'s news editor. He was previously global media editor, when he was based in New York and then London. Prior to that he spent eight years in California as Los Angeles correspondent.

LUCY KELLAWAY

Lucy is a secondary school teacher and a co-founder of Now Teach, a charity set up to persuade older professionals to retrain as teachers. For three decades she was an *FT* journalist.

ROULA KHALAF

Roula is deputy editor of the *FT*. She has worked for the *FT* since 1995, first as north Africa correspondent, then Middle East correspondent and most recently as Middle East editor. Before joining the *FT*, she was a staff writer for *Forbes* magazine in New York.

HANNAH KUCHLER

Hannah is the *FT*'s US pharma and biotech correspondent. She covered technology for the *FT* from San Francisco, specializing in social media and cyber security. She has reported for the *FT* from London, New York, Hong Kong and Silicon Valley.

SIMON KUPER

Simon joined the *FT* in 1994. He wrote the daily currencies column, before leaving the *FT* in 1998. He returned in 2002 as a sports column-ist and has been there ever since. Nowadays he writes a general column for *FT Weekend* on all manner of topics from politics to books, and on cities including London, Paris, Johannesburg and Miami.

LEO LEWIS

Leo is the *FT*'s Tokyo correspondent and has lived in a combination of Tokyo and Beijing for the past 15 years as a journalist. He has reported widely throughout Asia, covering politics, business and society. He grows peanuts in his garden and stares adoringly at the Pacific from his balcony.

VICTOR MALLET

Victor is a former Asia editor and Asia news editor of the *FT* and has been a foreign correspondent for more than 30 years. His latest book is *River of Life, River of Death: The Ganges and India's Future*. He is now the *FT*'s Paris bureau chief.

HENRY MANCE

Henry is a voracious Lunch interviewer, his guests ranging from Nigel Farage to Hilary Mantel. He joined the *FT* in 2010, and was named interviewer of the year at the 2017 British Press Awards. He is now chief features writer at *FT Weekend*.

RICHARD MILNE

Richard started at the *FT* on work experience in Paris before joining as a graduate trainee in 2003. He reported on the UK, French business, German industry, European companies and capital markets before his current role as Nordic and Baltic correspondent.

MALCOLM MOORE

Malcolm joined the *FT* in 2015 covering the sport and leisure business. He is now the technology news editor.

DAVID PILLING

David is the Africa editor of the *FT*. He was previously Asia editor, Tokyo bureau chief, pharmaceuticals correspondent, deputy features editor and Chile and Argentina correspondent. He is the author of *The Growth Delusion* and *Bending Adversity*.

ALAN RUSBRIDGER

Alan is Principal of Lady Margaret Hall in Oxford. He was editor-in-chief of the *Guardian* for 20 years from 1995. He chairs the Reuters Institute for the Study of Journalism.

ALEC RUSSELL

Alec is editor of *FT Weekend*. Previously he was the *FT*'s news editor, comment editor and world news editor. His editing roles followed a long career as a foreign correspondent based in Johannesburg (twice), Washington and the Balkans. He has written three books.

MAX SEDDON

Max is an *FT* correspondent in Moscow, where he reports on topics from oligarch intrigue to football and Russian rappers. In 2017, the *FT* awarded him the Jones-Mauthner Memorial Prize for outstanding reporting of international affairs by a journalist under 40.

ERIKA SOLOMON

Erika joined the *FT* in 2014 as its Middle East correspondent, based in Beirut. Before joining the *FT*, she was a staff reporter for Reuters news agency for five years, covering stories in the Middle East and north Africa.

MEHUL SRIVASTAVA

Mehul has worked for the *FT* since 2015, when he joined as Turkey correspondent. He grew up in Calcutta and studied journalism at Washington & Lee University in Virginia. He lives in Jerusalem, where he covers Israel, Palestinian issues and Jordan for the *FT*.

BARNEY THOMPSON

Barney is the *FT*'s legal correspondent, covering lawyers, criminal justice, white-collar crime and corporate litigation. Before that he was an editor on the UK and world news desks.

JOHN THORNHILL

John is innovation editor at the *FT*, writing a regular column on the impact of technology. He also hosts the *FT*'s weekly Tech Tonic podcast. In a 30-year career at the *FT*, John has – among other roles – been deputy editor, European edition editor, Asia editor and Moscow bureau chief.

JACKIE WULLSCHLÄGER

Jackie is the *FT*'s chief art critic. Among her books are the prize-winning *Hans Christian Andersen* and *Chagall: Love and Exile*.

Acknowledgements

I would like to thank all my colleagues at the *Financial Times* for their invaluable contributions to this special second edition of *Lunch with the FT*. In particular, I want to acknowledge the indefatigable Natalie Whittle at *Weekend FT* and the *WEFT* editor Alec Russell. Both drove and steered the project to a successful conclusion. Special mention too to John Ridding, CEO, and his team for supporting us, proving that there is such a thing as a second Lunch. Thanks to Peter Cheek and Bhavna Patel for library searches into the Lunch archive. They are the best in the business. Graham Tuckwell and John Bradley also gave help and guidance on artworks. Thanks to John Halton, Richard Pigden and Nigel Hanson, often unsung heroes, for their legal guidance; thanks too for advice from Leyla Boulton, who played the lead role in our first serving of Lunch. And finally, thanks to the Penguin team who saw the book patiently to press: Martina O'Sullivan, Lydia Yadi, Joanna Whitehead, Ellie Smith and Karen Whitlock, among others.

PENGUIN PARTNERSHIPS

Penguin Partnerships is the Creative Sales and Promotions team at Penguin Random House. We have a long history of working with clients on a wide variety of briefs, specializing in brand promotions, bespoke publishing and retail exclusives, plus corporate, entertainment and media partnerships.

We can respond quickly to briefs and specialize in repurposing books and content for sales promotions, for use as incentives and retail exclusives as well as creating content for new books in collaboration with our partners as part of branded book relationships.

Equally if you'd simply like to buy a bulk quantity of one of our existing books at a special discount, we can help with that too. Our books can make excellent corporate or employee gifts.

Special editions, including personalized covers, excerpts of existing books or books with corporate logos can be created in large quantities for special needs.

We can work within your budget to deliver whatever you want, however you want it.

**For more information, please contact
salesenquiries@penguinrandomhouse.co.uk**